Karen Brown'
SPAIN

Charming Inns & Itineraries

Written by
CYNTHIA SAUVAGE and CLARE BROWN

Illustrations by Barbara Tapp
Cover Painting by Jann Pollard

Travel Press
Karen Brown's Country Inn Series

Karen Brown Titles

Austria: Charming Inns & Itineraries

California: Charming Inns & Itineraries

England: Charming Bed & Breakfasts

England, Wales & Scotland: Charming Hotels & Itineraries

France: Charming Bed & Breakfasts

France: Charming Inns & Itineraries

Germany: Charming Inns & Itineraries

Ireland: Charming Inns & Itineraries

Italy: Charming Bed & Breakfasts

Italy: Charming Inns & Itineraries

Portugal: Charming Inns & Itineraries

Spain: Charming Inns & Itineraries

Switzerland: Charming Inns & Itineraries

Dedicated

to

Cyndi & David

and their sons

Michael & Evan

Editors: Karen Brown, June Brown, Clare Brown, Kim Brown Holmsen, Iris Sandilands, Gretchen DeAndre.

Illustrations: Barbara Tapp; Cover painting: Jann Pollard.

Maps: Susanne Lau Alloway—Greenleaf Design & Graphics; Back cover photo: William H. Brown.

Distributed by Fodor's Travel Publications, Inc., 201 East 50th Street, New York, NY 10022, USA.

Distributed in the United Kingdom by Random House UK, 20 Vauxhall Bridge Road, London, SW1V 2SA, phone: 44 171 973 9000, fax: 44 171 840 8408.

Distributed in Australia by Random House Australia, 20 Alfred Street, Milsons Point, Sydney NSW 2061, Australia, phone: 61 2 9954 9966, fax: 61 2 9954 4562.

Distributed in New Zealand by Random House New Zealand, 18 Poland Road, Glenfield, Auckland, New Zealand, phone: 64 9 444 7197, fax: 64 9 444 7524.

Distributed in South Africa by Random House South Africa, Endulani, East Wing, 5A Jubilee Road, Parktown 2193, South Africa, phone: 27 11 484 3538, fax: 27 11 484 6180.

A catalog record for this book is available from the British Library.

Library of Congress Cataloging-in-Publication Data

Brown, Clare.
    Karen Brown's Spain : charming inns & itineraries / written by
Clare Brown, Cynthia Sauvage, Ralph Kite ; illustrations by Barbara
Tapp ; cover painting by Jann Pollard. -- Totally rev. 7th ed.
    p.   cm. -- (Karen Brown's country inn series)
    Includes index.
    ISBN 0-930328-65-5 (pb)
    1. Hotels--Spain--Guidebooks. 2. Spain—Guidebooks. I. Brown,
Karen, 1956- . II. Sauvage, Cynthia, 1955- . III. Kite, Ralph.
IV. Title. V. Series.
TX907.5.S7B76   1997
647.9446'01--dc21   97-11560
                                                    CIP

Contents

Introduction

Once you fall under Spain's magical spell, there will be no breaking free, nor any urge to do so—only the desire to return, again and again. However, many seasoned travelers never experience its enchantment, since Spain is considered somewhat "off the beaten path." Outside the major cities, you quickly find yourself away from hoards of tourists and happily immersed in the magic of places that haven't changed for hundreds of years. You will be entranced by the beauty of the landscape, the rich selection of places to see, the diversity of the culture, and the warmth of welcome. We are constantly amazed that more people have not yet discovered Spain's many wonders and hope our guide will entice you to visit. You too will become addicted to its boundless charms.

About This Guide

Our goal in writing this guide is to share with you the most charming, historic hotels in Spain and to provide itineraries that will lead you to them by the most scenic and interesting routes. This book is designed for the traveler looking for a guide to more than the capital city and a handful of highlights, for the visitor who wants to add a little out of the ordinary to his agenda. We do not claim to be objective reporters—that sort of treatment is available anywhere—but subjective, on-site raconteurs. We have definite biases toward hotels with romantic ambiance, from charming stone farmhouses tucked in the mountains to sumptuous castles overlooking the sea. We believe that your choice of accommodation helps to weave the tapestry of your trip. The locations you select to spend the night can enhance your memories immeasurably. If you follow our itineraries (each one of which we have traveled personally) and trust in our hotel recommendations (every one of which we have visited personally), you will be assured of Spain's best lodgings while discovering the country's most intriguing destinations.

This book is divided into four parts. First, the *Introduction* gives a general overview of Spain. The second section, *Itineraries*, outlines itineraries throughout Spain to help you plan where to go and what to see. The third section, *Hotel Descriptions*, is our recommended selection of hotels in all price ranges with a description, an illustration, and pertinent information provided on each one. The fourth section, *Maps*, pinpoints the location of each of the recommended hotels.

About Spain

Spain is a country with something for everyone: from the birthplace of Don Juan to the birthplace of Hernán Cortés, Conquistador of Mexico, from the tomb of St. James the Apostle to the tomb of El Cid, Spain's medieval epic hero. You can visit the plains traversed by Don Quixote in search of "wrongs to right" and can admire the quixotic architectural achievements of Antonio Gaudí. You can drive the highest road in Europe and visit the largest wildlife refuge. You can see the youthful work of Picasso and the mature work of Salvador Dalí. To cap it all off, there are great beaches, spectacular mountains, stunning gorges, beautiful landscapes, fine dining, and, above all—a warm, welcoming people. Following are some facts about Spain, listed alphabetically.

BANKS

Generally, banks in Spain are open from 9 am to 1:30 pm, sometimes 2 pm, Monday through Friday. Some banks (most frequently in larger towns) maintain similar business hours on Saturday. Many, but not all, exchange foreign currency: look for a *Cambio* (exchange) sign outside the bank. Often your hotel or the local tourist office will exchange your dollars, though usually at a slightly less-favorable rate than at the bank.

CLIMATE

There are three distinct climates in Spain, dividing the country in thirds from north to south. The northern area is subject to the moderating Atlantic currents and has a relatively good climate for most of the year—too cold to swim in winter, but seldom bitterly cold either; summer is warm, but never extremely hot. The central plateau is cut off from those moderating currents and has what the Spanish call *nueve meses de invierno y tres de infierno* (nine months of winter and three of hell). The southern third of the country has a more Mediterranean climate: relatively warm, though with damp winters, and often brutal heat in midsummer, which is slightly alleviated along the coastal areas by sea breezes. If you venture to some of Spain's exotic islands, you will find still other climates. In fact, on some of the Canary Islands (just off the coast of Africa), it is so dry that sometimes it doesn't rain for the entire year.

CLOTHING

Standards of formality can be generalized: In the most elegant city restaurants, dresses and coats and ties are common, though only occasionally required. Skimpy summer attire, though common in resort areas, might make you feel conspicuous elsewhere. When visiting Spain's magnificent cathedrals, it is respectful to dress conservatively.

CURRENT–VOLTAGE

You will need a transformer plus an adapter if you plan to take an American-made electrical appliance. Even if the appliance is dual-voltage, as many of them are these days, you'll still need an adapter plug. The voltage is usually 220, but in a few places 110 is used. Occasionally a 110 outlet is provided in the hotel bathroom, but these should be used only for small appliances such as electric razors, since they usually can't handle things like hair dryers. Be sure to check with the manager if the outlet is not clearly marked.

DRIVING

CAR RENTAL: This guide is the perfect companion for the traveler who wants to experience Spain by car. Most of the major car rental agencies maintain offices in cities throughout Spain. It is usually possible to pick up a car in one city and drop it off in another, although sometimes a surcharge is made.

DRIVER'S LICENSE: You will need to have a valid driver's license from your home country.

GASOLINE: Gasoline is relatively expensive (perhaps double the USA price) and should be considered in your budget if you plan to drive extensively. Gasoline is available in any small town and at frequent intervals along the freeways. Diesel (called *gasoil* or *gasoleo* in Spain) is considerably less costly. With a little common sense, you should have no trouble finding fuel. Many of the major gas stations accept credit cards—if so, most display a sign with the credit card emblems.

ROADS: Roads in Spain run the gamut from superb freeways to barely two-lane country roads (and, as you might expect, our countryside itineraries find you more often on the latter). Travel on the freeways is swift, but as a rule-of-thumb, calculate that you will average only about 50–60 kilometers per hour on the country roads. However, the leisurely pace allows you time to enjoy your surroundings as you drive. The personality of the country does not lend itself to an accelerated pace, nor do the itineraries.

There is order to the Spanish road numbers. A (A6, for example) indicates freeways. N plus a Roman numeral (NIV) indicates major national highways that radiate like spokes from Madrid. N with an Arabic numeral (N403) indicates minor national highways that connect the major ones. C (C321) indicates regional roads, and two letters (which are the first two letters in the name of the province, e.g., TO1234 for Toledo) indicate provincial roads. Their size and the speed possible is usually correspondingly lower as you go down the list from freeways to provincial roads. Roads are constantly being upgraded, so you will encounter many pleasant surprises—a road that looks of questionable quality on a map might turn out to be wider than expected and freshly re-tarred.

Some of the longer freeways are toll roads and every so often require that you pass through a toll booth. When you enter the highway, usually you will be given a ticket with the point of entry marked and will pay according to the number of kilometers accrued when you leave the highway. If you don't know Spanish, look for the amount due on the lighted sign at the booth. While these freeways are excellent and generally uncrowded, the tolls take their "toll" on your wallet if you drive all day on them. Wherever there are freeways, there are also parallel non-toll highways, but you can expect them to double the driving time between two points. Most of the toll stations will take a credit card. This is a great convenience—just one quick swish of your card through their computer and you are on your way.

SEAT BELTS: The use of seat belts is mandatory in Spain, and the law is strongly enforced both in cities and in the countryside, so get into the habit of buckling up when you get into the car.

TRAFFIC: This is never a problem on the freeways. However, on smaller roads it can be ferocious. If you're trying to cover a lot of ground in a given day, we suggest that you try to drive during siesta time—between 1 and 4 pm—when many trucks and buses stop for lunch. In the large cities, unfamiliarity combined with traffic, parking problems, and the fact that almost no two streets are parallel, make driving a trial for all but the bravest of souls. Our preference is to leave the car in the hotel parking lot (or one recommended by the hotel) and take cabs or walk around the cities. Underground public parking areas are common and are designated by a rectangular blue sign with a large white "P." In Madrid and Barcelona try the excellent subway systems (called the Metro and marked with signs bearing a large "M"). If you're stopping to visit a town along an itinerary route, we suggest you park on or near a main square (for easy recall), then venture on by foot into those streets that were never designed with cars in mind. It is not uncommon for parking areas on central streets and plazas to be *vigilados* (overseen) by an attendant, usually wearing something resembling a uniform. He may direct you to a free spot and will approach you after you park—a small tip is appropriate.

ECONOMY

Though long known as a travel bargain, since its entry into the European Union (EU) Spain has made appreciable progress toward bringing the cost of its commodities (including tourist facilities) closer to the level of other EEC members. Tourism accounts for a large share of foreign income, with the number of tourists entering each year exceeding the native population of over 38 million. Fortunately, they don't all arrive at the same time—the vast majority of visitors comes in July and August.

ENGLISH

We suggest you tuck in your suitcase a Spanish phrase book (Berlitz has an excellent one). In the large hotels in the major cities, you will probably never use it, but elsewhere you might find situations where English is not spoken. Most hotels and paradors have someone on the staff who speaks English, but he/she is not always available. When this happens, just pull out your trusty phrase book and point—Spaniards are friendly and you'll eventually make yourself understood (and probably learn some Spanish while you're at it). If you make advance reservations, be sure to take your letters of confirmation and/or vouchers with you: it will save a lot of pointing.

FESTIVALS AND FOLKLORE

By far the six most internationally renowned Spanish festivals are *Semana Santa* (Holy Week), which is celebrated throughout the country; the *Feria* in Seville (the week leading up to Easter and the second week after it, respectively); the *Festival of San Fermín* in Pamplona, which features the running of the bulls (the second week of July); the *Fallas* in Valencia (the middle of March); the *Festival of St. James* in Santiago (the last two weeks of July); and *Carnival* in Cadiz (the week in which Ash Wednesday falls).

In addition, every Spanish town has its patron saint, and every saint its day of honor, so there are as many festivals as there are Spanish towns. If you know where you want to go ahead of time, write to the Tourist Office of Spain or the *Oficina de Turismo* (Tourist Office) in the town(s) you plan to visit for a list of festival dates so that you might arrange your visit to coincide with one or several of these colorful events. Be forewarned, however, that hotel space will be at a premium and room rates are almost always more expensive during festival time.

FOOD AND DRINK

Today, Spanish cuisine is approaching the international European standard. The government rates restaurants from one to five forks: however, its rating system is based on such matters as the number of choices on the menu and the wine cellar rather than the quality of the food, so it can be misleading. For instance, in order to receive three or more forks, the headwaiter must speak, and the menu must be translated into, several languages (which often makes for amusing reading)—an achievement that does not reflect upon the dishes served. A modest-appearing and reasonably priced restaurant will often offer good, regional fare.

A very important aspect of dining in Spain is to acclimate yourself to the national time schedule. Breakfast is at the same time as at home. The main meal, however, is almost exclusively eaten at around 2 pm. Most restaurants open around 1 pm and close about 4 pm and it is during this period that they offer their main menu that can be expected to have almost everything on it. They open again at about 8:30 or 9 pm for dinner, which is normally a light meal and is served until 10 or 11 pm, and, often, even midnight. Traditionally, restaurants have a reduced menu in the evening, although it seems that nowadays more and more establishments are offering the same fare at night as at midday, as Spain becomes increasingly "Europeanized," a process which is taking place rapidly and, logically enough, from north to south in the country. In Catalonia and the Basque country, you'll find that restaurants close earlier—a fact that astounds even many

Spaniards. Restaurants that cater to tourists—such as the parador dining rooms—are the most flexible and will normally offer a full menu in the evening. We feel it is most comfortable to adjust to the Spanish schedule if possible. You may find the service less than perfect if you take a table at a busy restaurant at 2 pm and order only a sandwich, and you may be disappointed if you expect to have a five-course dinner in the evening. Between the *tapas* (munchies) available at all bars at almost all times, and the numerous *cafeterias* where small, quick meals can be had at any hour, you won't starve.

By far the most common type of food on the Spanish menu is the wide variety of seafood. Many of these are totally unknown to most Americans (even where the menu is translated, it doesn't necessarily help). Items such as *angulas* (baby eels), numerous varieties of squid (*calamares*) and octopus (*pulpo*), and shellfish are best viewed as an adventure. You will find many of them excellent and should definitely experiment. Organ meats—such as brains and sweetbreads—are also common and, prepared in many different ways, can be delicious.

If there is any dish more common than seafood, it is the *tortilla española* (Spanish omelet) which is made with eggs and potatoes. It will be found on almost every menu as an appetizer or as a main course for the evening meal. It is also often available as a sandwich (*bocadillo*).

There are a few things you should note about the names of eating and drinking establishments. A *bar* is seldom what we call by that name. It is usually a place where everything from coffee to alcohol is served and is frequented by patrons of all ages. Continental breakfast is served there too, as are pastries and other desserts. Bars often also serve simple sandwiches. A *café* is about the same thing, and indeed, these places are often called *café-bar*—these are the spots that often have tables outside when the weather permits. A *cafeteria* offers a modest but complete menu and relatively fast service. This seldom involves self-service, but provides a less elaborate setting for a meal than the typical restaurant.

Wine is ubiquitous. In the large fancy restaurants a good selection of imported wines is usually available along with the extensive wines of Spain. In smaller restaurants the list is mostly Spanish, which is often a rich selection indeed, and fun to sample. Probably the best wines come from the Rioja region around Logroño. These are followed by those of the Valdepeñas area of La Mancha, which are slightly more astringent. But there are many other smaller wine-producing regions, some of which we'll point out in the itineraries. If you have no particular favorite, you'll rarely go wrong by requesting the *vino de la casa*, often a wine bottled especially for the restaurant, or else a *vino regional* (regional wine), either *tinto* (red), *blanco* (white), or *rosado* (rose), according to your preference.

Sangría is a national favorite, made from red wine mixed with fresh fruit and liqueur, with infinite variations on that theme, and served over ice. It's a great thirst-quencher and, even if it doesn't appear on the menu, any place will happily drum up a passable *sangría*.

If there is a more common drink than wine in Spain, it is coffee. Spanish coffee is usually served as what we call espresso in the United States. It is thus a small cup of very strong brew to which most people add a considerable amount of sugar. Here are some of the common terms used in ordering: *café solo*—a demitasse of espresso; *café solo doble*—a double portion of the same; *café con leche*—the same coffee with an equal amount of warm milk added to it; *café cortado*—espresso with just a splash of milk added.

Beer is another favorite, and is always good, sometimes excellent, especially on hot days in a shady plaza. Asking for *una cerveza* will get you a bottle of regional beer or a draught (*cerveza de barril*). *Una caña* will get you a small glass of draught, and the request for *un tanque* will result in a large glass of the refreshing brew.

Another very common beverage ordered in Spanish restaurants is, believe it or not, water: the bottled kind. Though there is nothing wrong with *agua natural* (tap water), *agua mineral* (mineral water) is popular in either *litro* or *medio litro* (liter or half-liter) sizes. It may also be ordered *con* or *sin gas* (with or without carbonation). You'll notice that Spaniards often dilute their wine with it.

Once you leave the large cities and tourist-frequented restaurants, you'll find that menus are poorly translated, or not translated at all. The following list includes some of the terms of traditional specialties to be found on most Spanish menus:

Desayuno (breakfast): This may be a Continental breakfast, consisting of *pan* (bread) and/or *pan dulce* (sweet rolls) along with *café* (coffee), *te* (tea), *leche* (milk), or *chocolate* (hot chocolate). Many hotels (and all the paradors) offer elaborate buffet breakfasts that include various fruits, cereals, breads, yogurts, cheeses, and meats plus sometimes extras such as *huevos* (eggs)—either *revueltos* (scrambled), *fritos* (fried sunny side up), *pasados por agua* (boiled), *poche* (poached), or in a *tortilla* (omelet).

Comida (lunch): This is the main meal of the day for most Spaniards and is taken around 2 pm. It normally consists of several courses: *entremeses* (appetizers), *sopas* (soup, usually of the thick variety), *carnes* (meat dishes), *pescados y mariscos* (fish and shellfish), *postres* (desserts), and, of course, *vino*. No one orders all these courses—three is most common.

Merienda (afternoon snack): This is taken around 6 pm by many people and may consist of any kind of light food. The most common are *pasteles* (pie or cake, not usually as good as they) and churros (deep-fried dough, somewhat like a stick-shaped donut) along with coffee or chocolate.

Tapas (hors d'oeuvres): This is as much a social tradition as a kind of food and is a feature of after-work bar hopping. Since the variety of *tapas* is apparently infinite, a good method is to search out a bar where they are on display so you can point to what you want. Also available at this time (8 to 10 pm, more or less) are *raciónes* (orders, approximately) which are the same things, but in larger portions (a ración will be a plateful of meatballs, for example, whereas a *tapa* will be just a couple).

Cena (supper): This meal has traditionally been taken in Spain after 10 pm and has been a light meal (one course of the same kinds of things as at lunch). Due to Spain's increasing contact with the rest of Europe in the last decade, customs are changing somewhat. Especially in the larger cities and along the French border, you'll find people eating earlier and restaurants offering a more complete menu at night. Most of the paradors and hotels begin serving the evening meal anywhere from 8 to 9 pm.

Aceite (olive oil): About the only kind of oil used to cook with in Spain and used in many, many dishes.

Carne (meat): *Ternera* (technically veal, but really closer to what we call beef) comes in *chuletas* (veal chop, but similar to a T-bone steak if it's thick), *solomillo* (sirloin), *entrecot* (ribeye), *filete* (thinly sliced and pan fried), and *asada* (roasted). *Cerdo* (pork) and *pollo* (chicken) are also commonly found on menus. In central Spain *cochinillo asado* (roast suckling pig) is a common specialty.

Ensalada mixta (tossed green salad): Besides lettuce, this usually contains any or all of the following: olives, tomato, onion, tuna, hard-boiled egg. But remember that there is only one salad dressing in the entire country: *vinagre* (vinegar) and *aceite* (olive oil).

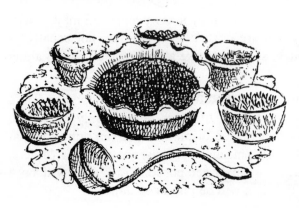

Gazpacho: Another justifiably famous Spanish dish, this is a cold tomato-based soup with various spices and olive oil, and garnished with bits of bread, bacon, green onions, celery, crumbled egg, etc. You are usually given a choice of garnishes at the table. Gazpacho is one of Spain's Moorish legacies, and has multiple variations even though it is usually called *gazpacho Andaluz*, which is the most popular kind. One common variation in the south is *gazpacho de almendras* (almonds), which is white and has thinly sliced almonds floating on top and raisins in it, but tastes pretty much like the regular kind. The soup is an absolutely wonderful cooler if you've been out in the summer heat seeing sights all morning.

Jamön serrano (cured ham, similar to prosciutto): A favorite of most Spaniards as a *tapa, a bocadillo,* or as an added ingredient to another meat dish. There are many varieties and qualities and you'll see them hanging from the ceiling in bars with little cups to catch the juice so it doesn't fall on the customers. *Pata negra* (literally "black foot," a darker variety) is considered the best.

Paella: Probably Spain's best-known dish, it has as many variations as there are Spanish chefs. Based on saffron-flavored rice and olive oil, it may contain any kind of fish, shellfish, chicken, sausage, green peas, beans, bell peppers, or any combination of these. Because it is complicated to make, it may be offered for a minimum of two people and the menu may warn you that there will be a 20- to 30-minute wait if you order it. Connoisseurs will tell you not to order it in the evening because it will be left over from lunch; but, in our experience, better restaurants make it fresh to order.

Pescados y mariscos (fish and shellfish): *Rape* (angler fish), *merluza* (hake), *mero* and *ubina* (sea bass), *lenguado* (sole), and *trucha* (trout) are the common fish varieties. *Pez Espada* (swordfish, also called *aguja* and *emperador*) is often offered thickly sliced like steak and can be superb. *Gambas* (shrimp), *langosta* (a small variety of lobster), *langostino* (large prawns), *almejas* (clams), and *mejillones* (mussels) are common shellfish. In the northern part of Spain there are also *vieiras* (scallops), *centollo* (spider crab), and *changurro* (sizzling crab casserole). A *zarzuela* is a commonly offered fish stew and has the usual infinite number of variations. Although not native to Spain, salmon is popular and frequently found on the menu.

Preparation: Many of the terms describing preparation are relatively meaningless because they simply refer to the origin—*a la Bilbaína*, for example, means Bilbao style, but it never seems to mean the same thing twice. A few terms which are reliable: *al ajillo* (sautéed in garlic), *a la plancha* (grilled), *al pil pil* (sautéed with garlic and olive oil, often with hot pepper), *frito* (fried), *cocido* (stewed), *a la brasa* or *a la parrilla* (charcoal broiled), *en brocheta* (skewered), *al horno* (baked in the oven), and *asado* (roasted).

GEOGRAPHY

Few people realize that Spain, tucked away on the Iberian peninsula, is actually one of Europe's largest countries (second only to France). Also surprisingly, Spain boasts one of the highest average elevations in all of Europe (second only to Switzerland). To continue its accolades, Spain has the highest capital in all of Europe—Madrid. Plus Spain is tops in other areas: her rich, red soil is perfect for growing olives (Spain leads the world in production) and her gentle hills are conducive to the production of grapes (Spain has more land planted in wine grapes than anywhere else in the world).

GOVERNMENT

The current government of Spain (dating from 1975 when Franco died) is a constitutional monarchy similar to Great Britain. The monarchy is hereditary and is balanced by a parliament (called the Cortés). The president is elected in somewhat the same fashion as the British prime minister. The traditional regions, such as Catalonia and Andalusia, which grew up during the Middle Ages, have been granted a degree of self control that might be compared to the powers held by the states in the United States. Strong regionalist identification has always been, and still is, characteristic of Spanish politics.

HISTORY

EARLY PERIOD: Traces of cave-dwelling prehistoric man—Neolithic, Megalithic, and Magdalenian—have been discovered all over the peninsula. Around the 6th century B.C. the area was widely inhabited by the Celts from the north and the Iberians from Africa. The Phoenicians, the Greeks, and especially the Carthaginians founded ports at Cadiz (1100 B.C.), Málaga, Huelva, and Ampurias (north of Barcelona). As a result of the Second Punic War (2nd century B.C.), the peninsula became a Roman colony.

ROMAN PERIOD: Hispania was the most heavily colonized of all Rome's dominions and, thus, the basis for modern Spanish culture. Its language, legal system, and religion all spring from that 600-year period. A number of Roman emperors were born in Spain of either Roman or Hispanic parents, and Julius Caesar himself served there and learned the art of bullfighting. When the entire Roman Empire was overrun by the Germanic tribes from the north, Spain suffered the same fate.

VISIGOTH PERIOD: By the 5th century A.D. the Visigoths had subdued the peninsula almost completely (the Basque area was an exception) and had adopted Roman Catholicism as their own. Their feudalistic system saw the origin of the traditional Spanish regions as kingdoms were combined and divided over the next centuries. Their political system involved a monarch who served at the pleasure of the feudal lords and was thus subject to considerable instability as the kaleidoscope of dynastic unions changed constantly. This characteristic strife provided the opportunity, in 711, for the Moors (Islamic Africans) to invade and sweep across the peninsula from south to north in the space of two decades.

MOORISH PERIOD: The Moors were tolerant people and allowed a diversity of religions to co-exist. At that point in history they represented the highest level of civilization in the western world and contributed greatly to Spanish culture—still evident today in Spanish architecture, painting, philosophy, and science. Córdoba, by the 10th century, was perhaps the most advanced city in Europe. Nevertheless, the Spanish Christians regrouped in the inaccessible mountains of Asturias to launch a crusade to retake their country from Moslem domination, an endeavor that was to last almost eight centuries.

RECONQUEST PERIOD: Legend has it that a Christian leader named Pelayo set up the Kingdom of Asturias after the first defeat of the Moors at Covadonga in 718. The Christians finally established their capital at León in 914. Under their control were Asturias and part of Burgos. The remains of St. James the Apostle were discovered in Galicia, and he became the patron saint of the Reconquest, as well as an object of devotion for millions of pilgrims who made the difficult journey along The Way of St. James (through France and across northern Spain) to venerate the holy remains. The pilgrimage to Santiago de Compostela is still made, albeit by more modern means. By the 11th century, as the frontier between the territories of the Christians and the Moors moved slowly southward, it became fortified with castles and, through various marriages and intrigues, the Kingdom of Castille (the name comes from "castle") had come into existence. During approximately the same period, the Basques began their own process of reconquest that included Catalonia and the eastern coastal areas. During this period border battles were constant, both between the Christian kingdoms themselves, and between the Christians and the Moors.

By 1248 the Castilian campaign had recaptured most of southern Spain from the Moors, including Seville, conquered by Ferdinand III (later to become known as St. Ferdinand). Castile, now united with León, included most of the western half and the south of the peninsula, except for Portugal, which had been established as a separate kingdom in the 11th century.

Meanwhile, the monarchs of Aragón had become supreme on the east side of the peninsula (not to mention in Sicily and Naples) and, when united with Catalonia, ruled from southern France to Valencia. The scene was now set for the transcendental step which would lead to the creation of the modern Spanish nation: the marriage of the heir to the Aragonese throne, Ferdinand V, to the heir to the throne of Castile, Isabella I, thenceforth known as *Los Reyes Católicos* (The Catholic Monarchs).

MODERN PERIOD: Ferdinand (who was a model prince in Machiavelli's famous work of that name) and Isabella spent most of their reign strengthening the monarchy and expanding their dominions, including financing the expedition of Columbus. Their daughter, Juana (the Mad), was too handicapped to rule and so her son Charles was elevated to the throne when Ferdinand died. Charles' father was Phillip the Fair of the Hapsburgs, the family who were in control of the Holy Roman Empire which included half of Europe and most of the western hemisphere, so Charles also gained the title of Emperor Charles V. His son, Phillip, to whom he abdicated the crown in 1556, soon added Portugal to his domain. Portugal held an empire of its own, including Brazil in the New World and Mozambique in Africa, as well as several high-powered trading enclaves in Asia. By the end of the 16th century, Spain's dominions literally ringed the world.

The 17th century saw, however, a serious decline in the monarchy with first Phillip III, then Phillip IV, then Charles II showing a decreasing capacity to rule wisely and an increasing desire to live licentiously on the vast income from their New World mineral riches. During this century, Portugal and many of the European territories were lost. When Charles II died in 1700 without an heir, the Bourbons of France took the throne because Charles's sister had married into that royal family. (The current king, Juan Carlos, is a Bourbon.) The series of Bourbons who ruled during the 18th century—Phillip V, Charles III, Charles IV, and Ferdinand VII—proved to be only marginally better than the Hapsburgs who preceded them, so Spain's holdings continued to dwindle, culminating in the loss of all the American possessions by 1825 (except the Caribbean islands and the Philippines). In 1808, Napoleon seduced the decadent Ferdinand VII with the good life in France, meanwhile installing his own brother on the Spanish throne. The Spaniards reacted swiftly, starting on the *dos de mayo* (the second of May) of the same year, and, with the help of the British (for the first and only time in history), soon regained the crown for Ferdinand. The scene was set for continuing conflict when Ferdinand's brother, Don Carlos, at the head of Basque and Navarrese extremists, disputed Ferdinand's claim to the throne.

The 19th century was thus characterized by three so-called "Carlist Wars" of succession and, in 1898, the Spanish-American War. The Bourbons did manage to hold the throne, but lost the remaining territory of the Empire (Cuba, Puerto Rico, Santo Domingo, and the Philippines). This loss gave rise to widespread intellectual speculation on the causes of Spain's decline by the so-called Generation of 1898.

The early years of the 20th century saw the rise of new populist ideas and continuing labor unrest. In 1923, General Miguel Primo de Rivera established a dictatorship with Alfonso XIII's support. The unrest continued, however, especially in Catalonia. In 1931 the King was forced to abdicate and go into exile by the Republican (essentially socialist) party, which, in the same year, proclaimed the government to be Republican. In 1936 the elections were won by the socialist forces and José Antonio Primo de Rivera, Miguel's son, was head of a rightist revolutionary party. In the same year the revolutionaries began an all-out civil war in the south under the direction of General Francisco Franco. Soon afterward, Germany joined the rebels (Hitler was planning to conquer Europe and used Spain as a testing ground for his weapons), whereas the Republicans were supported by the Soviet Union (allegedly in exchange for some 50 metric tons of gold reserves) and the International Brigade. American volunteers served in the Abraham Lincoln Brigade. Ernest Hemingway covered the war as a journalist and later immortalized the brutality of it in *For Whom The Bell Tolls*. By 1939, the Franco forces had won the war, over a million Spaniards had died, and another half-million were in exile.

As a means of gaining Hitler's support, Spain had promised to remain neutral in any wars he engaged in, and was thus not directly involved in World War II. After the war Spain found itself somewhat of an outcast in international circles because of its neutrality and generally perceived sympathy to Germany. It finally became a member of the United Nations in 1955 and returned to active diplomatic involvement, but with limited success due to the authoritarian regime headed by *El Caudillo* (The Chief), Generalísimo Francisco Franco.

In providing for his succession, Franco proclaimed that Spain was a monarchy and Juan Carlos (born in 1938), grandson of Alfonso XIII, would be the future king. When Franco died in 1975, the young king was installed and the process of creating a constitution began. The document was approved in 1978 and orderly elections have occurred since that time. The death of Franco did not signify the disappearance of rightist sentiment, however, and, as late as 1981, the right-wing military attempted a coup. Juan Carlos reacted swiftly to put it down and thus reassured the world that he was a firmly democratic ruler.

PLAZAS

It may be helpful to understand the general layout of most of the cities and towns of Spain. The "heart" of most of them is the main plaza, often referred to as the *Plaza Mayor*. Some larger cities like Madrid have a central plaza in the old quarter plus others in the more recently constructed sections of town. Small towns usually have just one main plaza in the center of the old quarter, the vicinity you probably most want to visit. The main plaza is frequently the most lively area of the city and is often surrounded by shops and outdoor cafés. This will typically be the site of the cathedral and other historic buildings and the area where the ancient custom of the *paseo* or evening stroll takes place. Plazas serve as excellent orientation points. There is usually parking either in the plaza itself or in a nearby garage which makes a good place to park your car since it will be easy to find and you are in the heart of the sightseeing area.

REGIONS AND PROVINCES

Spain is divided into regions, each of which has its own personality and distinct flavor. The landscape changes constantly and as you move from one region to another, you feel as if you are visiting totally different countries. The regions are further divided into provinces. On the last line of each hotel's description, we indicate the region where it is located while the province is shown in the hotel's address. The provinces are extremely important since there are many towns with identical names, so you need to know in which province your hotel is located in order not to get lost. Note: In the map section is a map showing the regions.

SIESTA

Except for restaurants, almost every place of business closes for two to three hours in the day, sometime between 1 and 5 pm. This includes all but the largest tourist attractions (e.g., the Prado), most stores (El Corte Inglés department store is an exception), and offices. (Banks don't reopen to the public in the afternoon.) So, about the only activities in which to engage during the siesta are dining, drowsing, or driving. You will most likely find "Spanish time" easy to adapt to.

TELEPHONES

Telephone calls made from your hotel room can be exceedingly expensive if you charge the call to your hotel bill. The easiest and least expensive method to call the USA is to use one of the readily available telephone calling cards that are issued by AT&T, MCI, and Sprint. With these credit cards, you dial a local number from the hotel, and then your long-distance call is charged to your credit card. Contact whatever telephone service you use and ask how to receive a charge card.

TIPPING

As everywhere, tipping is not a simple matter on which to give advice. Most restaurants and hotels include *servicio* in the bill, but a small tip is appropriate when the service is good, especially in restaurants frequented by tourists. "Small" means different things to different people, but certainly should not exceed 5%. In informal bars and cafeterias no tip is expected.

TOURIST OFFICES OF SPAIN

The Spanish tourist offices are a rich source for information about Spain. You can write in advance of your holiday for information. Their addresses are as follows:

USA: Tourist Office of Spain, Water Tower Place, Suite 915 East, 845 North Michigan Avenue, Chicago, IL 60611, USA, tel: (312) 642-1992, fax: (312) 642-9817.

USA: Tourist Office of Spain, 8383 Wilshire Boulevard, Suite 960, Beverly Hills, CA 90211, USA, tel: (213) 658-7188, fax: (213) 658-1061.

USA: Tourist Office of Spain, 1221 Brickell Avenue, Miami, FL 33131, USA, tel: (305) 358-1992, fax: (305) 358-8223.

USA: Tourist Office of Spain, 666 Fifth Avenue, 35th Floor, New York, NY 10103, USA, tel: (212) 265-8822, fax: (212) 265-8864.

CANADA: Tourist Office of Spain, 2 Bloor Street West, 34th floor, Toronto, Ontario, M4W 3EZ, Canada, tel: (416) 961-3131, fax: (416) 961-1992.

ENGLAND: Spanish Tourist Office, 57–58 St. James's Street, London SW1A 1LD, England, tel: (0171) 499-0901, fax: (0171) 629-4257.

SPAIN: Tourist Office of Spain, Princesa 1, Edif. Torre de Madrid, 28008 Madrid, Spain. Open 9 am to 6 pm Mondays through Fridays, and 9 am to 2 pm on Saturdays.

The Tourist Offices of Spain can provide you with general information or, at your request, specific information about towns, regions, and festivals. Local tourist offices (*oficina de turismo*) are found in most small towns throughout the country—they are well marked and usually located in the heart of the town or city. They offer an incomparable on-site resource, furnishing town maps and details on local and regional highlights that you might otherwise miss. Those in the regional capitals are especially well equipped to provide you with colorful and informative brochures on the surrounding area. Make the local *oficina de turismo* your first stop at each destination.

TRAINS

The Spanish National Railways (called RENFE) has an extensive network of trains throughout the country with various rail passes, round-trip fares, and special rates available for children and seniors. Trains connect almost every city in Spain. In addition to the normal trains, there are others that offer exceptionally fast, convenient service. One of these is a bullet train called the *AVE* that runs several times a day between Madrid and Seville with one stop en route in Córdoba. This once cumbersome journey now takes a mere two hours and forty minutes. The *AVE* is air conditioned, offers a choice of first- or second-class seating, and has cafeteria service. Another bullet train is the *Talgo 200*, which connects Madrid and Málaga. The train journey between these two popular cities used to take seven hours, but with the super-fast *Talgo 200*, the time is cut to under five hours. Both the *AVE* and the *Talgo 200* are sold in the USA by VE Tours, tel: (800) 222-8383. The telephone number for the RENFE office in Madrid is (1) 527.48.99, the fax number is (1) 528.99.98.

Also available are the *Estrella,* night trains with first- and second-class accommodation, sleeping compartments (berths or couchettes), and sometimes a restaurant or cafeteria service (depending upon the route and time of departure). For long-distance routes, the *Train-Hotel* offers a new dimension in train travel, providing top quality and comfort. These "traveling hotels" cover routes from Barcelona to Milan, Zurich, Paris, and Seville, and from Madrid to Paris, offering *Gran Clase* accommodation, superb restaurant service, and often such extras as individual videos in the carriages, private telephones, and personal attendants. Most rail tickets (except for the *Talgo 200* and the *AVE* trains) can be purchased in the USA through Rail Europe—tel: (800) 848-7245. Call to see if they can assist you with the train of your choice.

ANDALUSIAN EXPRESS: Spain's answer to the famous Orient Express is called the Andalusian Express (*Al-Andalus Expreso*). From the beginning of April to the end of October, this luxurious *belle-époque* train travels weekly on a six-night package. Starting in Madrid or Seville, passengers spend five nights aboard the train which travels through a landscape of olive groves and white towns, ending the trip in Seville or Madrid. A night in Madrid or Seville before the journey completes the package. This meticulously restored train from the 1920s has thirteen cars including two sumptuous dining cars, two bars (one resembles a London club, the other a chic European bistro), five richly paneled sleeping cars (each with six deluxe double cabins and two luxury suites), and two shower cars (with twenty showers, each with its own private dressing room). All of the cabins have their own washbasin (suites also have private toilet and shower). This train is expensive, but offers a nostalgic journey that combines sightseeing excursions along with your meals and accommodations. Reservations for the Andalusian Express can be made in the United States through Marketing Ahead—tel: (800) 223-1356, fax: (212) 686-0271. In Europe reservations can be made through Iberrail in Madrid—tel: (1) 57.15.815, fax: (1) 57.11.417 or (1) 55.61.795. Of course, your travel agent can also help you with tickets.

About Itineraries

The itineraries section of this guide features itineraries covering most of Spain. They may be taken in whole or in part, or strung together for a longer journey. Each of the itineraries highlights a different region of the country, and they are of different lengths, enabling you to find one or more to suit your individual taste and schedule. They are designed to accommodate customization.

HOW TO FIND YOUR WAY

ITINERARY MAPS: Accompanying each itinerary is a map showing the routing and places of interest along the way. These are an artist's renderings and are not meant to replace a good commercial map. Before departure, it is truly vital to purchase detailed maps showing highway numbers, expressways, alternate routes, and distances. There are many maps you can buy covering the whole of Spain, but these are not precise enough. Michelin has seven regional maps of Spain that are exceptionally reliable and tie in with the Michelin *Green Guide* for Spain (an excellent source for more detail on sights, museums, and places of interest). Because many of the places we recommend are off the beaten path, you will have difficulty finding them on most maps. However, the Michelin regional maps are so detailed and have such an extensive index, that you can pinpoint each place to stay and highlight your customized itinerary before you ever leave home.

We have intentionally not specified how many nights to stay at each destination—your personality and time restraints will dictate what is best for you. We strongly suggest concentrating your time in fewer locations in order to relax, unpack, and savor the atmosphere and novelty of the spot. We recommend choosing a few hotels that most appeal to you and using them as hubs from which to explore the surrounding regions.

If you're new to Spain and planning a trip there, we hope that upon reading through the itineraries and hotel descriptions, you'll get a feel for which places merit the most time and which can be done justice with an overnight stay. In other words, this guide should be a reference and not a prescription for your personalized trip. In each destination in the itinerary we have recommendations of places to stay. Look in the itinerary section to study the details of each hotel to make your selection. As you study the itinerary maps, note that there are stars locating hotels near the recommended overnight destinations. If you love staying in the countryside, look for stars representing hotels outside of the larger cities and consider "commuting" (you usually will find the price more of a bargain).

FAVORITE PLACES

As you read through our itineraries, you might become muddled as to choices. All of Spain is enchanting—filled with towns that brim with the romance of yesteryear. To assist you, we have described some of our favorite places. Many of these are so well known that they are probably already on your schedule to see, but others are gems that we were surprised to discover. The following list of "favorites" is very subjective— destinations that we think outstanding. Most of these are also featured in our individual itineraries. In the back of the guide (in the *Hotel Descriptions* section) you can find hotel accommodations in all of the following places:

ARCOS DE LA FRONTERA (Andalusia): Arcos de la Frontera is one of the many charming towns dotting the hills that rise from the Costa del Sol. Its setting is very special—the indisputably beautiful town is set on a rocky promontory with cliffs dropping down to the Guadalete river. The town has narrow, sloping streets lined by whitewashed houses, a magnificent cathedral, and several charming places to stay.

ÁVILA (Castilla y León): Ávila cannot help being on every list of special places. Located conveniently close to Madrid, the town is one of the best preserved in Spain. Try to approach from the west where you get the most impressive first impact of the town—you will be astounded by the perfection of the 12th-century crenelated walls punctuated by mighty stone towers surrounding the city. These medieval fortifications are without a doubt some of the finest remaining in Europe. Within the town are a maze of narrow streets and a splendid cathedral that must not be missed.

BARCELONA (Catalonia): Barcelona, the second largest city in Spain, is on the Mediterranean coast, not far from the French border. We have a complete chapter devoted to this delightful city (see *Barcelona Highlights* on pages 163–168).

CARMONA (Andalusia): Carmona is located just a short drive east of Seville and makes a delightful day's excursion, or overnight. The walled town crowns a small hill that rises out of the vast plains of the Guadalquivir. The main entrance is on the lower level through the old Moorish gates, leading to a maze of narrow streets which twist up the hill. Although there are several churches to peek into, the main attraction is the town itself. In its former glory, Carmona was obviously a town of great wealth—the streets are lined with 17th- and 18th-century palaces built by nobility.

CHINCHÓN (Madrid): Chinchón is just a tiny town, about an hour's drive south of Madrid. Being close to a major city makes Chinchón even more special—it's a surprise to find such a quaint, unspoiled town nearby. The fascinating feature of Chinchón is its Plaza Mayor, a real gem. The vast plaza is enclosed on all sides by picturesque three-storied, whitewashed houses with rustic red-tiled roofs. A double row of wooden balconies stretch out from the upper two stories, forming a perfect perch for watching the bullfights. Yes, bullfights: during the season, the plaza is completely sealed and transforms into a picturesque bullring.

CUENCA (Castilla-La Mancha): Cuenca is only about a two-hour drive southeast of Madrid, yet is not as well known as many of Spain's towns that, in our estimation, are not nearly as spectacular. If time allows, definitely include Cuenca—and plan to stay for several days because there is so much to see in the area: the dramatic castle at Belmonte, the Romanesque church in Arcas, the fanciful rock formations in *La Ciudad Encantada* (The Enchanted City), and the Roman amphitheater at Segóbriga. But Cuenca itself is the highlight. The town is perched high on the top of a rock formation that drops straight down to the River Huécar. Clinging impossibly to the cliffs are the *casas colgadas* (hanging houses) whose wooden balconies stretch out over open air. Narrow streets and steep stairways make walking an adventure. Spanning the deep gorge carved by the river, a narrow walking bridge connects the old town with the cathedral (now housing a parador) on the other side of the chasm.

GRANADA (Andalusia): Granada is instantly a favorite of all who visit. When you see the mountain setting, it is easy to understand why this was the last stronghold of the Moors. From its lofty perch, the Alhambra, a fairy tale of palaces built around courtyards filled with flowers, fruit trees, tranquil pools, and beautiful fountains, dominates the newer city. The interior walls are covered with tiny colorful tiles creating intricate patterns that are enhanced by slender columns, graceful arches, and fancy plasterwork. Obviously the Moors were great romantics—all the senses are rewarded from the fragrance of the gardens to the soothing melody of the fountains. As you meander through the enchanting inner courtyards, it is easy to imagine the women of the harem peeking out undetected from their hiding places behind the lacy plaster designs. You must not rush your time here.

GUADALUPE (Extremadura): Guadalupe was a marvelous surprise to us. We knew about its Franciscan monastery where pilgrims have come since the 14th century to worship the Black Virgin of Guadalupe, but we did not expect to find a town of such utter charm. Many of Spain's medieval towns are stunning in their central core, but modern civilization has crept right to their periphery. Not so with Guadalupe: the town exemplifies great architectural purity and there is nothing new to jar the senses.

Monastery of Guadalupe

HONDARRIBIA (Pays Basque): Hondarribia—on some maps named Fuenterrabía—is a picturesque coastal town in northern Spain almost on the border of France. Our preference always gravitates towards towns that are unspoiled and Hondarribia certainly fits the bill. Although close to traffic-congested San Sebastián, Hondarribia maintains the quiet ambiance of a small medieval town. It is located on a gentle hill overlooking a sparkling blue bay lined with modern holiday condominiums and dotted with colorful yachts. Yet within the walled town itself, time stops still. Starting at the lower gates, the streets lead up the hill, terminating in a large plaza with one side opening to a belvedere overlooking the bay. Another side of the plaza is faced by one of Spain's most special paradors, El Emperador, while the other two are lined by brilliantly colored houses with wooden balconies—quite unlike anything you expect to see in Spain.

Convento de San Marcos, León

LEÓN (Castilla y León): León—once the capital of Castilla y León—is a fascinating city dating back to the 10th century, just begging to be explored. Narrow streets spread like a maze in every direction, leading to quaint squares accented by colorful fountains. León's most outstanding sight is its gorgeous 13th-century Gothic-style cathedral with 125 splendid stained-glass windows that must not be missed. Another superb edifice is the *Antiguo Convento de San Marcos* (Monastery of St. Mark), one part of which unbelievably houses one of Spain's most spectacular paradors. If overnighting in León, you must stay here where you have the chance to step into living history.

MADRID (Madrid): Madrid needs no introduction. Spain's capital, located right in the center of the country, is usually the first stop for every tourist coming to Spain. Although a large city, it is a beautiful one, filled with parks and fountains and some of the finest museums in the world. Definitely not to be missed. We have a complete chapter devoted to this wonderful city (see *Madrid and More* on pages 145–156).

MÉRIDA (Extremadura): Mérida is a must if you have even the slightest interest in archaeology. The Roman ruins here are astounding and conveniently grouped together so you can wander from one to the other. Especially awesome is the theater built by Agrippa, the son-in-law of the Emperor Augustus. A semi-circle of tiered stone bleachers faces onto a huge stage backed by a two-storied gallery held up by slender columns interspersed with marble statues. Just across the street from the park where the ruins are located is a stunning museum—a modern edifice of admirable design with a massive arched brick ceiling pierced by skylights that set off to perfection the many Roman artifacts displayed within.

PEDRAZA DE LA SIERRA (Castilla y León): Pedraza de la Sierra became an instant favorite. We could not help pondering why it is not better known (and almost felt reluctant to share its enchantment and perhaps spoil its laid-back perfection). Obviously it is popular with Madridians who flock here on weekends to escape the heat of the city, dine in Pedraza's charming restaurants, and overnight in her pretty hotels. Weekends are busy, but if you go midweek, you will find a quiet, enchanting walled village built upon a small knoll with views out over the countryside in every direction. Walls encircle the lower part of the hill and a castle crowns the summit. The Plaza Mayor is a gem—almost like a stage setting with picturesque houses with wide balconies facing the square. The narrow side streets are lined with medieval houses, many with family crests above the stone doorways. Completely lacking are tacky tourist shops: instead you find pretty, small boutiques selling quality merchandise.

PICOS DE EUROPA (Asturias): Picos de Europa is a range of mountains just before you reach the coast going north from Madrid. What most people relate to when they think of Spain's mountains are the Pyrenees, but for sheer drama, in our estimation, they don't compare with the Picos de Europa. A national park has been set aside to protect these magnificent peaks and provide a paradise for those who want to enjoy nature at its finest. The jagged limestone mountains thrust straight up into the sky, a majestic spectacle reminiscent of the mighty Dolomites in Italy. Lush meadows enhanced by sparkling mountain streams complete the picture of perfection. This is a paradise for those who love hiking, mountain climbing, horseback riding, or fishing.

RONDA (Andalusia): Ronda is tucked high in the hills up a winding road from the Costa del Sol. A rich Arabic and Christian heritage has left its mark on the town that is filled with palatial houses. It was in Ronda that bullfighting first began, and even today bullfights are still held in the colorful bullring. However, it is the setting that makes Ronda stand out from many of the other white villages of Andalusia—the town is split by a deep gorge spanned by an incredibly high, 18th-century arched stone bridge.

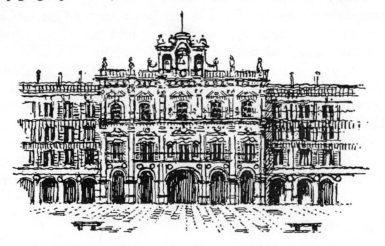

Plaza Mayor
Salamanca

Introduction–About Itineraries

SALAMANCA (Galicia): Salamanca is one of our favorite cities in all of Spain. If you are anywhere close, you must visit it and stay long enough to relish its many wonders. We had not expected to be so enraptured since a university town is not usually so special—but Salamanca is. The Tormes river flows below the city with roads leading up from the riverbanks to meet at the top of the hill in the Plaza Mayor. And what a plaza this is! The plaza is an architectural masterpiece built in the 18th century by Philip V and there is no prettier in all of Spain. It is enclosed by three-storied buildings built of a pastel ochre-colored stone whose ground levels are fronted by a series of identical arches that form a dazzling arcade all around the square. Although the highlight, the Plaza Mayor is not all that Salamanca has to offer. The beautiful old city is filled with buildings of merit, all within walking range. Start at the river and follow San Pablo up to the Plaza Mayor, then loop back down to the river by the Rua Mayor. Be sure to include the characterful buildings of the university, the *catedral nueva* (new cathedral), the *catedral viejo* (old cathedral), the *Casa de las Conchas* (House of Shells), and the *Convento de San Esteban* (St. Stephen's Monastery).

SANTIAGO DE COMPOSTELA (Galicia): Santiago de Compostela is a highlight of Spain and well worth a detour if you are anywhere in the northwestern part of the country. According to legend, Saint James's grave was found by simple shepherds guided to the site by a field of stars and his remains reside in a shrine in Santiago's magnificent cathedral. Since the 11th century the city has been the destination of millions of pilgrims who have made the perilous journey by foot across Europe to worship at the shrine. The first travel guide ever written was printed to help these pilgrims along their way and, to ease their journey, hospices sprang up along the route, several of which are now paradors featured in this book. Santiago's cathedral faces onto a stunning plaza, still bustling with pilgrims. Facing onto the same plaza is one of the original hospices, now housing one of Spain's most deluxe hotels, Los Reyes Católicos.

SANTILLANA DEL MAR (Cantabria): Santillana del Mar is a charming small town in the north of Spain. There is nothing of great tourist value to draw you here—no magnificent cathedrals or museums. Rather, it is the town itself that is the magnet. It is amazing that a town could remain so untouched—the whole town is like a living museum and as you wander along the charming streets, it is as if you have stepped back in time. There are no modern buildings, no hint of the 20th century. Stone mansions, many with the noble owner's crest above the door, line the narrow lanes. Just 2 kilometers away are the famous Altamira Caves with their incredible prehistoric drawings. These are almost impossible to visit for the average tourist, but in the vicinity there are many other similar caves open to the public.

Hotel Alfonso XIII, Seville

SEVILLE (Andalusia): Hands down, Seville is our favorite major city in Spain. It really has all the ingredients to make it special: a lovely setting, a manageable size for walking, a romantic old quarter, beautiful buildings, many parks, friendly people, good shopping, great restaurants, and excellent hotels. For more in-depth information on Seville, see our itinerary *Seville Highlights*, pages 157–162.

SIGÜENZA (Guadalajara): Sigüenza is a small village northeast of Madrid, tucked into the barren, rocky landscape. This picture-perfect town of pretty pastel-colored houses roofed with thick rustic tiles seems a world away from modern civilization, yet it is less than a two-hour drive from Madrid. As always, there is the Plaza Mayor in the center of town, and also a lovely 12th-century cathedral

Castle at Sigüenza

which is well worth a visit (be sure to see the exquisite statue of Martín Vázquez de Arce, squire to Isabella the Catholic). The houses in Sigüenza climb in tiers up the hillside to an imposing castle that has been converted into a dramatic parador.

SOS DEL REY CATÓLICO (Aragón): Sos del Rey Católico is one of the most charming towns in Aragón. This is an area of many desolate, windswept, rocky hills, often crowned by a ghost town piercing the sky. I don't know why so many of these walled towns were deserted, but a few have survived, including the delightful Sos del Rey Católico. The town is named for the Ferdinand the Catholic who was born here in 1452 and went on to unite Spain. Be sure to wear sturdy walking shoes for the town is built on a hill that is laced with cobbled streets and walkways that always seem to go straight up or down.

TOLEDO (Castilla-La Mancha): Toledo is justifiably popular: hardly any tourist visits Madrid without taking a side trip to Toledo. Most come for the day, but to enjoy the town to its fullest, try to spend the night so that you can settle in after the bus loads of tourists have left. The site itself is worth a journey—Toledo huddles on a plateau that rises steeply above the River Tagus which forms a steep ravine looping around the city. Within its mighty walls, Toledo is a virtual museum. Don't miss the spectacular Gothic cathedral with paintings by El Greco, Van Dyck, and Goya or the Church of Santo Tomé where El Greco's best work, the *Burial of Count Orgaz* is displayed. Also see the Alcázar, a huge 13th-century fortress converted by Charles V into a royal palace. Toledo is a treasure of monumental sights combined with intimate little squares and colorful winding alleys.

Bell Tower of San Martín, Trujillo

TRUJILLO (Extremadura): Trujillo is closely linked with the conquest of America since many of the explorers who ventured to the New World were born here. Most famous of these is Francisco Pizarro, the conqueror of Peru, whose impressive statue stands in the Plaza Mayor—there is an identical statue in Lima. The Plaza Mayor is especially interesting, with a distinct personality distinguishing it from those in many other towns. Its shape is irregular and the ground slopes so that the buildings border it on various levels. Be sure to take the trail up the hill to the 10th-century fortress which hovers above the town. Although the fortress is mostly in ruins, the vistas are lovely. While at the fortress, visit the tiny, sweetly simple chapel which is still in use.

Introduction–About Itineraries

About Hotels

There still exist in Spain numerous places where you may find yourselves the only English-speaking guests in the castle. Yes, *castle*! Private proprietors, as well as the government, have created some of the most romantic hotels in all of Europe in historical sites such as castles, palaces, convents, and monasteries—many found in locations boasting some of the most spectacular sights in all of Europe.

In the *Hotel Descriptions* section of this guide is a selection of hotels that we consider to be the most charming in Spain. A detailed description, an illustration, and pertinent information are provided on each one. Some are large and posh, offering every amenity and a price to match; others small and cozy (often with correspondingly smaller prices), providing only the important amenities such as private baths, personality, and gracious personnel. Our choices were not governed by room rate, but rather by romantic ambiance, location, and warmth of welcome. We have visited every hotel that appears in the book, and our selection covers a wide price range—tailored to fit every budget.

Sometimes we could not find an ideal hotel in an important sightseeing location where we felt it important to have a place to recommend. In such situations we have chosen for you what we consider to be the best place to stay in the area. We try to be consistently candid and honest in our appraisals. We feel that if you know what to expect, you won't be disappointed.

HOW TO FIND YOUR HOTEL

MAPS SHOWING HOTEL LOCATIONS: In the Maps section (the last section of this book) there is a key map of the whole of Spain plus seven regional maps showing each recommended hotel's position. In order to find which of our regional maps highlights the town where your hotel is located, the pertinent map number is shown on the *top line* of each hotel's description. To further ease the task of spotting the town, we divided the hotel location maps into a grid of four parts. The upper left segment is designated "a," the upper right segment "b," the lower left segment "c," and the lower right segment "d." As an example: Salamanca is located on Map 6 in the upper left segment of the map, so the *top line* of the hotel's description will read "Map: 6a."

SUGGESTED MAPS: As mentioned previously, our maps give you only a broad concept of where the hotels are located. You **must** buy detailed regional maps before leaving home. Because they are exceptionally accurate, have excellent indexes, and are readily available, we use Michelin maps as a cross reference. On the last line of each hotel's description, we also indicate the number of the Michelin map on which the town where your hotel is located can be found. If you can't find the maps you need, your local bookstore can order them for you. Please buy them! They will make planning your vacation so much easier and finding your hotels so much less stressful. Note: When you are looking in the map index for hotel locations, be aware that many towns in Spain have identical names. It is imperative to be sure that the town is in the proper province.

PARADORS

The Spanish government operates a system of hotels called *paradors* (literally "stopping places") which are widely acknowledged to constitute the most outstanding bargain in the country for quality received. The first paradors were created in 1928 in an effort to encourage tourists to those areas of Spain lacking adequate hotel facilities. Over the years, the number of paradors has grown tremendously as new ones have been added (periodically others are taken temporarily "off the market" while closed for renovation). A few of the paradors are situated in starkly modern buildings with no concession to an old-world theme; others are of new construction but built in a creative regional style. However, the great majority of paradors are imaginatively installed in remodeled historic buildings. Numerous paradors are simply stunning and in breathtaking locations such as the Parador San Francisco in Granada—imagine staying in a 15th-century convent literally **within** the Alhambra grounds, just steps from its fabulous palaces and gardens!

The paradors are not privately owned so do not expect the proprietor to be at the front desk to greet you warmly. The management is very professional and the quality of service dependable. The mood of each parador seems to reflect the talents of the individual in charge. The excellence of some of the paradors shows that there are indeed some extremely capable managers in the group—some of the best are women. Also, the amenities vary between the paradors: almost all that we visited had hair dryers, many had small refrigerators in the room, and some even had bathrobes and turn-down service

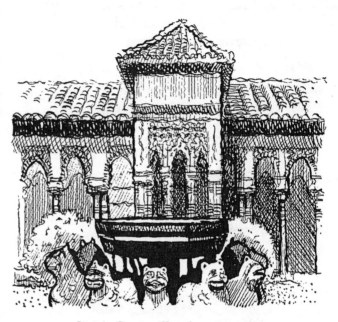

Lion's Court, Alhambra, Granada

While you could travel throughout Spain staying practically only in paradors, we also recommend a variety of other charming hotel accommodations. In the hotel section, we give in-depth descriptions of our favorite paradors, along with many other choices of exceptional places to stay. We have not included every parador in Spain in this book, although we have visited almost all of them. Sometimes we have rejected a parador because we have other hotels in the area that we think offer more charm. However, even though we have not featured them in our guide, you cannot go wrong staying at any of the paradors—for a complete list, contact one of the Spanish tourist offices in your area (see Tourist Offices of Spain on pages 21–22).

All paradors have good to excellent dining rooms serving regional culinary specialties from a set menu or *a la carte*. Local wines are also featured. They do not specialize in light fare, however, so be prepared to eat substantially. If you follow the Spanish tradition of taking your big meal at midday, paradors provide good stopping places en route. If you don't feel up to two large meals a day, at most paradors (and hotels) you can frequently purchase a sandwich or snack at the bar. The set menu for lunch or dinner usually features a three-course meal costing approximately 3,200–4,000 pesetas per person. Food-wise, another bonus is that all of the paradors serve a generous buffet breakfast with an attractively displayed assortment of meats, cheeses, breads, fruits, juices, yogurts, and even sometimes egg dishes. The cost for breakfast averages about 1,300 pesetas per person, similar in price to what other hotels charge.

Another advantage in staying at a parador is that there are almost always signs that lead you from the edge of the town (sometimes even from the freeway) to the parador. This may sound like a minor advantage, but it can save time and frustration.

Since the first edition of our guide, there have been astounding changes. Not only are stunning new paradors being opened (such as the sensational Parador de Ronda), but the "old timers" are radically improving. Although we love them dearly, we must admit that the decor in many of the paradors that have been around for a long time is, to put it kindly, a bit bland, with a great sameness to the furnishings. But, happily, all that is rapidly changing. Previously, the paradors had to take the furniture sent to them by upper management but a new policy allows the use of private enterprise, and what a difference it is making! As each parador takes its turn for renovation, the most talented interior designers in the country are being hired to plan the decor. The recently refurbished properties are emerging as real beauties—rivaling the finest private hotels in Spain.

Also, since the first edition of our guide the quality of the paradors' brochures has been constantly improving. Although it will be a gradual change as more brochures are printed, the latest goal is to have not only a photo of the hotel, but also a wealth of pertinent information: a map giving its location, city tours, excursions available, and cultural and natural places of interest to visit in the area.

In addition to being an overall good value, paradors offer some extremely appealing rates for travel off season. These special rates (which are not available at every parador) are most frequently offered mid-week and usually begin the first of November and last until the end of June. The exact dates and qualifications vary at each parador. Another terrific value (if you are over 60 years old) is the senior rates that give a whopping discount—35% discount for the first and second nights and 50% discount for the third night on. These senior rates are offered only off season, and at some hotels are valid only mid-week—the rules vary with each parador. So, if you are traveling off season (frequently the nicest time to travel anyway), be **sure** to ask if there are any discounts available. Important note: These special room rates are offered only when booked directly with the parador or with the Paradores de Turismo central reservation office in Madrid (see following paragraph).

PARADOR RESERVATIONS—PARADORES DE TURISMO: Although you can contact each parador individually, the response to your letter or fax is sometimes slow, and if you call, some of the paradors do not always have a person who is fluent in English available to answer the telephone. Therefore, it is more efficient to contact Paradores de Turismo's central reservation office (*central de reservas*) in Madrid where you can make reservations at any parador in the network without a booking fee. You can write, call, or fax for reservations. If you telephone, the travel consultants, who speak English, can often advise you immediately of availability, and will follow up with a written confirmation (office hours are 9:30 am to 1:30 pm and 3:30 to 5:30 pm, Monday through Thursday—on Fridays the office is open only from 9:30 am to 1:30 pm). A deposit can be made on your credit card to guarantee your arrival. For further information contact: Paradores de Turismo, Central de Reservas, C/Requena, 3, 28013 Madrid, Spain, tel: (1) 55.90.069, fax: (1) 55.93.233.

PARADOR RESERVATIONS—MARKETING AHEAD: If you live in the United States reservations for all the paradors (plus many of the other hotels featured in this guide) can be booked with Marketing Ahead, the Paradores de Turismo's representative in New York. This is a most convenient way to make a reservation. You can call or fax to reserve any of the paradors and there is no surcharge or service fee. Reservations are confirmed within 48 hours and a $50 deposit (per hotel) is collected; then reservations are prepaid 30 days prior to departure from the USA. The prepayment is for the room, tax and breakfast. The rate in dollars is only guaranteed once the prepayment has been made. Vouchers showing proof of payment will be mailed to you. For further information contact Marketing Ahead, 433 Fifth Avenue, 6th Floor, New York, NY 10016, tel: (800) 223-1356, fax: (212) 686-0271.

RATES

Although prices in Spain are playing catch-up with much of the rest of Western Europe, especially in the most popular tourist destinations, there remain many delightful hotel possibilities, reasonable enough to allow you the pleasure of indulging yourself.

The rates hotels charge are regulated by the Spanish government, with inflation causing periodic upward adjustments in prices (usually at the beginning of the year). Most hotels have an intricate system of rates, which vary according to season, local special events, and additional features such as sitting rooms, balconies, and views. Prices quoted in this book reflect the range of rates for a double room for two people in the high season. We state whether the rate includes breakfast and the 7% IVA (tax). Suites are often available for an additional cost. May through June and September through October are lovely times to travel and frequently offer slightly lower rates than July and August, which are the two hottest months in most of Spain. If you can travel in early spring, late fall, or winter, you can often realize substantial savings. Many hotels also have rates for *media pensión* or *pensión completa* which mean breakfast and either one or two meals, respectively. These are often an excellent value and should be investigated where convenient. Children are welcome virtually everywhere in Spain, and frequently there are special rates for those under 14 years old.

Breakfast in all the paradors (and at many of the hotels) is a bountiful buffet where you can have all you want to eat. If you are in the habit of sleeping late, breakfast might appease your hunger until dinner—allowing you to skip lunch. However, if you are on a tight budget, you might consider skipping breakfast (which in the paradors is usually about Pts 1,300 per person) and instead stopping for a cup of coffee and a pastry at one of the bars along the way. This will be much less expensive. However, before you decline breakfast, be sure it can be broken down separately on your bill—in a few places it must be included.

RESERVATIONS

Whether or not to reserve ahead is not a question with a simple answer: it depends upon the flexibility in your timetable and your temperament. It also depends to a large extent on the season in which you are traveling. For example, during the peak season, all hotel space is at a premium and a super star (such as the Parador San Francisco in Granada) frequently mandates reservations six to eight months in advance. Other popular hotels with limited rooms are similarly booked, especially those located in towns of particular touristic interest. Prudent travelers make arrangements months in advance to secure desirable accommodations during a local festival. On the other hand, throughout much of the year, space can be obtained in most places with a day's notice, or less. For those who prefer the comfort of knowing where you are going to lay your head each night, following are various ways of making reservations:

FAX: If you have access to a fax, this is an efficient way to contact a hotel. Many of them now have fax machines, and if so, we give the fax number in the description of the hotel. The method of faxing is the same as telephoning—dial the international access code (011), followed by the country code for Spain (34), then the city code, followed by the local telephone number. When faxing from within Spain, you need to put a 9 in front of the city code. Be sure to specify your arrival and departure dates and what type of room(s) you want. And, of course, include your fax number for their response. In the back of the book on page 309 (immediately after the map section) there is a reservation request letter written in Spanish with an English translation. You can photocopy this to use for either your faxes or letters to Spain. When you receive a reply, send the deposit requested (if any) and ask for confirmation of receipt. Some hotels will take a credit card guarantee or offer to hold the room until a certain time of the day instead of a requiring a deposit. Note: When corresponding with Spain be sure to spell out the month since Europeans reverse the U.S. system—to them 7/8 means the 7th of August, not the 8th of July.

LETTER: If you start early, you can write to the hotels directly for your reservations. Because the mail to Spain tends to be slow, especially outside the large cities, you should allow six weeks for a reply. Although most hotels can find someone able to understand a letter in English, we have provided on page 309 (directly after the map section) a reservation request letter written in Spanish with an English translation. Following this format you can tailor a letter in Spanish to meet your requirements. The translation includes phrases that will enable you to request specific features, such as sea view, terrace, extra bed, etc. Check the hotel's description for recommendations in this regard before writing. See comments above under FAX about deposits and dates.

TELEPHONE: We provide all the telephone and fax numbers in the *Hotel Descriptions* section. A convenient method of making reservations is to call (although you might not always find someone at the other end of the phone who speaks English). The cost is minimal if you dial direct on a weekend (business days for hotels), and the advantage is great since you can have your answer immediately (though you should still request written confirmation) or, if space is not available, you can look right away for an alternative. Remember that Spain is six hours ahead of New York for most of the year so time your call accordingly. Basically, the system from the United States is to dial the international access code (011), followed by the country code for Spain (34), then the city code, followed by the local telephone number. Note: When dialing from within Spain, you need to put a 9 in front of the city code.

TRAVEL CONSULTANT: A travel agent can be of great assistance in giving you professional advice and handling all of the details of your holiday. Your travel agent can tie all your arrangements into a neat package, including hotel reservations, airline tickets, boat tickets, train reservations, and sightseeing tours. For your airline tickets there is usually no service fee (unless you are using mileage coupons or some kind of special promotional fare) but most travel agencies do charge for their other services. The best advice is to talk with your local consultant. Be frank about how much you want to spend and ask exactly what he or she can do for you and what the charges will be. If your travel consultant is not familiar with the places in this guide (some are so tiny that they appear in no other major reference source), lend him or her your book—it is written as a guide for travel agents as well as for individual travelers.

PAYMENT BY CREDIT CARDS

Most hotels and many restaurants in Spain accept plastic payment. All paradors accept all major cards. In the *Hotel Descriptions* secton we indicate which hotels accept cards with the following abbreviations: AX—American Express, MC—MasterCard, VS—Visa, or simply, all major. Some hotels accept a credit card to guarantee a reservation, but do not accept final payment by credit card.

RESPONSIBILITY

Our goal in this guide is to outline itineraries in regions that we consider of prime interest to our readers and to recommend hotels that we think are outstanding. All of the hotels featured have been visited and selected solely on their merits. Our judgments are made on charm, setting, cleanliness, and, above all, the warmth of welcome. However, sometimes hotels do not maintain their standards. If you find a hotel is not as we have indicated, please let us know, and accept our sincere apologies—we are sorry when hotels have changed and are no longer as we describe them. The rates given are those quoted to us by the hotel for the year of 1998. These rates are not guaranteed, but rather given as a guideline. **Be sure** to ask at the time of booking the exact price for the room, and what it includes (such as breakfast, tax, etc.). We are in no way affiliated with any of the hotels or hotel representatives mentioned in this book, and cannot be responsible for any reservations made nor money sent as deposits or prepayments.

Overview of Itineraries

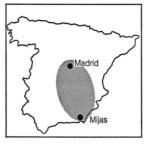

Moorish Memories

Pilgrimage to Santiago

Treasures Off the Beaten Track

Cradle of the Conquistadors

Old Castile and the Cantabrian Coast

The Costa Brava and Beyond

Andalusian Adventures

Madrid and More

Seville & Barcelona Highlights

45

Don Quixote and Sancho Panza

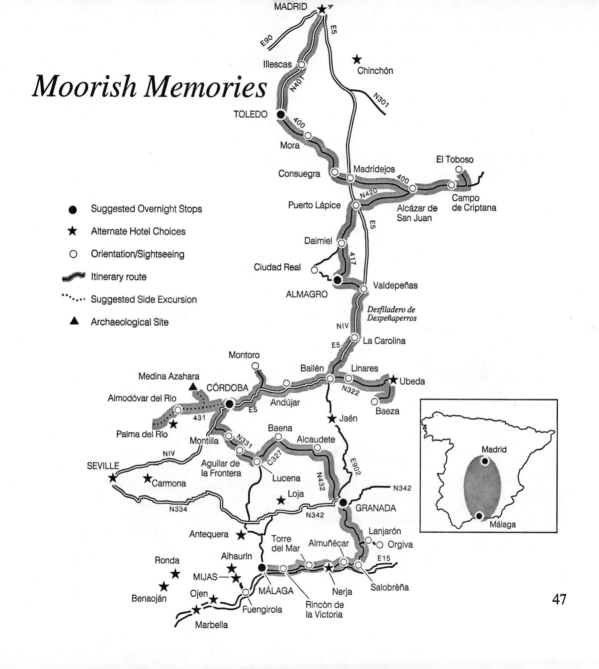

Moorish Memories

Suggested Overnight Stops

★ Alternate Hotel Choices

○ Orientation/Sightseeing

Itinerary route

····· Suggested Side Excursion

▲ Archaeological Site

MADRID

Illescas

Chinchón

TOLEDO

Mora

Consuegra

Madridejos

El Toboso

Campo de Criptana

Puerto Lápice

Alcázar de San Juan

Daimiel

Ciudad Real

Valdepeñas

ALMAGRO

Desfiladero de Despeñaperros

La Carolina

Montoro

Bailén

Linares

Ubeda

Medina Azahara

CÓRDOBA

Andújar

Baeza

Almodóvar del Río

Jaén

Palma del Río

Baena

Montilla

Alcaudete

SEVILLE

Aguilar de la Frontera

Lucena

Loja

GRANADA

Carmona

Lanjarón

Orgiva

Antequera

Torre del Mar

Almuñécar

Ronda

Alhaurín

MIJAS

Nerja

Salobreña

Benaoján

Ojen

MÁLAGA

Rincòn de la Victoria

Marbella

Fuengirola

Madrid

Málaga

47

Moorish Memories

The culture of contemporary Spain is a rich mixture of its prehistoric Celtic-Iberian, Roman, Visigothic, and Moorish heritage. When the last of the Moors (Moslems) were expelled from Granada in 1492, after almost 800 years of war known as the Reconquest, the modern nation of Spain was born. Each of the cultures left its mark; however, and nowhere is the variety of modern Spain more evident than in the area covered by this itinerary: from cosmopolitan Madrid to the glamorous Costa del Sol, playground of the jet set. You visit historic Toledo, capital of Visigothic Spain from the 6th to the 8th centuries and of Christian Spain from 1085 to the mid-16th century. Chosen home of the renowned painter, El Greco, Toledo is perhaps the most Spanish of all Spanish towns and a veritable open-air museum of history

Windmills in Don Quixote Country

Moorish Memories

Next you traverse the plains and pass the windmills of La Mancha, wandering ground of Don Quixote, to Córdoba—capital of Moorish Spain and, in the 10th century, second in wealth and luxury only to Baghdad. Córdoba still recalls the glory of the Moslem empire on the peninsula. Next you visit the Moors' last stronghold, Granada, where the most spectacular architectural monument of that culture, the Alhambra, towers majestically over the city. This itinerary ends on the sunny beaches of the Costa del Sol (Coast of the Sun), where European royalty and Hollywood stars moor their yachts.

Your route passes many kilometers of olive groves and vineyards and winds through small towns spilling down mountainsides under the remains of ancient castles. Be sure to sample the regional wines (Valdepeñas), the delicious cold gazpacho soup (there is nothing so refreshing on a hot day), and the varied seafood specialties.

ORIGINATING CITY   MADRID

Whether before or after your stay in Spain's capital city, a journey to her southern cities, steeped in Moorish heritage and graced with Mudéjar mementos, should not be missed. So, when you are ready to leave the hustle and bustle of Madrid, head south to follow in the footsteps of Don Quixote and the warriors who reclaimed Spain for the Christians.

DESTINATION I   TOLEDO

Take N401 south from Madrid to **Toledo**, passing through the medieval town of **Illescas**. Fortified Toledo is lovely to come upon, and you may wish to take a turn around the walled city (bear right just before entering the Bisagra gate) when you first arrive. When you witness the incredible views of the city from the hillside across the River Tagus, you understand what inspired El Greco's famous painting, *View of Toledo* (now in the Prado).

Puente de San Martin, Toledo

There is a modern parador on a hill outside town with a stunning view of Toledo from across the river. But our preference is to be right in the heart of the city where our favorite place to stay, the **Hostal del Cardenal**, former summer residence of Cardinal Lorenzana (Archbishop of Toledo in the 18th century), is built into the walls themselves. It is easy to find as it is located just 91 meters from the Puerta de Bisagra, one of Toledo's main medieval gates. Besides the romance of its historical setting, the convenience of its location, and lovely accommodations, the Hostal del Cardenal also boasts one of the finest restaurants in town, so you will definitely want to enjoy a leisurely *al fresco comida* on the garden patio (roast pig and lamb are the specialties) after exploring the town.

Be prepared for wall to wall tourists as you tour the abundance of sights in Toledo. When the capital was moved to Madrid in the 16th century, Toledo remained the center of the Catholic hierarchy in Spain and the cathedral (13th to 15th centuries) reminds you

Moorish Memories

of the great cathedrals of France, but is even more richly adorned. In **Santo Tomé** church you can view El Greco's famous *Burial of the Count of Orgaz* in its original setting (the sixth figure from the left is said to be a self-portrait of the artist) and the **El Greco House and Museum,** which lends an idea of how he lived. Also noteworthy is the startling Mudéjar decoration of the **El Tránsito** and **Santa María la Blanca synagogues.** The **Santa Cruz Museum,** with its fine 16th- and 17th-century art, includes 22 works by El Greco. But above all, roaming the ancient, winding streets of the city, pausing for refreshment in a pretty town square (such as the Plaza de Zocodover), soaking up the essence of Spanish history, and sitting on the terrace of the parador bar to watch the city turn golden in the setting sun, are the highlights of Toledo's offerings.

Toledo is loaded with souvenir shops and is famous for its swords and knives—you find both decorative and real ones in all shapes, sizes, and prices—and for its damascene-ware: gold, silver, and copper filigree inlaid in black steel.

DESTINATION II	ALMAGRO

Leave Toledo on C400. You are soon in **La Mancha** (from *manxa,* an Arabic word meaning parched earth), the land of Cervantes' Don Quixote, famous for its wine, cheese (*queso manchego*), windmills, saffron, olive trees, and ceramics. Above Consuegra, you pass the romantic sight of a ruined 12th-century castle surrounded by 13 windmills. (The best picture-taking spot is after you leave the town to the east.) Between here and Madridejos look for *alfares,* the pottery studios for which this area is known.

If you are a Cervantes (or a *Man of La Mancha*) fan, you should take the short side trip (about 50 fairly fast kilometers each way) east from Madridejos on C400 toward the wine-trade town of Alcázar de San Juan which you bypass continuing east to reach **Campo de Criptana** where, it is claimed, Don Quixote had his tryst with the windmills. A few kilometers farther east brings you to the **Criptana Hermitage** at the junction of N420 and TO104 and another splendid view of the countryside dotted with windmills.

About 15 kilometers northeast is **El Toboso**. Just southeast of the church in the center of town is a reproduction of the home of the peerless Dulcinea, reluctant recipient of the knight-errant's undying love. The house supposedly belonged to Ana Martínez whom Cervantes renamed Dulcinea (*dulce* = sweet + Ana). You will enjoy touring the house which contains 17th-century furniture and an intriguing antique olive-oil press on the patio in the back. Across the street from the church is a collection of over 300 editions of the novel in everything from Japanese to Gaelic. A number of interesting facsimiles and signed and illuminated editions are housed there, too. If you know some Spanish, you see that there are signs which are quotations from the novel all around town pointing the way to the church.

Return to **Alcázar de San Juan** and from there head for Puerto Lapice, where you can follow the signs to the delightful **Venta del Quijote**—a well-restored example of the type of inn where Don Quixote was dubbed knight. The Venta has a charming restaurant and bar, as well as some cute little shops. Continuing southwest, you pass through the fertile plains of the **Campo de Calatrava** on the way to Daimiel. Take C417 south to the lovely town of **Almagro**, once the main stronghold of the knights of the military Order of Calatrava who battled the Moors during the Reconquest.

Almagro's unique, oblong Plaza Mayor is surrounded by wooden houses, and the restored 16th-century **Corral de Comedias** (in the southeast corner) is where the plays of the Spanish Golden Age were performed. It is similar in style and epoch (as were the plays) to the Elizabethan theaters of Shakespeare's time. You will enjoy exploring the town's cobbled streets and alleyways with their marvelous whitewashed houses, sculptured doorways, and shops selling the renowned, locally tatted lace. A number of other historic buildings are in the process of restoration.

Our hotel recommendation is the graceful **Parador de Almagro**, installed in a 16th-century convent, whose Moorish arches, patios, and musical fountains will prepare you for tomorrow's entrance into the delights of Andalusia. The building is mostly new, but

Parador de Almagro, Almagro

the manager says he has trouble convincing people of that because of the incredible attention to detail in the re-creation of the original.

As a side trip from Almagro, visit the wine center of Valdepeñas, a short drive to the east. As you leave Almagro, you are likely to see women outside their homes bent over their work of lace-making. After a short drive through vine-laden flatland, you arrive in **Valdepeñas**, which has made a name for itself with its good light table wine. Wine-harvest festivals are held here in September. Valdepeñas has a charming central plaza, and the Victory Monument hill north of the town on NIV offers a splendid panorama of vine-covered plains. Another worthwhile side trip from Almagro is 21 kilometers southwest where, outside the town of **Calzada de Calatrava**, are the fascinating ruins of the 13th-century castle of **Calatrava la Nueva**.

When you are ready to leave Almagro, rejoin NIV and head south, climbing gradually into the pine-forested Sierra Morena until, at the **Despeñaperros Gorge** (*despeña perros* means throwing off of the dogs, i.e., Moors), you officially enter **Andalusia**. The Andalusians are fond of saying that this is where Europe ends and Africa begins. This is not a total exaggeration—Andalusia has a markedly different culture and a much stronger Moorish tradition than the rest of Spain.

You pass through La Carolina before coming to Bailen, where you head east on N322 through Linares to **Ubeda**. Recaptured from the Moors in 1234, it once served as an important base in the Reconquest campaign. The heart of all Spanish towns is the plaza, and Ubeda's striking oblong **Plaza Vázquez de Molina** was designed for lingering, lined with palaces and mansions with classic Renaissance façades, grills, and balconies and the beautiful El Salvador chapel. You can also spot the remains of old town walls and towers around town. Ubeda's elegant parador (on the plaza in a 16th-century palace) offers an imaginative lunch menu, if the time is appropriate.

From Ubeda it's a short drive to captivating **Baeza**, the seat of a bishop during the Visigothic period and a prominent border town between Andalusia and La Mancha during the Reconquest. Golden seignorial mansions testify to its importance as a Moorish capital before 1227, when it became the first Andalusian town to be reconquered. Make time to drop by the tourist office in the enchanting Plaza de los Leones, pick up a town map, and wander on foot from there to visit this open-air museum of architecture, from Romanesque through Renaissance.

Return to Bailen, then head west toward Córdoba. You pass **Andújar**, with a pretty little plaza dominated by an ochre-colored Gothic church and an arched Roman bridge across the Guadalquivir. You are in the major olive-producing region of Spain now, and drive by seemingly unending, symmetrical rows of olive trees (*olivos*). After passing Villa del Rio, on the left bank of the river is the fortified town of **Montoro** just off the main road to the north. This was an important stronghold during the Moorish period, and you may wish to take time to wander across the 14th-century bridge to the old town and explore its picturesque Andalusian streets. The remaining 55 kilometers to Córdoba passes through a sea of olive trees parted occasionally by cotton fields.

Córdoba was the most opulent of the Moorish cities in Spain and boasted a university to which scholars from all over Europe came to study in the 11th and 12th centuries, when it was the largest city in Europe. Most of the former opulence is gone, but the city preserves one of the architectural marvels of that period, the **Mosque** (*Mezquita*). A vast square of apparently endless red-and-white-striped arches, with a second level above the first to provide a feeling of openness, it is a fantastic example of Moslem construction. The only discordant note is the 16th-century cathedral carved out of the middle of it. Even though the Emperor Charles V had approved the idea, he is said to have lamented "the destruction of something unique to build something commonplace" when he saw the result.

Just northwest of the Mosque is the old **Jewish Quarter** (*Barrio de la Judería*), a virtual maze of twisting streets, modern and ancient shops, and colorful bars and cafés, often punctuated at night by the intricate rhythms of spontaneous flamenco dancing. Don't miss the **Street of Flowers** (Passage des Fleurs), a favorite of tourists because of its profusion of potted flowers dotting the dazzling whitewashed walls of the houses lining the narrow street. This area should not be entered by car. Even on foot, it is very easy to lose your sense of direction in the tiny streets as each one begins to look like the rest. This is especially true if you allow darkness to catch you—which you should let happen if possible, since the area takes on a very different, magical aspect when lit by its quaint lanterns.

Córdoba is such a popular destination that it sometimes seems that every person who comes to Spain stops here. Unfortunately there are numerous shops selling rather tacky souvenirs that have grown up to service this tourist trade. Nevertheless, the town has much character and the setting and old-world ambiance are noteworthy.

Our recommendation for lodging in Córdoba is the **Hotel Albucasis**. If you are looking for deluxe accommodations, this two-star hotel might not fit your needs, but it is one of our favorites because of its quiet central courtyard, friendly owner-management, spotlessly clean rooms, and super location in the heart of the Jewish Quarter. Although it is only a few short blocks from the Mosque, you will need a map to find your way since this fascinating section of Córdoba is a maze of twisting streets. Although the hotel has a parking garage available, it is almost impossible to drive to the hotel without help, so we suggest parking your car somewhere close to the Mosque, then finding the hotel on foot and asking for help.

Hotel Albucasis, Córdoba

If time permits, a side trip to **Medina Azahara** (watch for signs off C431 west of town) would prove interesting. In 936, Moorish King Abdu'r Rahman III began construction of an immense palace on three terraces (mosque, gardens, then the Alcázar at the top) of a hillside outside Córdoba, and named it after his favorite wife, Azahara. It took decades to complete the sophisticated project, and it was sacked and destroyed by Berbers shortly thereafter. But today, thanks to careful excavation and restoration, the delightful palace can be more than just imagined. Not far east on C431 is the tiny town of **Almodóvar del Rio**, above which floats one of the most stunning castles in the region.

Today head south out of town on NIV to follow the Wine Road (*Ruta del Vino*) on a journey to Granada at the foot of the Sierra Nevada. At Cuesta del Espino bear southeast through **Fernan Nuñez** and Montemayor—with 18th- and 14th-century castles, respectively—to **Montilla,** an ancient town perched on two hills. A short time later **Aguilar de la Frontera** appears, an old hilltop town, whose whitewashed, octagonal plaza of San José is particularly charming. Before turning northeast to **Cabra** you see **Monturque,** with fragments of its ancient town walls, and **Lucena,** a center of the Andalusian wine trade (in whose ruined Alcázar, Boabdil, last Moorish king in Spain, was once held prisoner). Near Cabra are the ruins of the **Castillo de los Condes** and **San Juan Bautista church,** one of the oldest in Andalusia.

Continue northeast on a beautifully scenic stretch of road to **Baena,** tiered gracefully on a hillside. In the upper, walled part of town are some wonderful Renaissance mansions. From here you can look forward to a lovely, if not speedy, drive through **Alcaudete,** dominated by a ruined castle, and **Alcala La Real,** overseen by the **Fort of La Mota,** before reaching **Granada.**

Granada fell to the Moors in 711. After Córdoba was recaptured by the Christians in the 13th century, Granada provided refuge for its Moslem residents under whom it flourished until, in 1492, the city was recaptured by Ferdinand and Isabella, marking the official end to almost eight centuries of Moorish presence in Spain.

All of our hotel recommendations are within walking distance of and share the park-like hill with the Alhambra—the only place to be. The **Parador San Francisco** is stunning, but securing a room is almost impossible unless you start planning far in advance. Also deluxe and with great Moorish ambiance is the **Alhambra Palace Hotel,** with its delicate arches, colorful mosaics, and magnificent city views. For a budget selection, the **Hotel America** has the prime location in town, just steps from the entrance to the citadel.

Alhambra Palace, Granada

If you are ready to jump right into sightseeing, the place to see in Granada (indeed, one of THE places to see in the world), the **Alhambra** with its **Generalife Gardens**, is within easy walking distance. Alhambra comes from the Arabic words for "Red Fort" and, though it is red, its somewhat plain exterior belies the richness and elegance of its interior. After your visit to this magical place, we are sure you will agree with the poet Francisco de Icaza who, after experiencing the Alhambra, then seeing a blind beggar, wrote: *Dale limosna mujer, que no hay en la vida nada como la pena de ser ciego en Granada*, meaning "Give him alms, woman, for there is no greater tragedy in life than to be blind in Granada." Look carefully to see a plaque with this inscription set into the Torre de la Vela on the palace grounds.

Moorish Memories

Most of the Moorish part (the **Alcázar**) dates from the 14th century, and the palace of the Emperor Charles V, one of the finest Renaissance structures in Spain, was designed and begun in the 16th century. It now houses a museum of pieces from the Alcázar and a fine-arts collection of religious painting and sculpture.

The magnificent tile-and-plaster geometric decoration is an expression of Moslem art at its zenith. The stunning patios and gardens with their perfectly symmetrical design will dazzle you as you stroll through the various halls and chambers. Equally appealing are the cool, green gardens of the Generalife, the summer palace. Countless fountains—now, as then, moved by gravity only—surrounded by sumptuous flower gardens, orange trees, and cypresses testify to a desert culture's appreciation of water.

Several spots on the north side of the grounds offer splendid views of the old Moorish quarter (the Albaicín) across the River Darro, as well as of the city of Granada. The same is true of the towers of the Alcazaba (fortress), which is the oldest part of the complex.

Try to schedule a nocturnal visit to the Alhambra grounds. Some nights it is totally illuminated and others only partially (ask at the hotel for the current schedule). Either way, the experience is unforgettable and dramatically different from a daytime visit. Also, inside the grounds are two good dining spots located in hotels: the Parador de San Francisco and the Hotel America.

But your visit to Granada should not end here. The **cathedral**, in the center of town, with its adjoining Royal Chapel (*Capilla Real*) was ordered built by the Catholic monarchs Ferdinand and Isabella for their final resting place and their tombs have been there since it was finished in 1521. Subsequently, their daughter, Juana the Mad, and her husband, Phillip the Fair, plus Juana's son, Prince Miguel, were buried here. Juana's other son was Emperor Charles V of the Holy Roman Empire and King of Spain in the 16th century.

The **Alcaicería** (the old silk market) around the cathedral is now a tourist area full of souvenir shops. At its west end is Granada's most attractive plaza, Bibarrambla. It is a marvelous place to sit with a cold Spanish beer—*una caña* (cahnya) is a glass and *un* *tanque* (tahnkay) is a mug—and watch the Granadinos (including the many gypsies who live nearby) go about their daily business. For the Granadinos, as for all Spaniards, this includes plaza-sitting, and for the gypsies includes begging from the plaza-sitters.

The old **Albaicín quarter** retains much of its former flavor. For an unbelievable view of the Alhambra and Generalife, try the terrace of the **Church of Saint Nicholas** in the Albaicín at sunset, and do not forget your camera. Though it is something of a walk, we do not recommend that you try to drive into the Albaicín's maze of tiny streets (although an experienced Granadino cabbie can manage it). Beyond the Albaicín to the east is the gypsy cave-dwelling area called **Sacromonte**, famous for its gypsy dancing and infamous as a tourist trap.

If time permits and you like mountain scenery, you should definitely take the 60-kilometer round trip to the peaks of the **Sierra Nevada** southeast of the city. An excellent road (at its highest levels, the highest in Europe) winds its way to the winter-sports area of Solynieve (sun and snow) in the shadow of the two highest mountains on the Iberian Peninsula, the **Cerro de Mulhacen** (3,480 meters) and the **Pico de Veleta** (3,428 meters). (There is a 37-kilometer road that ascends to the summit of Mulhacen and down the other side to Prado Llano, but it is open only in early fall.)

DESTINATION V   MÁLAGA

Leave Granada on N323, which runs south to the coast through the wild terrain of the **Alpujarras**—the mountains to which the Moors fled, and from which they launched their futile attempts to retake Granada. After about 15 kilometers, you pass over the **Puerto del Suspiro del Moro** (Pass of the Moor's Sigh) where, it is said, Boabdil, the last of Granada's Moorish kings, wept as he turned to take a last look at his beloved Granada upon his leave-taking. The contrast in scenery on the Motril road is breathtaking: green valleys, rows of olive and almond trees, and the towering, snow-capped peaks of the Sierra Nevada.

If you get an early start, this scenic detour is well worth the hour or so it adds to the journey: About 40 kilometers from Granada, turn left on C333 and continue to **Lanjarón**, a lovely small spa with mineral springs in a gorgeous mountain setting with a ruined castle perched on a shelf above it. The water is supposed to cure various ailments and is bottled and distributed nationally—if you order mineral water with your meals, you have probably tried it already. Continue on C333 to **Orgiva** at the edge of the Alpujarras. This is the area the Moors occupied for more than a century after Granada fell to the Catholic monarchs. In this picturesque little mountain village you find fine views of the Alpujarras, the Sierra Nevada, and the smaller Sierra de la Contraviesa to the south. Leave Orgiva on C333 toward the south and turn right after 3 kilometers on L451. Thirteen scenic kilometers later, you arrive back at N323 which you follow to the coastal highway N340.

Turn right and you soon have the pleasure of coming upon **Salobrèña**, a picturesque, white-walled village crowning a rocky promontory surrounded by a waving sea of green sugar cane. These *pueblos blancos* (white towns) are typical of the warmer areas of Andalusia and you see several as you drive along. Park at the edge of the town and stroll up to its partially restored Alcázar to enjoy the splendid view of the surrounding countryside and the Mediterranean.

As you head west from Salobreña, there are numerous lookout points with fabulous views of the sea and the beautiful coastline. The road winds along the coast through the small seaside resort of **Almuñécar**, with its ruined Castillo de San Miguel. A bit farther on, near the village of Maro, are the impressive **Nerja Caves** (*Cuevas de Nerja*), definitely worth a visit—vast stalactitic caves with prehistoric paintings and evidence of habitation since Paleolithic times. Its archaeological revelations (including parts of Cro-Magnon human skulls) can be seen at the small museum nearby. The caves are efficiently run and offer a cool break from driving. Continuing west, you reach the resort and fishing port of **Nerja**, known for the Balcón (balcony) de Europa, a terrace-promenade with wonderful views rising high above the sea near the center of the charming little town.

Before reaching the final destination, you pass through the seaside port of **Torre del Mar**, with its pretty lighthouse, and the village of **Rincon de La Victoria**, where another, smaller cave (Cueva del Tesoro) with prehistoric drawings can be visited in a park above town. Unlike the Nerja caves, this one was formed by underground water and presents a quite different impression. The area is popular with local Malagueños for weekend beach excursions. Follow the coast road and you arrive in **Málaga**, the birthplace of Pablo Picasso, the provincial capital and one of the oldest Mediterranean ports.

A prime place to stay in Málaga is the **Parador de Gibralfaro**, which reopened in the summer of 1995 after being closed for several years while it underwent a massive renovation that included adding more guestrooms and a complete face lift by Spain's top interior designers. It boasts excellent views of the city and the sea from its perch on top of the hill. Nearby are the ruins of the Moorish **Castillo de Gibralfaro** with beautiful gardens. There are numerous accommodation options along this strip of the Costa del Sol. The **Parador de Golf** (on the sea just west of Málaga) offers an excellent beach and golf facilities. Look in the hotel description section in the back of the guide and see what appeals to you in **Mijas**, **Alhaurín**, **Ronda**, **Ojen**, **Marbella**, and **Benaoján**—all are within easy driving distance and offer accommodation to suit any fancy.

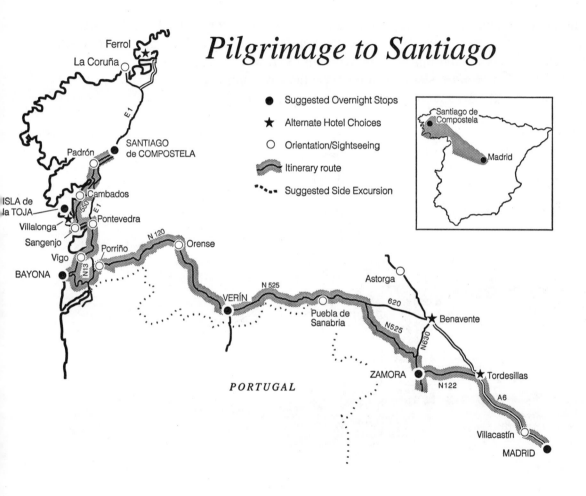

Pilgrimage to Santiago

● Suggested Overnight Stops
★ Alternate Hotel Choices
○ Orientation/Sightseeing
〜〜 Itinerary route
••••• Suggested Side Excursion

Ferrol
La Coruña
SANTIAGO de COMPOSTELA
Padrón
ISLA de la TOJA
Cambados
Villalonga
Pontevedra
Sangenjo
Porriño
Vigo
BAYONA
Orense
N 120
N 525
VERÍN
Puebla de Sanabria
Astorga
620
Benavente
N525
N630
ZAMORA
N122
Tordesillas
A6
Villacastín
MADRID
PORTUGAL
E 1
550
E 1
N13

Santiago de Compostela
Madrid

63

Pilgrimage to Santiago

This itinerary takes you to a hallowed spot that was once the most popular destination in Spain—Santiago de Compostela, site of the tomb of Saint James the Apostle and goal of countless religious pilgrims for a millennium. You will even be staying in one of the places they stayed in (modernized a bit since then, of course, and rather more expensive now). Most of the destinations described are in the region of Galicia: basically, that part of

Cathedral
Santiago de Compostela

Spain directly north of Portugal (the provinces of Lugo, Pontevedra, La Coruña, and Orense). It was at one time part of Portugal but, as a result of some royal intrigues, was separated from that kingdom in 1128. Although everyone speaks Spanish, Galicia has its own special language (somewhat of a mixture of Portuguese and Spanish). Because of this, you will notice some spelling variations in town names, depending on whether the Galician or the Castilian spelling is used. The area is separated from the rest of the country by several mountain ranges. Perhaps for that reason, Galicia seems to have kept its face turned to the sea and has developed a strong seafaring tradition and economy. It is also the region that has maintained the strongest Celtic influence since the Celts invaded the peninsula around 3,000 years ago. Galician folk music still has the sound of bagpipes—called here the *gaita*—and the name Galicia is from the same root as Gaul and Wales. Galician cuisine, like that of Portugal, puts a lot of emphasis on cod (*bacalao*) prepared in many ways. *Empanadas* (folded meat or fish pies) are a typical dish, as is *lacón con grelos*, consisting of smoked pork shoulder and turnip greens. Shellfish are also commonly available: be sure to try *vieira* (scallops), a regional specialty prepared in many delicious ways.

ORIGINATING CITY   MADRID

This itinerary begins in **Madrid**, a most convenient starting point, and a city worthy of a visit time and again. Be sure to spend a few days enjoying the many museums (the exhibits are constantly changing), taking advantage of fine dining, and, if the weather is pleasant, don't miss a stroll through the beautiful **Buen Retiro Park** before heading off to northwestern Spain. This part of the country is too often foregone by the visitor who views it as relatively inaccessible, and has time only for the more well-known tourist attractions. But this region has its share of the best sights in the country and a flavor all its own. Note: For more in-depth suggestions on sightseeing in and around Madrid, see our chapter titled *Madrid and More*, pages 145–156.

Leave Madrid heading northwest on the A6 freeway until it turns into NVI, on which you continue north toward the first destination. After a few kilometers you pass **Arevalo**, one of the oldest towns in Castile, in whose 14th-century castle Isabella spent her early years. She was born in nearby **Madrigal de Las Altas Torres** whose lovely Plaza de la Villa is typical of Spain, dominated by the Church of Saint Martin's two Mudéjar towers. The **Convent of Saint Francis** was founded by the saint himself in 1214. If church architecture is your interest, you should see the beautiful **Our Lady of the Lugareta Nunnery** 2 kilometers south of town. It constitutes one of the major Romanesque structures in Spain.

Next you come to **Medina del Campo,** historically a very important Castilian market town, but now not really worth a stop. However, the historic market town of **Tordesillas,** where you cross the Duero, one of Spain's major rivers, does make an interesting stop. Juana the Mad (Ferdinand and Isabella's daughter) locked herself away in the **Santa Clara Convent** here for 44 years after the death of her husband, Phillip the Fair, in 1506. The convent has a beautiful patio, and the nearby church has a fabulous artesonado ceiling which you should not miss. This is also the place where the Spanish and Portuguese signed a treaty in 1494 that divided the world between them. Setting a line some 1,620 kilometers west of the Cape Verde Islands, it resulted in Spain's ownership of all of America except Brazil.

From Tordesillas turn west through the small fortified town of **Toro**—picturesquely situated above the Duero and well known for its wines—then to **Zamora,** where we suggest you overnight at the **Parador "Condes de Alba y Aliste"** overlooking a pretty, untouristy, small plaza. The parador boasts fantastic tapestries, coats of arms, and suits of armor, and has one of the prettiest interior patios in Spain, overlooked by an arcaded stone gallery. The Parador "Condes de Alba y Aliste" makes a perfect base for exploring the narrow, picturesque streets of the old quarter of Zamora.

Parador "Condes de Alba y Aliste," Zamora

Zamora, which figured prominently in *El Cid*, has been a point of contention between various warring factions since the time of the Visigoths. Castile and Portugal battled for possession of the strategic town and it was occupied by first one and then the other in the heyday of the struggle. The fortified town seems to be wall-to-wall churches, but if you can see only one, visit the impressive 12th-century **cathedral**, whose tower dome, ringed by arched windows, should not be missed, and whose museum has a stunning collection of 15th- and 16th-century Flemish tapestries. The town, with its many beautifully preserved Romanesque monuments, is a great place for simply strolling and poking down narrow streets and alleyways. Its wealth of beautiful mansions and quaint little plazas add greatly to the charm and atmosphere.

When you are ready to continue the pilgrimage, head north out of Zamora, then bear left after a bit on N525, which takes you through the **Sierra de la Culebra** (snake) National Reserve. At **Mombuey** watch for the lovely 13th-century church—now a national monument. Several mountain ranges converge in the area you pass through, forming a gloriously scenic setting. Rustic stone houses with slate roofs and iron or wood balconies are characteristic of this region.

The landscape grows increasingly rugged as you near **Puebla de Sanabria**. If time allows, stop to see this fine example of a small Castilian hill town that dominates the countryside. Visit the plaza at the tiptop of town, ranking among the most remarkable we have seen. It perfectly preserves a medieval atmosphere, flanked by hunkering whitewashed houses, the old city hall with its wooden gallery, and a reddish 12th-century granite church. The plaza can be reached by car by crossing the river and bearing left, or, for the hardier among you, on foot from the east side. Either way you will love the atmosphere and panoramic views from the top.

We also highly recommend an especially scenic side trip, less than 20 kilometers, to the gorgeous mountain-lake area to the northwest of Puebla de Sanabria. The big, blue lake is over 915 meters above sea level and surrounded by craggy, green mountains and dotted with small towns. This is an ideal spot for a picnic outing—you can rent paddle boats (*patines*) if you are feeling adventurous, taking along one of the good local wines for company. **Ribadelago**, at the far end of the lake (bear left at the fork), is a new town built in the late '50s when floods destroyed the existing town. It has swimming areas and pretty views, combining to make a refreshing interlude. If you bear right at the fork, you will climb to the high mountain town of **San Martin de Castaneda**, whose wonderful 11th-century church overlooks cultivated hillsides dropping to the lake.

Our recommended destination for tonight is the **Parador Monterrey**, a convenient breaking point from Zamora to the coast. Drive through the rather drab city of **Verín** and, as you leave town, you spot on a hill to your right a castle and a small road marked with the parador sign. Weave up the hill and you find your night's lodging, not in the castle, but in the hotel constructed below it. Ask for a room (such as 107) with a romantic view of the castle.

DESTINATION III BAYONA

DEVIATION NOTE: If you are planning to head for Portugal, there are two ways to go about it. The first is to head south from Verín on C532 to the border crossing and to Chaves in Portugal. The other, more common route, is to follow this itinerary as far as Porriño and head south on N550 to the Spanish border town of Tuy. This brings you to the scenic coast of Portugal.

Continuing west from Verín, you pass over numerous viaducts with splendid views of the surrounding countryside. The earth changes from red to white before your eyes, and the hillsides are sprinkled with granite-colored towns. At the 915-meter pass of **Portillo de la Canda**, you officially enter Galicia, characterized by rocky landscape and its equally rocky buildings constructed from the native stone. Continue on toward Orense, passing between green hillsides dotted with red-roofed stone houses.

The provincial capital of **Orense**, famed for its sulfur springs, has an enchanting old quarter with twisting, stepped streets overhung by old houses, and delightfully punctuated with picturesque plazas. This was an important capital of the pre-Visigoth Suevi in the 6th and 7th centuries. An old bridge (near the newer one) across the Miño was constructed on the foundations of the Roman bridge in the 13th century. Take time out to stop here to see the Plaza Mayor and its Romanesque Bishop's palace. Park in one of the plazas and walk around the old quarter to visit the shops.

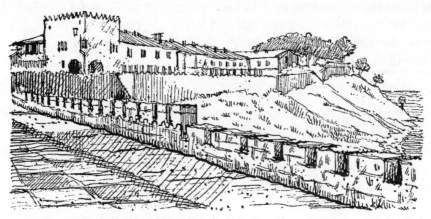
Parador Conde de Gondomar, Bayona

Continue in the direction of Vigo, passing through the beautiful **Miño Valley** (legend has it that gold existed here, thus the name of Orense from the Spanish *oro*, meaning gold). The highway borders landscape carpeted with vineyards and parallels the river Miño as far as Ventosela. When you reach the industrial city of Porriào, turn east on PO331 and continue through Gondomar and A Ramallosa. The road is narrow and winding, but the slow going gives you time to enjoy the incredibly lush forest, interspersed with some spectacular views over the valleys below. At A Ramallosa you turn left and, after a few kilometers, you come to a bridge (paralleling an ancient Roman bridge on your left) leading into **Bayona**, whose former inhabitants were the first to hear the news of the discovery of the New World when the *Pinta* put in here in 1493 (the *Santa María* sought refuge in Lisbon after a storm). Subsequently, it continued to be a major port for the many gold- and silver-laden ships that followed thereafter from America. Thoughts such as these will not seem at all out of place as you stroll on the perfectly preserved seaside battlements which encircle the **Parador Conde de Gondomar**, your suggested resting spot for tonight on this heavenly peninsula.

Since you are staying in the castle, which is the premier tourist attraction in town (non-guests of the parador pay for visiting privileges), you do not have to go far to explore the site or enjoy the little inlet beach at the foot of the drive. The castle ramparts are 3 kilometers in length and parts of them date from the 2nd century B.C. (other parts are as recent as the 17th century). The walk around them affords bird's-eye views of the

crashing sea, the picturesque fishing port, and the coastline stretching into the horizon. If you crave more, however, you can venture out to see Bayona's 12th-century collegiate church or drive the 30 kilometers down the coast to the Portuguese border. About halfway you pass the little fishing village of **Oya**. At the end of the road is the port of **La Guardia**.

DESTINATION IV ISLA DE LA TOJA

If time is at a premium, from Bayona follow the quickest route back to the freeway and drive north to the pearl of this itinerary, Santiago de Compostela, but, if you are in no hurry and would like to dawdle along the way, we suggest a stop at Isla de la Toja to give you yet another insight into this region of Spain. If this is your choice, drive from Bayona along the craggy coast to **Vigo**, situated on the **Ría de Vigo** (*ría* means inlet or estuary) and the most important fishing port in Spain. In the 15th and 16th centuries English buccaneers preyed upon Spanish galleons returning here from the rich Spanish colonies—Sir Francis Drake the most famous among them. You pass some nice beaches south of Vigo, notably **Alcabre, Samil**, and **Canido**. Though Vigo has become quite industrial, it has managed nonetheless to retain old-world charm. It surrounds Castro hill, topped with two castles (and a restaurant appropriately called El Castillo), from which there are extensive views of the city and the bay. Driving in the city is a challenge, particularly as you near the old quarter. Probably the best approach is to drive to the port area, park your car, and walk up into the old quarter. You find interesting shops and ancient houses in a maze of stone-paved streets in the Berbes fishermen's quarter, which has been declared a national historical monument.

If you are a seafood fan, you will be delighted with the dozens of colorful bars and cafés offering everything from full meals to *tapas* featuring the day's catch. Speaking of the day's catch, you will find it in unbelievable variety in the busy fish market (you can find it by the smell) between the Berbes area and the port.

From Vigo head north on the freeway to **Pontevedra**. Signs lead you through town (if you follow them carefully) and out again on the road to **Isla de la Toja** (*A Toxa* in Galician). You now take a scenic drive along the coast through small resort areas, the inevitable condominium complexes, and quaint fishing villages. There are many beaches along here, but they are a few hundred meters off the road. After you round the tip of the peninsula, you come upon the beautiful 6-kilometer-long **La Lanzada**, a gorgeous beach with pale sand and cool, clear water which you will find difficult to resist. And you need not forego this splendid beach for long, for your hotel is nearby. You soon cross a pretty stone bridge with tall stone lamp-posts which connects the idyllic, pine-covered little island of La Toja with the mainland. Here stay in the turn-of-the-century **Gran Hotel**. This large, old-fashioned hotel will satisfy just about your every whim—from gambling in the casino to dining in true splendor, your indoor time will be catered to in style. Outdoors, there is golf, a splendid pool, and tennis, or you can walk, drive, or ride a rented bike to La Lanzada, where you can enjoy exploring the immense expanse of sandy beach, or perhaps consider renting horses for a morning ride.

From Isla de la Toja, continue your pilgrimage on to Santiago de Compostela. Cross the bridge, turn left, and soon you come to **Cambados**, whose colorful little Plaza de Fefiñanes is lined with old stone mansions—a good spot to stretch your legs and take some pictures.

Farther on you join N550 (note the change in letter) and arrive in legendary **Padrón** where, tradition has it, the boat carrying Saint James's remains put in, and in whose parish church you can see the mooring stone upon which the saint's body was placed after the boat docked. The town was formerly called Ilia Flavia, but *padrón* is the word for commemorative stone, hence the name change.

Heading north from Padrón you soon arrive in **Santiago de Compostela**, one of Spain's most famous cities. Justifiably touted as one of the finest hotels on the continent, the **Hostal de Los Reyes Católicos** was built, at the order of Ferdinand and Isabella, as a hospice for the pilgrims who made the arduous journey to this sanctified spot. Today it lacks nothing to help the modern pilgrim thoroughly enjoy and fondly remember his stay here, surrounded by antiques and catered to in medieval splendor. Its location on the main plaza makes it a little difficult to reach by car: you come into the plaza from the north, on the east side of the hotel, and drive down a street with a barrier seemingly prohibiting your entry. Enter anyway (slowly), turn right, and you are in front of the hotel.

According to legend, Saint James (in Spanish, Santiago or Sant Yago) the Apostle came to Galicia and spent seven years preaching there. After he was beheaded in Jerusalem, his disciples brought his remains back to Spain by boat, mooring in Padrón and, after some difficulty, he was finally buried. Seven centuries later, in the year 813, mysterious stars appeared in the sky above his grave and led the Bishop Teodomiro to the spot. The traditional explanation for the name Compostela is that it comes from the Latin *Campus Stellae* or field of stars. The city that grew up around the area was named Santiago de Compostela, and Saint James became the patron saint of all Spain. From that time pilgrimages began, and continue—although not quite so massive as in those times—to the present day. Most pilgrims from Europe took the Way of Saint James through modern-day Vitoria, Burgos, and León. Another route, considered dangerous because of highwaymen, ran closer to the northern coast. As many as two million pilgrims per year made the exhausting journey in the Middle Ages.

The magnificent **Plaza de España** (also called the Plaza del Obradoiro) is bordered on the north by your hotel, on the east by the baroque cathedral, on the south by the Romanesque College of San Jerónimo, and on the west by the neoclassical city hall. The plaza is without a doubt one of the most majestic in Spain.

The **cathedral** dates from the 11th to 13th centuries and was built on the site of Saint James's tomb (and several earlier churches). An unusual feature of the building is the existence of plazas on all sides, which allow encompassing views—of the cathedral from the plazas and vice versa. There is a breathtaking panorama over the red-tiled Santiago rooftops from the upper floor of the cathedral. Be sure to take a stroll around the cathedral through the Plaza Inmaculada (north), the Plaza de la Quintana (east), and the beautiful Plaza de las Platerías (Silversmiths) on the south side. Probably the most impressive artistic element of the cathedral is the Pórtico de la Gloria, just inside the main entrance, where millions of pilgrims have touched the central pillar upon their arrival. A thousand years of loving touches have left the stone worn and smooth. You will discover your hand will fit naturally into a favorite spot on the pillar where millions have touched it before you.

There is often a line of devout pilgrims waiting to enter the cathedral. You will also notice a few modern-day pilgrims throughout Spain walking to Santiago along the Way of Saint James—following the same roads that have been trod by millions before them. As might be imagined, the journey used to be a treacherous one with bandits and various fiefdoms at war along the route. Pilgrims wore a hat adorned with three scallop shells and carried a tall staff. These symbols identified them as pilgrims on a religious journey and was supposed to guarantee them safe passage through dangerous lands. The pilgrims today usually carry a tall staff and frequently wear a badge of scallop shells.

Santiago has one of the most industrious *tunas* we have ever encountered. The tradition of the *tuna* dates from the Middle Ages when university students from a single college— such as the medical school—would form a musical group and frequent bars and

Los Reyes Católicos, Santiago de Compostela

restaurants singing for their supper. They are characterized by their black medieval costumes consisting of hose, bloomers, and capes (each colorful ribbon hanging from their cloaks supposedly comes from a female admirer). You find *tunas* in many of the larger cities of Spain, especially in the tourist areas. Today they are more often just strolling musicians who entertain in restaurants and plazas for contributions. The group in Santiago, however, has elaborated the tradition to the point where they not only sing in the plaza but afterwards go around individually, offering their own records and tapes for sale. You are not likely to escape being approached to buy a memento of the experience.

As for the rest of Santiago, most of it can be seen by walking straight out of your hotel, across the plaza, and (on Calle del Franco) into the streets to the south. While Spaniards seem to be able to navigate the streets in an automobile, we strongly recommend that you leave yours in the underground parking lot of the Reyes Católicos (for a fee per day) and hoof it around the old city. Marvelous old buildings, many small plazas, shops of all kinds, and numerous restaurants and cafés line the narrow streets, which should be explored at leisure for a taste of northern-Spanish atmosphere. If you continue about 400 meters down Calle del Franco, you come to the Paseo de la Herradura, where a calm time can be spent wandering on the wooded hill and enjoying the views back to the city.

SIDE TRIPS: If you need an excuse to extend your stay in the Hostal de los Reyes Católicos, there are some interesting side trips from Santiago.

If quaint fishing villages and gorgeous scenery appeal, get some bread, some smooth Galician San Simön cheese, and some slightly sparkling, white ribeiro wine and head west on C543 to **Noya**, turning north on C550 to explore the coastal road along the *rías*.

If more history of the Way of Saint James intrigues you, drive east on C547 to **Arzua**, then on to **Mellid**—both stops on the medieval pilgrims' route.

If large cities attract you, the major city in Galicia, **La Coruña**, is only an hour away via the A9 freeway. This was Generalísimo Franco's home town, and, understandably, became an important industrial center during his regime.

Treasures off the Beaten Track

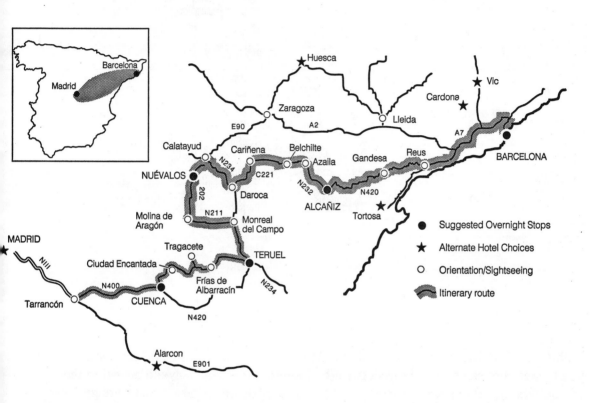

Madrid · Barcelona

Huesca

Vic

Cardona

Zaragoza

Lleida

E90

A2

A7

Calatayud

Cariñena

Belchilte

Reus

N234

Azaila

Gandesa

BARCELONA

NUÉVALOS

C221

202

N232

Daroca

N420

Molina de
Aragón

ALCAÑIZ

N211

Monreal
del Campo

Tortosa

MADRID

Tragacete

Ciudad Encantada

TERUEL

NIII

N400

Frías de
Albarracín

N234

Tarrancón

CUENCA

N420

Alarcon

E901

● Suggested Overnight Stops

★ Alternate Hotel Choices

○ Orientation/Sightseeing

〰 Itinerary route

Treasures off the Beaten Track

*Hanging Houses
Cuenca*

This itinerary starts off in New Castile, traverses Aragón and winds up in Barcelona, the sophisticated, seaside capital of Catalonia. Most of the route, as its name suggests, takes you to areas not so commonly frequented by foreign tourists, and should appeal to those of you who are anxious for a more intimate taste of Spain. It heads east through New Castile, which holds in store the beautifully rugged Cuenca Range and Cuenca, one of Spain's most enchanting medieval towns, famous for its "hanging houses." Then the route continues on to Aragón with its small, earth-colored, hidden villages nestled in gorgeous, scenic mountain valleys or in the midst of olive groves and vineyards. It is easy to understand why these are considered some of the most ancient settlements in the country: the medieval and Moorish past is evident at every turn.

Starting in the 11th century, Aragón began to expand its dominions. Within three centuries, it included parts of southern France, Catalonia, Navarre, and all of southeastern Spain, Sicily, and Naples. Thus, when Ferdinand II of Aragón married Isabella I of Castile (which included the eastern half of Spain) in 1464, the modern nation state was born. No longer so extensive, the old kingdom is now characterized mostly by agricultural activity. The final stop, Barcelona, provides considerable contrast: it is Spain's second largest city and one as glamorous and worldly as any in Europe.

ORIGINATING CITY MADRID

Almost all tourists fly into or out of Madrid when visiting Spain. After a few days enjoying this lovely city, many then drive on to Barcelona, another of Spain's jewels. It is possible to take a freeway most of the way from Madrid to Barcelona—possible but not very interesting. This itinerary outlines a much more engaging way to make the journey from Spain's largest to its second-largest city. By following this route you enjoy some fabulous sights that are truly "off the beaten track." Note: for more in-depth suggestions on sightseeing in and around Madrid, see our chapter titled *Madrid and More* on pages 145–156.

DESTINATION I CUENCA

Make your way to the southeast side of Madrid and head out of town on the A3 freeway (which becomes NIII when you leave the city). Continue through Arganda del Rey, then wind through lovely scenery to **Tarrancón**, a little country town with a Gothic church and a mansion built by Queen María Cristina. As you drive, you get a strong feel for one of Spain's major geographical features, the central meseta, or plateau. The drive east between here and Cuenca is one of the loveliest in Spain—through pretty rolling hills of wheat and sunflowers contrasting with pale, golden hay fields.

Posada de San José, Cuenca

Cuenca was originally constructed on the top of the cliff. This is the part known today as the old town, the area of most interest to the visitor. The best way to reach this district is to turn sharply right just after you cross the river as you head into town. The road climbs steeply and enters a small plaza through a massive stone gate. Park here and explore this engaging town by foot.

Ask directions to the hanging houses *(casas colgadas)*, seemingly perched in midair at the edge of the cliff. Inside one of these ancient structures, in impressive and tasteful surroundings, is Spain's most important **Museum of Abstract Art**. The extensive collection of Spanish masters is a must to visit. Also situated in one of the old, cliff-top houses is the restaurant **Meson Casas Colgadas**. If it is not mealtime, you still might want to stop for a cool drink and to savor the views over the ravine. Be sure to save some time for a leisurely walk through the picturesque streets and alleys of this old quarter, and to sit in the lively plaza to soak up the typical Spanish flavor of the town.

The Gothic **cathedral**, parts of which date from the 13th century, is a national monument: be sure to go in to see the elaborate interior. The treasury is also worth a visit—among other works of art, there are two paintings by El Greco.

We recommend two choices of accommodation: if you choose the **Posada de San José,** it is just a short walk from the plaza. As you face the cathedral, look for signs to your left marking the way to your hotel (if you don't see the signs, ask someone). The posada is easy to miss. As you tread the cobbled lane, look for a massive doorway on your right, adorned by a niche with a statue of San José—this is the entrance to the hotel. The Posada de San José is not a deluxe hotel, but ideally situated in the heart of Cuenca with the added advantage of breathtaking views across the gorge to the dramatic Convento de San Pablo, perched on the rocky cliffs opposite your hotel. In the evening, when the convent is softly illuminated, the vista is even more romantic. You can easily walk to the picturesque convent by taking the suspension bridge that links the two sides of the gorge. If you prefer a fancier hotel than the Posada do San José, our other highly recommended place to stay is actually in the **Convento de San Pablo,** which, following meticulous restoration, has become one of the latest historical buildings to be added to the chain of paradors.

Convento de San Pablo, Cuenca

When you are ready to leave, head north on CU921 through the Júcar river ravine (Hoz). Take the turnoff toward Valdecabras for a gorgeous drive through rugged mountain terrain to the **Ciudad Encantada** (Enchanted City). This eerie scene has been created by wind and water erosion which has separated large rock formations from their surrounding mass and carved them into shapes which resemble (with a bit of imagination) buildings, animals, and monsters. You buy your ticket from the booth and follow a well-marked footpath for about an hour through the interesting rock formations. The tour makes a cool and refreshing break from driving.

Continue on the same road, passing through Una and La Toba, at the end of a lovely turquoise reservoir surrounded by green pines. Follow the meandering Júcar river, then the signs to Teruel, climbing through the Puerto de El Cubillo Pass in the **Montes Universales**. This scenery is wonderful, with pine trees lining the narrow road and the sharp gray mountain crests in the distance.

By descending the other side of the pass, you come to a large monument on your left. This area is where the Tagus river begins its long journey to the Atlantic through Toledo and Lisbon in Portugal. It is amazing to see that this important river's origin is a tiny spring flowing out from under a pile of rocks. Continue winding amidst marvelous scenery with expansive views of the valley below until you arrive at the little town of Royuelo where you bear left and then turn right on TE903 for the 7-kilometer drive to the spectacularly situated little mountain town of **Albarracín**. Designated a historical monument by the national government, this whimsical town looks as if it were carved into the living rock below the ruined castle whose towers reach toward the sky.

Albarracín is a medieval gem with narrow, twisting, cobblestoned streets (almost exclusively pedestrian) and ancient brick, stone, and wooden houses whose roofs practically touch each other over the tiniest alleyways. The atmosphere cannot have changed much over the past several hundred years. The handsome **cathedral**, with its collection of 16th-century Brussels tapestries, is interesting to visit, and it is fun to explore the numerous ceramics shops selling their locally made wares. Since you are only a 30-minute drive from the next destination, you should have leisure time to explore this little Aragonese town: if time is short, do not fail to make the excursion from Teruel.

A short distance south of Albarracín are some **Paleolithic caves** with prehistoric paintings. You can get near only one of them by car and to visit the others requires considerable walking, a visit that might best be done as a side trip from Teruel, since it takes half a day. Follow the signs leading to the Pinturas Rupestres. (You see signs as you approach for Cueva del Navazo.) A little rock-climbing brings you to the shallow caves protected by an iron grating. Inside are paintings of hunters and bulls. The other caves are farther along the same increasingly impassable road, but we do not recommend you attempt to proceed by car.

A pretty easterly drive takes you to **Teruel**, surrounded by the gorges of the Río Turia. (Soon after leaving Albarracín, glance up to your left for the dramatic sight of ancient castle ruins crowning a rocky vantage point.) Our hotel recommendation, the **Parador de Teruel**, is located on the left just before you enter Teruel. The parador is restful and comfortable, providing the best accommodations available from which to base your explorations of this region, rich in history and archaeology, and of Teruel, rich in Mudéjar monuments.

Besides its remarkable natural setting, Teruel is noteworthy for the dominance of its Mudéjar architecture. Mudéjar is the style created by the Moors who continued to live in Christian-dominated areas even after they were reconquered. The Moors remained in Teruel a particularly long time, hence the prevalence of the style here. The five Mudéjar towers spread around town are truly of special interest: they are detached belfries with obviously Oriental ornamentation. Two of the delicate structures grace the entrance to the old town.

Parador de Teruel, Teruel

The 13th-century **cathedral** has an artesonado ceiling of intricately carved wood, with numerous other Mudéjar motifs in the sculptured plaster and in the domed ceilings. The tile decoration is of the same style. One of the five towers is the belfry for the cathedral.

Next to **Saint Peter's church** (which has another of the towers as a belfry) is the funerary chapel of the "**Lovers of Teruel.**" The legend of Isabel and Juan Diego, who lived in the 13th century and who died of grief at being unable to marry because of her father's disapproval, has inspired numerous famous literary works, the best-known by the 19th-century romantic dramatist Hartzenbusch (thus the name of the street). They were buried in a single grave and their remains are on display here in a glass coffin topped by a recent alabaster relief of the lovers reaching out to touch hands. To visit the chapel, ring at a nearby door (indicated by a sign) and someone will come down to open it for you. (Tip a couple of hundred pesetas.)

Just east is the triangular Plaza del Torico (baby bull), a popular gathering place with a tiny statue of, logically enough, a baby bull in the center.

When you are ready to move on, travel north on what must be one of Spain's best country roads towards the tidy farming center of **Monreal del Campo**, at the foot of the Sierra Menera, and bear left by the impressive, tiny fortified town of **Pozuel del Campo** with its crumbling walls and huge, imposing church. Continue to **Molina de Aragón**, an ancient, pre-Moorish village, once a hotly disputed strong point between warring Aragón and Castile. Perched above the town is a dramatic, red-tinged fortress surrounded by extensive crumbling walls and several restored towers, of which one, the 11th-century Torre de Aragón, is a national monument. This fortress was one of several, including Sigüenza and Alarcón, which served as a second line of Christian defense during the Reconquest.

Turn north in Monreal del Campo, first along a flat road through farmland, then on a more scenic drive through rugged countryside toward Nuévalos, a little south of which you encounter your hotel, the **Monasterio de Piedra**, just across the Piedra river. Remember the size of this river as you cross it because it will amaze you when you see what it does in the nature park ahead. Your first view of the monastery is of the lengthy, sturdy old walls around the grounds, which you follow to the entrance. The 12th-century Cistercian Monasterio de Piedra is situated, thanks to the River Piedra, in a green oasis surrounded by red, arid countryside. Your room is a former monk's cell, but a 12th-century monk would hardly recognize it. Most rooms have a sunny balcony with views of the wooded countryside.

Besides the hotel part of the monastery, there are other interesting remains attached to it and on the surrounding grounds. The 12th-century keep (Torre del Homenaje) is an excellent example of Romanesque-Byzantine-style construction. Off the beautiful cloister is a fascinating old kitchen and, next to it, the large monastery dining hall. On the other side of the cloister is the old church, which has not been restored.

Hotel Monasterio de Piedra, Nuévalos

The hotel is situated next to the **Monasterio de Piedra Park,** the lush park watered by the river which flows through the grounds in capricious ways, forming waterfalls and pools of great beauty. Be sure to visit the series of waterfalls La Caprichosa (the whimsical lady) and the 52-meter Cola de Caballo (horse's tail)—you can see both from a vista point and from underneath in the Iris Grotto. In contrast to the rushing cascades, the lake properly carries the name of Mirror Lake, a truly spectacular natural sight. Buy a ticket at the entrance and follow the arrows for an unforgettable stroll.

While at the monastery, drive to the pretty little town of **Nuévalos**, sitting in a valley surrounded by the deep-red hills. Another worthwhile side trip for scenery lovers is to the spa of **Jaraba**, reached by going south to the tiny village of Campillo de Aragón and turning right on Z452. You have a 12-kilometer drive through a red, green, and gold

Treasures off the Beaten Track

patchwork quilt of fields as you go over the Campillo Pass, then you descend into steep canyons lined with dark-red cliffs. This is a dramatic excursion.

DESTINATION IV   ALCAÑIZ

Leave this gorgeous setting by heading northeast to Calatayud. Today you drive through alternately dusty gray plateaus and deep-red earth planted with fruit trees, vines, and olives, along with occasional hay and wheat fields. **Calatayud** is built up against a hillside, crowned by the minaret of an old mosque and the ruins of the Moorish **Kalat-Ayub** (Castle of Ayub). You might want to stop for a closer inspection of the Mudéjar tower sitting impressively atop its rocky ridge above the hillside covered with tiny houses. You can see the castle on the mountain well before you reach the town, but it blends in so well with the stone ridge that you may not notice unless you are watching.

From here drive southeast, passing the dramatic ruins of a castle near the little village of Maluenda, then drive through **Velilla**, **Fuentes de Jiloca**, and **Montón**, all picturesque towns on hilltops overlooking the lush Jiloca river valley. As you leave Montón, notice that vines are beginning to replace fruit trees on the red landscape.

Turn right on N330 to reach the town of **Daroca**. This beautifully situated medieval town is still enclosed by crumbling 13th-century walls with 114 towers. Park near the first gate you come to and take time to stroll along the Calle Mayor and visit Saint Mary's church and the Plaza Mayor.

Back on N330, drive northeast over the winding **Puerto de Paniza Pass**. As you descend from the pass, you come to **Cariñena**, a little walled town famous for its wine.

Head east on the C221 driving through seemingly endless vineyards on the undulating, reddish-brown hills. A short drive brings you to **Fuendetodos**, the birthplace of Francisco de Goya y Lucientes, one of Spain's greatest artists. It is definitely worth a short stop to see the simple house where he lived. The house is furnished with 18th-century pieces in an effort to re-create the way it must have looked when Goya lived there. You can even see the room where he was born. Signs direct you to Goya's house and there is no admission charge, but a donation (perhaps 100 pesetas per person) is appropriate.

Continue east, through scrubby hills occasionally alternating with lush green vineyards, to **Belchite**, which was extensively destroyed during the Civil War (1936–39). The rebuilt town stands next to the ruins of the former one, a grim monument to the horror of that conflict. The old town soon appears on the right as you leave: an eerie moonscape of bombed-out buildings, houses, and church.

A short drive farther, after a stretch of fairly flat pasture land, lies Azaila, where you turn south on N232 to **Híjar**, another beautiful, small hilltop town overlooking the Martin river from behind its ruined walls. The terrain around the town changes to reflect the ravines carved by the river. From Híjar it is a short drive across flat farmland to **Alcañiz**.

As you enter town, you see the impressive cathedral ahead and, above on the right, dominating the town, your hotel, the **Parador de la Concordia**, itself a national historic monument. Part of the 12th-century castle was converted to a palace in the 18th century, and that part now houses the parador. Behind the palace remain some of the original castle buildings, dating from the 12th and 13th centuries. The tower, chapel, and cloister can also be visited.

Alcañiz is a delightful little town in the middle of an olive- and almond-growing region. The Plaza Mayor is flanked by the town hall with a Renaissance façade, the arcaded 15th-century Lonja (trade hall), and the highly elaborate baroque façade of the colossal Saint Mary's collegiate church. Due to its relative isolation, the town has maintained a serene, medieval atmosphere.

Parador de la Concordia, Alcañiz

DESTINATION V   BARCELONA

Head southeast on N420 and N232 and take N420 east towards Tarragona where the roads separate. As you leave Alcañiz, you see the olive trees slowly give way to vines on the rolling hillsides. About 8 kilometers past Calaceite, at Caseres, you officially enter Catalonia. Since Catalonians speak (in addition to Spanish) their own language, Catalan, you find a number of words spelled differently from the way you may be used to (e.g., river is *riu* instead of *río*).

Gandesa, rebuilt since it suffered severe destruction during the Civil War and thus a relatively modern town, is at the end of a pretty drive. After crossing one of Spain's most important rivers, the Ebro, at Mora de Ebro, you arrive at the new town, from where the best view of the old quarter, built right up to the river's edge on the opposite bank, is presented. Now the grape dominates completely as you enter the rich wine-growing valley around Falset. The vast vine-clad hills are dotted with tiny villages that seem to float above the vineyards on their little hillocks. Look back as you leave Falset, for there is an enchanting view of the town.

The highway follows a winding downward course through a number of passes to Reus, the birthplace of architect Antonio Gaudí and also known for its wool-weaving. The town is now mostly industrial and not particularly appealing to tourists. Just past Reus join the A7 freeway for a short drive into Barcelona. **Barcelona** has a rich selection of places to stay—look in the back of the book in the *Hotel Descriptions* section to see what suits your fancy. Note: For more in-depth suggestions on sightseeing in and around Barcelona, see our chapter titled *Barcelona Highlights* on pages 163–167.

Hotel Gran Vía, Barcelona

Treasures off the Beaten Track

Cradle of the Conquistadors

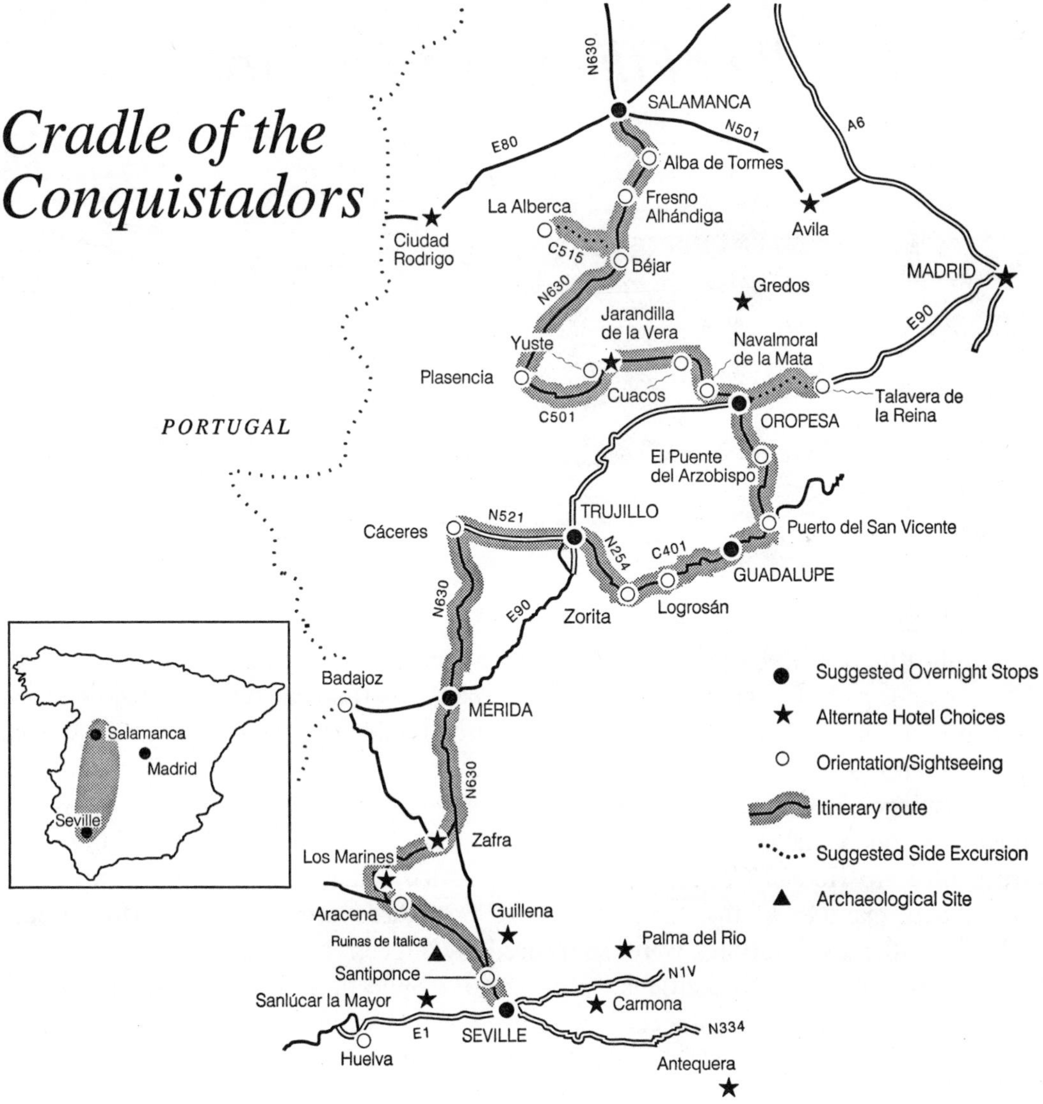

SALAMANCA
N630
E80
N501
A6
Alba de Tormes
Fresno
Alhándiga
La Alberca
Ciudad
Rodrigo
Avila
C515
Béjar
MADRID
N630
Gredos
E90
Jarandilla
de la Vera
Yuste
Navalmoral
de la Mata
Plasencia
Cuacos
Talavera de
la Reina
C501
OROPESA
PORTUGAL
El Puente
del Arzobispo
TRUJILLO
N521
Cáceres
Puerto del San Vicente
N254
C401
GUADALUPE
N630
E90
Zorita
Logrosán
Badajoz
MÉRIDA
N630
Zafra
Los Marines
Aracena
Guillena
Ruinas de Italica
Palma del Rio
Santiponce
N1V
Sanlúcar la Mayor
Carmona
SEVILLE
E1
N334
Huelva
Antequera
Salamanca
Madrid
Seville
Suggested Overnight Stops
Alternate Hotel Choices
Orientation/Sightseeing
Itinerary route
Suggested Side Excursion
Archaeological Site

Cradle of the Conquistadors

Guadalupe

Most of this itinerary finds you in Extremadura—an area of Spain less frequented by tourists, which is part of its appeal. The name *Extremadura* originated during the Reconquest period and translates as "land beyond the river Duero" (which runs across the country from Soria to Valladolid to Zamora). Historically somewhat at the periphery of national life, and less privileged economically, the area was rich in young men eager to seek their fortunes in the New World, as the name of this itinerary suggests. Some famous Extremadurans you may recognize are Hernán Cortés, conqueror of Mexico; Francisco Pizarro, conqueror of Peru; Orellano, explorer of the Amazon; and Balboa, discoverer of the Pacific Ocean. Indeed, since the explorations were sponsored by Queen Isabella of Castile, which included Extremadura, only Castilians were given the opportunity to make the journey to the New World during the 16th century. The area is still resplendent with fine old mansions built with the treasures found in Mexico and Peru.

Typical cuisine of Extremadura includes one of our favorite Spanish specialties: raw-cured ham (*jamón serrano*), as well as lamb stew (*caldereta de cordero*), fried breadcrumbs with bacon (*migas*), and numerous game dishes such as pheasant (*faisán*) and partridge (*perdiz*). The major local wine is a simple white called Almendralejo.

The last destination brings you into Old Castile and the enchanting medieval university city of Salamanca.

ORIGINATING CITY　　　SEVILLE

It is never easy to leave Seville, Spain's most romantic city, but, if you fall under its spell, you will be back. However, Spain offers many additional enchantments and much more of it remains to be seen, so set your sights north. Note: for more in-depth suggestions on sightseeing in Seville, see our chapter titled *Seville Highlights*, pages 157–162.

DESTINATION I　　　MÉRIDA

Leave Seville heading west across the bridge and turn north toward Mérida. After about 24 kilometers look for N433 which takes you northwest to the little hill town of Aracena, a popular escape from the heat of the Andalusian summer. The **Sierra de Aracena**, the western part of the Sierra Morena, is known for copper and pyrite production, as well as the justifiably famous and delicious *jamón serrano*, which must be sampled—especially if you are a prosciutto-lover. It is a ubiquitous and favorite *tapa* throughout the country, and you will have more than likely seen the hams hanging from the ceiling of many a Spanish bar. (Enjoy it while you are here, but do not try to take any home with you, as you will not be allowed through US customs with it.)

About halfway between Seville and Aracena is the dazzling white town of **Castillo de las Guardas** nestled against a green mountainside. As the drive approaches the pretty town of **Aracena**, the air gets cooler, the earth redder, and the hills are covered with cork trees. Aracena is tiered up a hillside, dramatically crowned with the 13th-century church of the Knights Templar and the 12th-century ruins of a Moorish fort with a beautiful brick mosque tower. Directly beneath the castle, within the hill itself, is the **Gruta de las Maravillas** (Cave of Marvels), hollowed out by underground rivers and an amazing sight to behold. Limpid pools and rivers and an underground lake reflect magnificent and multicolored stalactites and stalagmites. The guided visit takes about 45 minutes, but you may have to wait for a group to form for the tour: if so, wile away the time in the quaint shops around the entrance to the cave that offer a surprisingly good-quality selection of regional ceramic ware.

Continue west on N433 for 16 kilometers and turn right on N435 to **Zafra**. Zafra preserves one of the most impressive fortified palaces in the region, now the **Parador de Safra** (see the hotel listing), on one of the prettiest little plazas in the area. Actually the former palace of the Duke of Feria, it was the residence of Hernán Cortés just before he embarked for the New World. Its conversion to a parador has not spoiled it in the least, and it's worth a short visit to see the fabulous chapel and the other faithfully restored public rooms. Leave Zafra on N435 and you have quite a fast drive to today's destination—**Mérida**, caretaker of the richest Roman remains in Spain.

You find Roman antiquities among those decorating your next hotel suggestion, the **Parador Vía de La Plata**, elegantly installed in an old convent that was built on the site of a Roman temple at the top of town. It has also seen duty as a hospital for the plague victims of 1729, and briefly as a jail. The combination of authentic Roman, Arabic, and Spanish architectural features (most discovered on the site) within the hotel make it unique, indeed, and interesting to explore. The parador fronts onto a plaza where it is practically impossible to park, but you will gratefully discover that the hotel has provided parking in back, next to its pretty Mudéjar gardens, as well as an underground parking garage.

Parador Vía de La Plata, Mérida

Founded in 25 B.C., the Roman town of Emerita Augusta, now Mérida, was so well situated at the junction of major Roman roads that it was soon made the capital of Lusitania. Outstanding Roman remains dot the city: bridges, temples, a racecourse, two aqueducts, an arena, and a theater—all attesting to Mérida's historical importance under Roman occupation. If your time is limited, you must not miss the **Roman Arena** (built in the 1st century B.C. with a seating capacity of 14,000) and next to it, the **Roman Theater** (built by Agrippa in the 1st century B.C. with a seating capacity of over 5,000). The astounding theater alone, with its double-columned stage, is worth a detour to Mérida. (If you are here in late June or early July, check at the hotel to see if the Classical Theater Festival is offering live performances.) Just across the road from the arena and theater is a stunning modern museum that you must not miss, **Museo Nacional de Arte Romano**. In this spectacular brick-vaulted, sky-lit building many Roman artifacts and panels of mosaics are displayed. Be sure to also see the **Casa Romana del**

Anfiteatro (1st century A.D. with mosaics and water pipes) and the **Alcazaba** at the city end of the Roman bridge (built by the Moors in the 9th century). If your time and archaeological knowledge are limited, you might want to arrange for a guide who can take you to all the interesting places more efficiently than you can do it on your own. Inquire at your hotel, the Teatro Romano, or the tourist office for information. A few blocks southeast of the parador, you find the **Plaza de España**, Mérida's main center of activity. It is a wonderful place to sit with a drink at one of the outdoor cafés and watch the world go by.

Mérida, Roman Theater

Cradle of the Conquistadors

Today's route includes a visit to one of the most fascinating cities of the region and ends up in another. Head north out of Mérida toward **Cáceres**. Shortly before reaching the golden city, keep your eyes open for some terrific castle ruins on your right. Soon after is Cáceres, the second largest city in Extremadura and a national monument.

Although surrounded by a congested, not-too-attractive, modern city, the totally walled-in section called **Old Cáceres** (Barrio Monumental) has abundant medieval atmosphere. Cáceres was hotly disputed during civil wars between Castile, León, and Extremadura, which explains its extraordinary fortifications. Incredibly well-preserved, the walls are mostly of Moorish construction, although they were built on and incorporated bits of previous Roman walls. Tradition has it that the most glorious of the military orders in Spain, the Knights of Saint James (Santiago) was founded here and for centuries Cáceres was renowned for the number of knights in residence. Many of the mansions were built in the 16th century with money brought back by the conquistadors from the American colonies.

A few hours wandering along the winding, stepped streets and visiting a museum or two richly reward the effort. You can park in the Plaza del General Mola (also known as the Plaza Mayor) where the main entrance gate sits. To the right of the largest of the dozen remaining wall towers (called the Bujaco tower), you enter through the Arco de la Estrella (Star Arch). The many handsome family mansions testify to the austere mood of the 15th and 16th centuries. None has much decoration save the family escutcheons that are mounted above the doors—silent testimony to the nobility of the residents.

As you walk along the narrow streets, which often lead into small, light-filled plazas, do not forget to look up at the church towers where you often see storks nesting precariously above the rooftops. The important thing, though, is to sample the ambiance of this truly medieval Spanish city.

When you are ready to move on, head east on N521 to the most famous cradle of conquistadors, **Trujillo**, a charming city, still pure in its medieval atmosphere which is uncontaminated by modern construction. Its most famous sons were the Pizarro brothers, ingenious and tumultuous conquerors of the Inca Empire in Peru in the middle of the 16th century. The quantities of gold and silver mined there and shipped home in just 50 years created chaos in the economy of all of Europe.

Parador de Trujillo, Trujillo

Our hotel suggestion is the **Parador de Trujillo**, which is installed in the former Convent of Santa Clara. Opened in 1985, it occupies a building dating back 400 years. Its former residents were cloistered nuns who now occupy a smaller convent nearby. Because they sold sweets as a means of support, to the right of the entrance to the parador you see a *torno*, a sort of revolving shelf, which allowed them to send the product out and bring the money in while obviating visual contact with the customer.

Trujillo also boasts a number of splendid mansions constructed with the booty of the travelers to the Americas. Most of the old quarter centers around the spectacularly beautiful Plaza Mayor where there is a large statue of **Pizarro**. The irregular shape and different levels of the plaza make it one of the most charming and appealing in the country. On the plaza, among the many monumental buildings, is the **Palace of Hernando Pizarro**. The mansions here were built a bit later than those of Cáceres and thus are not quite so austere. The **Church of Santa María la Mayor**, a block off the plaza, contains a pantheon of several of Trujillo's illustrious sons. The winding, stone streets around the plaza impart an unusual degree of charm and tranquillity, inviting you to linger and wander around town.

Before leaving Trujillo, stroll up the hill to see the partially-in-ruins castle which towers over the town. There is a pretty little chapel, lovely views, and always a refreshing breeze.

DESTINATION III   GUADALUPE

From Trujillo take C524 south through beautiful countryside which in spring displays a carpet of green laced with flowers and dotted with cork trees. For accommodations along this route, the **Finca Santa Marta** makes an excellent choice (details are given in the hotel descriptions at the back of the book under Trujillo). Turn in left at the tidy little town of Zorita toward Logrosán, and soon begin to climb into the gray ridges of the Guadalupe mountains. A drive of 20 kilometers, through mountainous landscape changing from gray to green, takes you over Puerto Llano pass (unmarked) and exposes some fabulous panoramas of the fertile valleys below. Be on the lookout for the town of **Guadalupe**, because your first glimpse of the tiny white village will take your breath away. Crowned by a golden fortified monastery—which also happens to be one of our suggestions for where to spend the night—it nestles in the shadow of its ancient ramparts.

The Virgin Mary is supposed to have appeared to a humble cattle-herder in this vicinity in 1300 and to have indicated where he should dig to unearth her image. When the pastor arrived home, he discovered his son had died, so he immediately invoked the aid of the Virgin and the boy revived. He and his friends dug where she had indicated and discovered the famous black image in a cave. They then built a small sanctuary for her on the spot. In the 14th century, Alfonso XI had a Hieronymite monastery built there after his victory over the Moors at the Battle of Salado, which he attributed to the **Virgin of Guadalupe**. The monastery has been a popular pilgrimage destination ever since, and the Virgin of Guadalupe has come to be one of the most important religious figures in Spain and Spanish America. Columbus named one of the islands in the Caribbean (now French) after her because he had signed the agreement authorizing his expedition in Guadalupe. When he returned from his voyage with six American Indians, they were baptized here. A short time later, the Virgin appeared again to a Mexican peasant and she became the patron saint of Mexico.

In 1972, the resident Franciscan order officially established an hospedería (hotel) in the monastery's Gothic cloister (though the monastery has sheltered visiting pilgrims and religious dignitaries for ages). It is a hotel, the **Hospedería El Real Monasterio**, through which you actually need a guided tour. This remarkable hotel, filled with antiques of all kinds, is a marvelous lodging choice. Our other highly recommended accommodation in Guadalupe is the **Parador de Guadalupe**, which was built in the 14th century as a hospital and resting place to shelter the pilgrims coming to worship the Virgin of Guadalupe.

Parador de Guadalupe, Guadalupe

When you tour the monastery, be sure to see the Camarín, with the image of the Virgin and her 30,000-jewel headdress, the Moorish Cloister with its two stories of graceful arches, and the church with its Zurbarán paintings and many other objects of art. The positively charming main plaza in Guadalupe has an ancient stone fountain at its center and old mansions huddled around it. Take time to just sit and watch the world go by from this vantage point. As for shopping, this

Cradle of the Conquistadors

is an area known for ceramics, and Guadalupe is no exception. A local specialty is worked copper and brass.

El Real Monasterio, Guadalupe

DESTINATION IV   OROPESA

If you enjoy ceramics and embroidery, note that this region is the national font for their manufacture (it used to be that you knew where tiles had been made by the colors used), so you might want to do a little shopping along your route today. Even if not, you will enjoy seeing the locals working at their ancient crafts. Return to C401 and turn left toward Puerto de San Vicente pass (follow the signs to Talavera de La Reina). The rocky crests of the Sierra de Guadalupe become sharply pronounced on the approach to the pass. As you drive through the tiny villages beyond, you are likely to spot women sitting outside their homes embroidering (if it is summer). Bear left to **La Estrella** and **El Puente**

del Arzobispo, a traditional ceramics center with many shops. The graceful old hump-backed bridge that takes you across the River Tagus (Tajo) dates from the 14th century. You see a beautiful hermitage on your right as you leave town. From here it is a quick hop to **Oropesa** and your marvelous hotel, the Parador de Oropesa Toledo.

Parador de Oropesa, Oropesa

Installed in a 15th-century castle-palace, the **Parador de Oropesa** was the birthplace of **Don Francisco de Toledo**, one of the early Viceroys of Peru. In addition, the management proudly boasts a dining room that is a cut above the normally fine parador standard. They host a Spanish cooking school here for culinary afficionados and have a small classroom next to the kitchen.

The quiet village, spilling down the hillside below the castle, is noted for its embroidery, and has retained a captivating medieval flavor and numbers of handsome noble homes. You find many opportunities to buy local products both here and in nearby Lagartera. You are treated to some panoramic views of the valley of the Tagus and the Gredos mountain range.

Just east of Oropesa is the ancient ceramics center of **Talavera de la Reina,** where there are many ceramic shops and factories. If you are still scouting for ceramics, your needs are sure to be satisfied here. The best shops are near the west end of town on the road from Oropesa. (Talavera was traditionally known for its blue tile, while Puente del Arzobispo was recognized by its green tile, but this distinction is no longer strictly observed.) Another interesting stop is the **Santa María del Prado** sanctuary at the other end of town. Situated in a park, the sanctuary, park benches, and fountains are all decorated with ceramic tiles, some from the 17th century.

DESTINATION V   SALAMANCA

When you are ready to depart from Oropesa, go west NV E90 to Navalmoral de la Mata, where you turn north on CC 904 for a pretty drive through rich green tobacco fields dotted with drying sheds to **Jarandilla de la Vera**, overlooking the Vera plain. You might stop for lunch in the 15th-century castle that houses the **Parador Carlos V** and, upon closer inspection, you will discover it to be complete with towers and drawbridge. It was once owned by the Count of Oropesa, and is where Emperor Charles V resided in 1556 while waiting for his apartments to be completed at the monastery of Yuste, just west of town on C501. **Yuste** is famous as the last retreat of Charles V. Mentally and physically burned out after more than three decades at the head of the world's greatest empire, this is where he died in 1558. You can visit his small palace and share the view he loved of the surrounding countryside. It is easy to imagine the serenity he must have found in this solitude near the end of his otherwise stormy life.

Go on to Plasencia from Yuste, turning north on N630. If you have time, we heartily recommend a detour to **La Alberca**, northwest on C515 beyond Bejar. This tiny, isolated town has preserved its historic charm to an unusual degree, and the sight of its picturesque stone houses overhung with timbered balconies richly rewards the effort.

Back on N630, bear right at Fresno Alhandiga onto SA120 to **Alba de Tormes**, dominated by the 16th-century Torre de la Armería, the only remnant of a former castle of the Dukes of Alba—among the greatest land barons of their time. This small town is one of the most popular pilgrimage destinations in Spain because Santa Teresa of Ávila, important church reformist and mystic, founded a convent and died here over 400 years ago. In the **Carmelite Convent** you can visit the cell where she died and view her relics in a coffer beneath the altar. Her small, ornate coffin is in a place of honor above the high altar. And before leaving town, you should peek into the beautiful Mudéjar-Romanesque **Church of Saint John** on the central plaza.

Cross the River Tormes and head northwest to **Salamanca,** a picture-perfect Castilian town so special in appearance and rich in history that it is now a national monument. We have two recommendations for places to stay. One is the small, elegant, family-owned **Hotel Rector,** conveniently located near the river within walking distance of all the major sights. This intimate, friendly hotel offers some of the finest accommodations in Spain.

Hotel Rector, Salamanca

Cradle of the Conquistadors

If your budget doesn't stretch to staying at the Hotel Rector, our other choice, the **Hotel Don Juan**, offers simple, attractive rooms and a superb location just off the Plaza Mayor.

After getting settled, put on your most comfortable shoes and walk to the **Plaza Mayor,** in our opinion the most exquisite plaza in all of Spain. Be sure to set time aside to linger in the very large golden, arcaded plaza with its symmetrical arches and many enticing outdoor cafés. One reason for its beauty is that it was built as a whole in the 18th century and is thus highly integrated in design.

Hotel Don Juan, Salamanca

Next pay a visit to the 12th-century **Saint Martin's Church**. Not far from here, down the Rua Mayor, you find the **Casa de las Conchas** (conch shells), a 15th-century mansion whose entire façade is covered with carved stone shells, with the motif repeated in the grillwork and elsewhere. At the next corner is the Plaza de Anaya, and beyond on the left are the **"New" Cathedral** (16th century), and the **"Old" Cathedral** (12th century). The former is Gothic, the latter Romanesque with an apparently Byzantine dome—quite unusual in Western Europe. Both are good examples of their periods and contain many worthy treasures.

Across from the Plaza de Anaya and the cathedrals is the back of the university. Go around to the opposite side to discover the **Patio de las Escuelas** (Patio of the Schools). Salamanca's major claim to fame is its **University**, the first in Spain, founded in 1218 by Alfonso IX de León. By 1254, when Alfonso X "the Wise" established the Law School,

Salamanca was declared one of the world's four great universities (along with Paris, Bologna, and Oxford). Columbus lectured here, as did San Juan de la Cruz and Antonio de Nebrija. Fray Luis de León, one of Spain's greatest lyric poets, was a faculty member here when he was imprisoned for heresy by the Spanish Inquisition. After five years in prison, he was released and returned to his classroom (which you can still visit). His first words back were *"Dicebamus hesterna die..."*:"As we were saying yesterday..." In the 20th century Miguel de Unamuno taught here and served as rector. Not to be missed is the patio itself with the statue of Fray Luis, and the entrance to the university, perhaps the premier example of Plateresque art in Spain. Finished in 1529, it serves as an elaborate façade for the basic Gothic edifice. If you look carefully, you can find a small frog carved into the doorway. A student pointed it out to us on our last visit, and neither she nor we have the slightest idea why it is there nor what the artist must have had in mind when he included this incongruous subject.

As you continue back down to the river, you see the **Puente Romano** with its 26 arches: the nearest half are actually from the 1st century, the others are later reconstructions. On the bridge you discover the stone bull which played a devilish part in the original picaresque novel *Lazarillo de Tormes*.

Cradle of the Conquistadors

Old Castile and the Cantabrian Coast

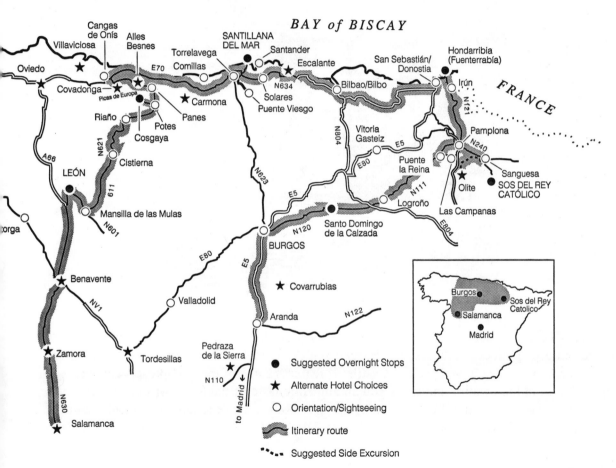

BAY of BISCAY

Oviedo
Villaviciosa
Cangas de Onís
Alles Besnes
Covadonga
Picos de Europa
Riaño
Potes
Cosgaya
Cistierna
LEÓN
Mansilla de las Mulas
orga
Benavente
Zamora
Tordesillas
Salamanca

Torrelavega
Comillas
Carmona
Panes

SANTILLANA DEL MAR
Santander
Escalante
Solares
Puente Viesgo

San Sebastián/ Donostia
Bilbao/Bilbo

Hondarribia (Fuenterrabía)
Irún

FRANCE

Vitoria Gasteiz
Puente la Reina
Logroño
Las Campanas

Pamplona
Sanguesa
SOS DEL REY CATÓLICO
Olite

Santo Domingo de la Calzada
BURGOS
Covarrubias
Valladolid
Aranda
Pedraza de la Sierra
to Madrid

● Suggested Overnight Stops

★ Alternate Hotel Choices

○ Orientation/Sightseeing

Itinerary route

Suggested Side Excursion

Burgos
Sos del Rey Catolico
Salamanca
Madrid

E70
N634
N804
N621
611
A66
N601
NV1
N630
E80
E5
N623
N120
N110
N122
E5
E80
N111
N240
N121
E5
Puente la Reina

107

Old Castile and the Cantabrian Coast

Sos del Rey Católico

This itinerary takes you through the north-central section of Spain. Beginning in Old Castile, it includes Asturias, the Basque region, then Navarre (originally Basque, but later "Romanized"), and back to Castile. It features some of the best-preserved medieval villages in the country and gives you an authentic taste of the Spain of the 11th through the 15th centuries, in addition to amazing you with some of the most spectacular natural landscape on the continent. This is an area filled with ancient cities, even more ancient caves, seaside resorts which are favorites of Spaniards on their summer vacations (because of the cooler climate), and, in the Basque region, Spain's premier cuisine. (The Costa Brava runs a close second.) Along the way, you will enjoy some of Europe's best hotels and some of Spain's finest scenery.

The coastal areas of Asturias and the Basque provinces were the only areas to escape Moorish occupation, and it was from there that the Reconquest (led by the legendary Pelayo) began in 718. The region similarly resisted Roman domination and thus retains the most remarkable prehistoric sites to be found in Spain. Castile traces its beginnings to the 9th century when the Christians built fortress-castles to establish and hold their frontier against the Moslems. Soon it was joined with the kingdom of León, and became the major power in the Reconquest, and ultimately in the creation of the modern nation. The Spanish language is still called *Castellano*, after Castile. Geographically, the itinerary includes the high central *meseta*, or large mesa, the spectacular Cantabrian mountain range, and the coast along the Cantabrian Sea.

ORIGINATING CITY   SALAMANCA

After allowing yourself ample time to sit in the Plaza Mayor and absorb the ambiance of the old university city of Salamanca, head north into the older part of Old Castile: the traditional Spain of castles and earth-colored towns in the vast meseta.

DESTINATION I   LEÓN

Leave Salamanca heading north to **Zamora**, on the bank of the Duero river. Visit the **cathedral** on the main plaza and take a peek inside the marvelous **Parador de Zamora** parador across the square. It is magnificently installed in the 15th-century palace of the Counts of Alba and Aliste, and the public rooms are decorated with beautiful tapestries, coats of arms, and suits of armor.

Continue north, following the signs for **León** as you bypass Benavente. This 70-kilometer drive is relatively uneventful, but the destination is worth the distance. Upon arriving in León, look for your hotel on the left just after crossing the Bernesga River.

Hostal San Marcos, León

The **Hostal San Marcos** is a pure delight—a luxury parador in a former 16th-century monastery with period furniture. This world-class hotel occupies a massive stone building with a fantastic Plateresque façade—itself one of the main tourist attractions in the city. As is often the case, you are staying in one of the major sights in town—the **Convento de San Marcos**, with its interesting archaeological museum and justifiably famous 11th-century ivory Carrizo crucifix. The adjoining church and, of course, the public rooms of the hotel itself are extremely impressive.

León, now a busy provincial capital, was the heart of the ancient kingdom of the same name and the center of Christian Spain in the early days of the Reconquest. As the Christians drove the Moors ever farther south, León was united with Castile and thereafter began to lose its power and importance.

León is a great pedestrian town so procure a map of the city from the hotel desk and head for the **Cathedral Santa María de la Regla**, one of the country's outstanding Gothic edifices, and an important stop on the Way of Saint James pilgrimage route. It features some of the most fabulous stained-glass windows in all of Europe (hope for a sunny day), which should not be missed. There are 125 windows of every period since the 13th century, said to total some 1,800 square meters of glass. If you are lucky enough to be there when the choir is practicing, you will have a thrilling experience. North of the cathedral are portions of the old city walls. South of it is the medieval quarter of the city and the small, colorful Plaza Mayor overhung by ancient buildings, mixed with new shops.

DESTINATION II COSGAYA

Upon departure from the Hostal San Marcos, take N601 in the direction of Valladolid. In the middle of the little town of Mansilla de las Mulas follow the sign pointing to the left to Villomar and the Picos de Europa and you find yourself on a flat, straight road paralleling the Esla river through numerous quaint little villages. The first glimpse of the sharp, gray **Picos de Europa** (European Peaks) into which you will soon be climbing appears and beckons as you leave the town of Cubillas de Rueda.

The Picos de Europa are indeed spectacular. They rise to almost 2,743 meters within 25 kilometers of the coast and provide stark, desert-like landscapes that contrast vividly with the humid lowland zone. Sheer cliffs broken only by huge slabs of jutting granite pierce the sky. The Torre de Cerredo is the highest peak at 2,648 meters. The entire range, rivaling the Dolomites in dramatic mountain splendor, occupies some 1,330 square

Picos de Europa

kilometers of northern Spain. This region is a haven for mountain climbing and has very controlled policies on hunting and fishing. Inquire in any of the numerous guide centers in the towns for information about these activities.

In Cistierna take the N621, following signs to Riaño, and start your ascent into one of the most scenic natural landscapes in Europe. From Riaño continue on the N621 for about 50 kilometers to Potes. At Potes turn left (west) and follow the Deva river as it winds its way through the valley to **Cosgaya**. Here you find the **Hotel del Oso**, a hotel that is not old, but brims with the charm and comfort of a meticulously run, small hotel. Settle here for a few days to savor the natural beauty of the magnificent region. On one day's excursion, continue west from Cosgaya to the end of the road and have lunch at the dramatic Parador Fuente Dé and take the cable car to the top of the mountain. Note: If

Hotel del Oso, Cosgaya

accommodation at Hotel del Oso is not available, study our other hotel suggestions on Map 2. There are several excellent choices of places to stay in this area.

HOTEL DEL OSO DESTINATION III   SANTILLANA DEL MAR

When you leave Cosgaya, return to Potes and continue north on N621 to Panes, then turn left and follow C6312 west in the direction of **Cangas de Onís**. This scenic drive follows the crystal-clear Cares river. Along this stretch of road are numerous picturesque mountain villages. No apartment blocks around here: the architecture is strictly local. Old stone houses with red-tile roofs and wooden balconies, usually hung with drying garlic, are the typical sight. About 23 kilometers after leaving Panes, you come to **Arenas de Cabrales**, noted for its blue cheese. Cabrales cheese is made in these mountains from a mixture of cow's, goat's, and ewe's milk. If you want to sample some, watch for the signs found all along here for *queso de Cabrales*. The cheese can also be found in other towns of the area. It has become so popular, however, that "counterfeit" cheese has begun to appear, causing its real manufacturers to put an official seal on the genuine article. You probably will not run into the false cheese here, since this is its place of origin.

In this region you will also notice many *horreos*, or grain-storage sheds, raised above the ground outside the farmhouses. These *horreos*, supported on pillars of rock, are especially colorful when viewed with the Picos de Europa in the background.

Leaving Arenas de Cabrales, continue west for about 26 kilometers until you see a road heading south marked to **Covadonga**. On the approach to the town is a breathtaking view on the right of the Romanesque-style **Basilica of Our Lady of the Battles**, built in the late 19th

Horreos (Grain storage sheds)

century. This tiny town is touristy but its setting is spectacular. Tourists also come to visit the **Santa Cueva,** a shrine tucked into a cave in the mountain, dedicated to the Virgin of Battles. It is the legendary place where Pelayo initiated the Reconquest of Spain from the Moslems in 718. The religious war raged on and off until 1492. Inside is the famous image of the **Virgin of Covadonga,** patron saint of Asturias, along with the sarcophagi of Pelayo and several of his relatives. In the treasury are the many gifts presented to the Virgin. Beneath the cave is a small pool, with a spring on one side, where you see visitors to the shrine collecting "holy" water.

If you are faint of heart, read no further. The area's main attraction is reached by a very steep, incredibly narrow, one-way road uphill from Covadonga. About 7 kilometers along is the **Mirador de la Reina** (overlook) with views of the **Sierra de Covalierda** and the sea. If you persevere about 5 kilometers farther, you come to **Lago Enol** and **Lago Ercina**, crystal-blue mountain lakes in a spellbinding setting in the **Montana de Covadonga** nature reserve. Though the road is tortuous, it is worth every twist and turn. You pass through green fields strewn with boulders before you reach the icy lakes. At a point called, logically enough, **Entre Dos Lagos** (Between Two Lakes), both lakes are visible from the top of a hill. This would make a fantastic spot to settle for an afternoon (or a whole day) for a picnic.

From Covadonga, return by the same road and join again the C6312 where you turn left to **Cangas de Onís**. As you cross the river, be sure to look to your left to see the picture-perfect 13th-century, humpbacked Roman bridge.

After Cangas de Onís you soon come to the N634 where you turn right in the direction of Santander. After Unquera you start to see signs announcing the availability of *corbatas*. While this word normally means neckties, in this case it refers to a small pastry folded to resemble a necktie, a specialty of this area. Sample them here or in Santillana del Mar.

A brief, scenic drive beyond Unquera brings you to **San Vicente de la Barquera**, a fishing village where the ocean appears for the first time. You are now on the beautiful Cantabrian coast of Spain. It is a picturesque spot with boats in the harbor and outdoor cafés along the waterfront—inviting if you need a break. At La Revilla turn left on the small road C6316 for the short hop through the green Cantabrian countryside to **Comillas**, a quaint old resort perched above the sea, which was the summer home of the Spanish royal court in the 19th century. It has a pretty beach and some handsome old homes. The large structure overlooking the sea is a seminary.

The road now turns slightly inland, through still more beautiful landscapes. As you drive through the village of **Orena**, you will be charmed by the little church and cemetery on the hillside overlooking the sea. Shortly afterward you reach enchanting and historic **Santillana del Mar,** with hunkering stone mansions bearing coats of arms, recalling the lifestyle of Spain's former nobility.

Parador Gil Blas, Santillana del Mar

Our first choice to stay is the 400-year-old **Parador Gil Blas**. It is ideally located in the heart of this perfectly preserved medieval jewel. If the parador is not available, we also recommend the **Hotel Altamira** (which is just around the corner from the Gil Blas) and the **Hotel Los Infantes** (which is on the edge of the old town). In Santillana del Mar the major attraction is atmosphere. It could fairly be called the most picturesque village in Spain and has retained its harmonious old-world feeling to an uncommon degree. The highly pure Romanesque architecture—from the Collegiate Church to the houses along Calle de las Lindas—will delight and amaze you. Just walk around and soak it in, not being too shy to glance discreetly into the ground-floor patios of the old houses, which occasionally shelter stables or shops. When you leave, you will know at least what it looked like to live in the Middle Ages.

Santillana is not on the ocean, but there is a large beach at **Suances** only 11 kilometers away, and it is only 30 kilometers farther to **Oyambe beach** at **Comillas.**

Another attraction of this area is its rich archaeological heritage. When we were there, a group of archaeologists were spending ten days based in Santillana to do nothing but visit regional caves. You can get a map (at the hotel) which shows where they are. It is true that the most famous one—the **Altamira Cave** with its 14,000-year-old paintings of bison and other animals—is practically closed. Its huge number of visitors were damaging the ancient paintings with the large quantities of carbon dioxide they exhaled in the caves every day. Currently, 20 people per day are allowed to visit (though the possibility of increasing the number is being considered), and most of those have either a professional interest or have written months in advance for the privilege. If you write at least six months in advance to the Director del Museo de Altamira, 39330 Santillana del Mar (Cantabria), you might be able to get on the list. If you do not have permission, check with the *conservador* at the museum in case there have been last-minute cancellations. But do not be too disappointed if not, for there are many more caves—just explore the possibilities.

One example is **Las Cuevas del Monte del Castillo** at Puente Viesgo. Head southeast from Santillana to Torrelavega, then east to Vargas, where you take the Burgos road to Puente Viesgo. Signs for the caves on the hill above the town can be seen. Discovered in 1903, the caves have drawings some 20,000 to 25,000 years old. There are actually three caves you can visit: the tour (in Spanish only) of the main one takes about 45 minutes; for all three plan on about four hours. They are closed during siesta time.

DESTINATION IV HONDARRIBIA

When you have finished sampling the unforgettable atmosphere of Santillana, head east toward **Santander,** a mostly modern provincial capital whose old city was destroyed in 1941 by a tornado and the resulting fires. The road turns south to skirt the bay and continues inland through cultivated farmland to Colindres, where you regain sight of the sea. Shortly afterward, you reach **Laredo,** a popular seaside resort with a beautiful, large beach on Santona Bay (with a much larger resort development in the town of **Santona** out on the peninsula). The road again moves away from the coast for a bit, through green rolling hills. You become aware of how close the Cantabrian range comes to the coast during this stretch.

As you continue east, you soon enter the **Basque Region** (*Vizcaya*), where you notice many of the town names indicated in both Basque and Spanish. Unlike the other languages in Spain, Basque is not a "Romance" or "Neo-Latin" language. Indeed, no one is sure where it comes from. Here you pick up the freeway towards **San Sebastián**, bypassing (thankfully) the industrial city of **Bilbao**. If you are interested and time permits, take the exit that goes north to **Guernica y Luno**, the town bombed by Germans during the Civil War (1937) and immortalized by Picasso in his painting *Guernica*. The town has been rebuilt since the bombing, but still serves as a symbol of the brutality of the Civil War, which killed over a million Spaniards when Germany and Russia used it as a testing ground in preparation for World War II.

After you clear San Sebastian (following the signs for Irun and Francia), watch for the exit for **Hondarribia** (called Fuenterrabía in Spanish) and the airport (*aeropuerto*). The road continues 7 kilometers farther before passing under the massive stone gate into Hondarribia.

We recommend several hotels in Hondarribia. Look in the *Hotel Descriptions* section for details of each. However, if you can secure a room, our first choice for accommodation is at one of Spain's finest paradors, **El Emperador**. Not only is this hotel ideally situated on the main plaza, but since its renovation, the interior decor rivals any of the finest hotels in Spain. There is also a spectacular terrace that captures a sweeping view of the harbor. The Parador El Emperador is a 10th-century castle that was considerably remodeled in the 16th century by the Holy Roman Emperor, Charles V. It has served as host (while a palace) to numerous monarchs in its long history. Reflecting the fact that Hondarribia was often coveted by the French because of its strategic position, the castle was constructed with stone walls, many meters thick. When you look out your window through these walls, you really get a feel for what it was like to live in a medieval castle. Note: There is no restaurant at the parador (breakfast is the only meal served), but catty-corner across the square in front of the hotel is a charming, inexpensive place to eat, the **Restaurant/Bar Antxina**.

The small, intimate plaza in front of the parador is unforgettable. Though you almost do not notice it, you are only a stone's throw from the ocean. Walk to the north end of the plaza which overlooks a very blue and very pretty little port filled with colorful sailboats. On other sides of the square are brilliantly painted mansions with iron or wood balconies draped with colorful flowers,

Parador El Emperador, Hondarribia

accentuating the stern façade of the parador. The most interesting and charming stroll from your hotel is down the Calle Mayor. The narrow, cobblestoned streets, often too small for anything but pedestrians, impart a feel for life in long-ago times. There is a country-town atmosphere to the many splendid mansions with their escutcheons in this most picturesque quarter. There are also numerous other small plazas with similarly enchanting buildings.

Your next destination is the birthplace of one of Spain's most famous monarchs, Ferdinand of Aragón. He was a model for Machiavelli in his classic study of governing in the days of monarchy. He was also the husband of Isabella and the two were known as the "Catholic Monarchs" (Los Reyes Católicos) because of their strong support of the Church during the time of the Protestant Reformation.

Head south from Hondarribia into the lush green valley of the River Bidasoa toward Pamplona. Along here the river forms the Spanish-French border until you cross the bridge at Enderlaza, where the river returns to Spain and you officially enter the region of **Navarre**. The beautiful, winding stretch of road takes you through the **Spanish Pyrenees** and numerous quaint little mountain villages with stone-trimmed red-roofed houses sitting in this heavily forested region. **Sumbilia, Santesteban,** and **Almandoz** are all charming towns situated in the midst of magnificent natural scenery. After Oronoz-Mugaire you wind your way up to the **Puerto de Velate Pass**, through some impressively rugged mountains, then down the **Valley of the Rio Ulzama** into **Pamplona**. Pamplona was the capital of the ancient kingdom of Navarre from the 10th to the 16th centuries, and now best known for the "running of the bulls" festival of San Fermín (July 6–20), made famous by Ernest Hemingway's depiction in *The Sun Also Rises,* published in Britain as *Fiesta.*

If you would rather make Pamplona an excursion from your hotel, you can follow the signs which lead you around the city and toward the south where you bear left on N240. Besides the views from the **Puerto de Loiti Pass**, watch for a lookout about 36 kilometers over the **Lumbier Defile**, a gorge cut by the Irati river through the **Sierra de Leyre**. The vast fertile valley can be seen spreading to the horizon in all directions. Bear right to Sanguesa and, just before reaching the town, you see to your right the ruins of **Rocaforte**, a mountain where the people of Sanguesa fled in the face of the Moorish invasion. They later came back and settled in the area where the town is now. Also on your right is a giant paper mill that is the origin of the smell that you cannot fail to have noticed by now, and which certainly discourages a long stay.

You next cross the Aragón river, enter Sanguesa and follow the signs past a 13th-century church toward **Sos del Rey Católico,** a few kilometers farther on through fields of sunflowers on rolling hills. Just before arriving, you cross the line between Navarre and Aragón. Since Sos is perched atop a hill in the middle of the large flat plain, you will see it long before you arrive. It seems as though it might blend into the brown mountain if it were not for the square tower that juts up above the town. As you get closer, you see that it spills down the hillside under the **Sada Palace** where Ferdinand the Catholic was born in 1452. The **Parador Fernando de Aragón** provides you with a fitting introduction to the town's medieval atmosphere.

Plan some time to walk around the picturesque little village, which is a national monument and has undergone much restoration. You can also tour the Sada Palace and see the very bedroom (or so it is claimed) where Ferdinand was born. There are splendid views of the fertile countryside from the castle and church at the top of the hill.

You might also want to make a short side trip to **Javier Castle** (return to Sanguesa and bear right). It is an 18th-century castle built on the site of the birthplace of Saint Francis Xavier (1506), one of the early members of the Jesuit order and a very effective missionary to Japan in the service of the Portuguese. If you happen to be there on a Saturday night in the summer, you can see a sound and light show.

Another worthwhile trip is to the town of **Olite** (head west from Sanguesa). Passing through beautiful agricultural land with greens and golds predominating, you also see a number of small, fortified villages clinging to the hillsides. Olite itself is known as the "Gothic city," and you see why as you approach it from the east. In the center of town is the 15th-century fortress of Charles III that now houses the **Parador Principe de Viana.**

Return to N240 via Sanguesa and bear left for about 19 kilometers. Watch for the signs indicating Campanas and turn left. At Campanas go south and turn right to Puente la Reina. You pass the **Ermita de Eunate Hermitage**, a Romanesque chapel where pilgrims on the Way of Saint James were ministered to and sheltered. It was in **Puente la Reina** that two major French pilgrim roads joined before continuing on to Santiago de Compostela. As you leave town notice on your right the ancient medieval stone bridge over the Arga river, worn smooth by millions of pilgrims' feet.

Continue west on N111, which was the Way of Saint James, to **Estella** where, in the Middle Ages, pilgrims stopped to venerate a statue of the Virgin reportedly found in 1085 by shepherds guided by falling stars. The Kings of Navarre chose this as their place of residence in the Middle Ages. Be sure to see the **Plaza San Martín** with, among many beautiful historic edifices, the 12th-century palace of the Kings of Navarre, one of the oldest non-religious buildings in Spain.

As you continue southwest toward the wine center of Logroño, you pass the 13th-century monastery (on your left) at Irache and, as you approach **Torres del Rio**, you have a splendid view of the late 12th-century church towering above the town. This area is known as La Rioja Alta (Upper Rioja) and, as you will no doubt deduce from the quantity of vineyards, is the major wine-growing region in Spain. Navigate your way carefully through **Logroño**, whereafter the vineyards begin to be mixed with wheat and potato fields.

Soon after Logroño is the rampart-encircled **Santo Domingo de la Calzada** whose most impressive 12th-century cathedral has a live rooster and hen in residence in commemoration of a miracle supposed to have occurred when a young pilgrim's innocence was proved by the crowing of an already roasted cock. (They are replaced each year on May 12th.) On signs leading into town you see the brief poem summing up the legend, which says, *Santo Domingo de la Calzada/ cantó la gallina/ después de asada.* Although the legend says a cock, the poem says a hen was involved. Maybe it just rhymed better. In any case there is one of each in the cathedral. Its 18th-century belfry is famed as the prettiest in La Rioja.

It makes a good breaking point for your journey to overnight at the very atmospheric **Parador de Santo Domingo,** housed in a former pilgrims' hospice, right across the plaza from the cathedral. The saint was a local hermit who took in pilgrims on their way to Santiago de Compostela.

DESTINATION VII MADRID

From Santo Domingo continue on the N120 through undulating wheat and potato fields (still following the Way of Saint James) to **Burgos.**

Burgos is a large, not particularly charming city, but of historical interest. The capital of Old Castile from 951 to 1492, when it lost its position to Valladolid, Burgos has strong associations with the victorious Reconquest. Spain's epic hero, El Cid Campeador (champion), was born Rodrigo Díaz in nearby Vivar in 1026. His exploits in regaining Spain from the Moslems were immortalized in the first Spanish epic poem in 1180 and subsequent literary works. He and his wife Ximena are interred in the transept crossing of the cathedral.

The **cathedral** is without doubt the leading attraction of Burgos. Surpassed in size only by the cathedrals of Seville and Toledo, the flamboyant Gothic structure was begun in 1221 by Ferdinand III (the Saint) and completed in the 16th century. The artworks in the many chapels inside constitute a veritable museum. The two-story cloister contains much stone sculpture of the Spanish Gothic school. Do not fail to walk around the outside to see the marvelous decoration of the various portals.

On the south side of the cathedral, if you walk toward the river, you pass through the highly ornate city gate called the Santa María arch. After crossing the river, you continue down Calle Miranda to the Casa de Miranda, an archaeological museum. North of the cathedral you can ascend the hill that harbors castle ruins and affords excellent city views. Enjoy the pretty pedestrian street along the riverfront, with its shops and lively bars and cafés.

When it is time to leave Burgos, head south on the N2 to **Madrid**. We recommend several hotels in Madrid in various price categories. Look in the back of the guide in the *Hotel Descriptions* section to see what most appeals to you. For details of what to see and do in and around Madrid, refer to our itinerary *Madrid and More*, pages 145–156.

Note: If you are weary of cathedrals, skip Burgos altogether and stop instead at one of our favorite petite towns in Spain, **Pedraza de la Sierra**. If this is your choice, approximately 120 kilometers after leaving Burgos, watch for the N110 where you turn right toward Segovia. After about 24 kilometers, turn right again in Matabuena, following signs for Pedraza. This medieval hilltop town is truly a gem, right out of a fairy tale. There is a wealth of marvelous restaurants. If you want to spend the night, we recommend two hotels, **La Posada de Don Mariano** and **El Hotel de la Villa**, both with rates far below what you pay for comparable comfort in Madrid. For details of these hotels, see the *Hotel Descriptions* section in the back of the book.

The Costa Brava and Beyond

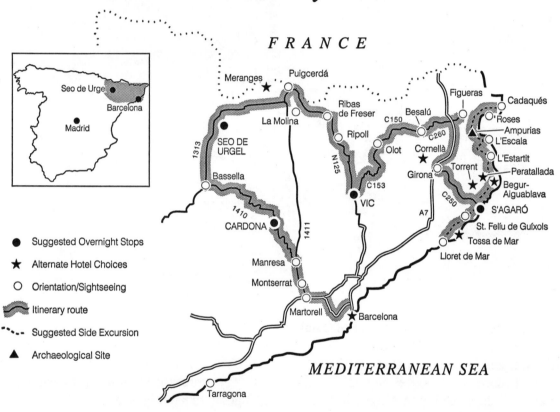

FRANCE

MEDITERRANEAN SEA

Seo de Urgel
Barcelona
Madrid

Meranges
Puigcerdá
Ribas de Freser
Besalú
Figueras
Cadaqués
La Molina
Ripoll
C150
C260
Roses
1313
SEO DE URGEL
Olot
Cornellà
Ampurias
L'Escala
N125
Girona
Torrent
L'Estartit
Bassella
C153
Peratallada
Begur-Aiguablava
1410
VIC
CARDONA
1411
A7
S'AGARÓ
Manresa
C250
St. Felíu de Guíxols
Montserrat
Tossa de Mar
Martorell
Lloret de Mar
Barcelona

Tarragona

● Suggested Overnight Stops
★ Alternate Hotel Choices
○ Orientation/Sightseeing
〰 Itinerary route
‑‑‑ Suggested Side Excursion
▲ Archaeological Site

125

The Costa Brava and Beyond

Tossa de Mar, Costa Brava

This itinerary is essentially a tour of Catalonia, and it includes a sampling of the multiple delights to be savored in this region: spectacular mountains, lovely old towns and castles, and beautiful sea coasts that alternate cliffs and beaches. Catalonia has been settled continuously since the Greeks landed in the 6th century B.C. In the 15th century Catalonia combined with Aragón to form a vast kingdom extending to Naples, Italy, and it became, somewhat reluctantly, part of the new kingdom created by the marriage of Ferdinand, King of Aragón, to Isabella, Queen of Castile.

Catalonia has fiercely defended its autonomy during its entire history. As a Republican stronghold in the Civil War of 1936–1939, the region experienced a great deal of the bloodshed. When the Nationalists (under Francisco Franco) won, regional autonomy was suppressed. Only after the adoption of the new constitution of 1978 were the various regions allowed to regain a measure of autonomy, and Catalonia was the first to do so.

In addition to Spanish, the regional language of Catalan is widely used. As in Galicia and the Basque country, you often see things spelled in the regional dialect and since 1978, most official signs have been replaced with bilingual ones. Cuisine in Catalonia vies with that of the Basque region for the title of best in the country. It includes many seafood and meat dishes with a variety of sauces, reminiscent—and imitative—of French culinary style. In Catalonia the mixture of sandy beaches, rugged coastlines, gorgeous mountain scenery, and fine food offers something for everyone.

ORIGINATING CITY   BARCELONA

Barcelona is an impressive and prosperous city with much to see and do. But the rest of Catalonia also has much to offer, so when you have completed a tour of Barcelona, head into the interior to see another side of this lovely region. Note: For suggestions on sightseeing in Barcelona, see our chapter titled *Barcelona Highlights,* pages 163–168.

DESTINATION I   CARDONA

Leave Barcelona by going south on the A2 freeway to exit 25 just outside of town. Turn right on NII to **Martorell,** an ancient town where the Llobregat river is spanned by the Puente (bridge) del Diablo, said to have been built by the Carthaginian general Hannibal in 218 B.C. He erected the triumphal arch in honor of his father Hamilcar Barca. Continue on NII to Abrera and bear right on C1411 to reach **Montserrat,** whose ragged, stark-gray silhouette makes you see instantly why it is called "serrated mountain." After entering the village of **Monistrol**, follow the signs to the monastery on top of the hill—about 7 kilometers, along a zigzagging road offering ever-more-magnificent views. You can opt for the cable car (funicular) from a clearly marked point just before Monistrol, if you would rather avoid the mountain driving and the sometimes severe parking problem up top. Taking the cable car certainly makes the trip more enjoyable for the driver.

The golden-brown **monastery** at the crown of Montserrat contrasts strikingly with the jutting gray peaks of the mountain. The setting is ultra-dramatic, and it is claimed that on a clear day you can see the Balearic Islands in the Mediterranean. The monastery church is home to the famed Moreneta, or Black Madonna. The figure, reportedly made by Saint Luke and brought to Barcelona by Saint Peter, was hidden in the Santa Cueva (holy cave) at the time of the Moorish invasions, then found by shepherds in the 9th century. This is the patron saint of Catalonia, and is venerated by thousands of pilgrims annually. Numerous marked paths and cable cars take you to various viewpoints as well as the monastery along the 22-kilometer massif.

After you have visited this marvelous mountain, one of the most famous in the world for its unusual appearance and the inspiration for Montsalvat in Wagner's *Parsifal,* return to Monistrol and turn left to **Manresa**. Visit the elaborate 14th-century collegiate **Church of Santa María de la Seo** on a rocky cliff above the town. Follow the signs for Solsona and, as you leave town, do not fail to look back to catch a spectacular view of Montserrat in the distance. Follow the Rio Cardoner through red, pine-covered ridges, punctuated with little farming towns, to **Cardona**, beautifully situated and crowned by an outstanding fortress/castle, which just happens to be our hotel suggestion, the **Parador Duques de Cardona**. This magnificent parador retains much of its 10th- and 11th-century construction, and the purely Romanesque Collegiate Church of Saint Vincent is in the center.

Cardona's earliest significance was as a source of salt for the Romans. The conical mountain of salt to the south of town has been mined for centuries. The town itself is very quiet unless you happen to be there on Sunday, market day, when things are considerably busier. If you time your visit for the first half of September, you can experience the annual festival with a "running of the bulls," similar to that of Pamplona.

A lovely side trip is to the ancient brown-and-red village of **Solsona**, about 15 minutes away, which is entered through a stone gate in the old town wall. It has a salt and craft museum, and a quaint old quarter for wandering. The parador in Cardona is wonderful, but Solsona is a more interesting town.

Parador Duques de Cardona, Cardona

DESTINATION II   SEO DE URGEL

Head northwest out of Cardona following a lovely stretch of road through rugged hillsides, dotted with ruins of castles and monasteries, through Solsona (worth a stop if you did not make the side trip above).

Continue to Basella, then turn north, following the Segre river for the 50-kilometer drive to Seo de Urgel. At this point, the Pyrenees begin to make their brooding presence known in the distance ahead. Cross the Segre to reach the beautiful aquamarine Oliana reservoir. From the banks of the reservoir you get splendid views of the lake surrounded by its gray-green sheer cliffs, which occasionally seem almost man-made—like giant stone edifices. At the other end of the reservoir is **Coll de Nargo**, then **Organya**, both tiny villages stacked on the hillside like layer cakes. Beyond Organya, the cliffs become steeper and closer as you traverse the deep Organya gorge. The gray cliffs rise to 610 meters here and make an impressive backdrop before you come out into the fertile valley where **Seo de Urgel** (named for its Episcopal see, founded in 820) is located. The town's modern parador, the **Parador de Seo de Urgel**, is constructed on the 14th-century site of a church and convent. The generally contemporary decor is enhanced in the public rooms by the stone arches that remain from the original cloister. You will enjoy strolling through the old quarter around the parador.

A suggested excursion includes travel from Spain to **Andorra**, across into France, and then back again to Spain, all in the course of a day. Just 9 kilometers north of Seo you reach the border of the tiny principality of Andorra, which is under the joint administration of the Bishop of Urgel and the French government. Recognized throughout history for the fierce independence of its residents, Andorra is now known mostly as a duty-free zone, and thus a shopper's paradise. You see an infinite number of stores selling imported goods lining the streets of the capital, **Andorra La Vella**. Besides shopping, Andorra offers mountain scenery *sans pareil*. You ascend through pine forests crowned by the barren, blue-gray, snow-dotted peaks of the Pyrenees. It is truly a breathtaking drive. You see numerous ski areas as you cross the Envalira Pass and descend the mountainside to the French border. From here it is a short drive through the French Pyrenees to the quaint little town of **Bourg Madame**. Just outside of town you cross back into Spain at **Puigcerdá**, a small fortified border town. From here head west through the pretty valley of the Segre river back to Seo.

DESTINATION III   VIC

When you are ready to move on, more beautiful mountain vistas await. Leaving Seo, head east to Puigcerdá tracing the Segre river. Follow the signs for Puerto de Toses and Barcelona and head south on N152 along a mountainside with terrific views of the deep valley below where you soon spot the ski resort of **La Molina**.

The road winds through green mountains as you approach **Ribas de Freser,** a charming little village of pastel-colored buildings. In a short while, if you keep an eye out to your right, you see a waterfall bursting from the hillside. It is not far to **Ripoll,** a pretty town with pitched red-tile roofs topping tall, narrow buildings on the Ter river, and the home of a 9th-century **Benedictine monastery** founded by Visigothic Count Wilfred "the Hairy." Wilfred was responsible for freeing Catalonia from the domination of Charlemagne. The Ripoll Library was once one of the largest in the Christian world.

As you approach the ancient town of **Vic,** watch for a castle on the hill to the right. Your hotel is about 15 kilometers northeast of town, off the C153 to Roda de Ter. Watch for signs in Vic directing you to it. The **Parador de Vic** is a new parador built in the regional *masia catalana* style that is supposed to resemble an old Catalonian manor house (although to us it just looks like a large hotel). The nicest aspect of the parador is its setting on a high shelf offering a panoramic view of dramatic red-and-white stone cliffs surrounding the blue reservoir.

Although on the whole Vic appears to be a rather uninteresting town, at some point during your stay here go into the town of Vic and visit the pretty Plaza Mayor, surrounded by the 15th-century town hall and a 16th-century palace. A short distance down the Calle de Riera is the neoclassical cathedral.

DESTINATION IV   S'AGARÓ

After leaving the Parador de Vic, return to the C153 and turn right to begin the next stretch of your journey. A short drive brings you to the turnoff to the exquisitely preserved, 16th-century town of Rupit, which you reach past a huge gray mesa, itself a dramatic sight. **Rupit** is an utterly charming, typical northern-Spanish town. Park outside the gate and stroll through the age-old cobblestoned streets and plazas with their stone houses and iron balconies hung with colorful flowers. It is a perfect place for pictures and an old-world atmosphere pervades. There is a restaurant on your left just before you enter town where you can stop for coffee.

The drive from Vic to the medieval town of Olot is particularly lovely. The variety of scenery is incredible—vast forests crowned by rugged gray cliffs and mesas give way to equally beautiful, vast fertile plains with the blue Pyrenees as a backdrop. The spectacular scenery and poor road surface dictate a leisurely pace.

Besalú

Just beyond Olot, where the road improves considerably, you drive through **Castellfollit de la Roca**, which on your approach appears ordinary. Be sure, however, to stop and look back at it from the other side, where you realize that it is built on a giant rock at the very edge of a deep ravine.

Your next stop, **Besalú**, requires similar treatment. Go through town, cross the bridge, then turn around and come back for a spellbinding view of this perfectly preserved medieval town. Stop here for a while because the lovely little Plaza de la Libertad is wonderfully typical of ancient Spanish towns. It is an atmospheric and picturesque place to sit for a while and watch the activity in the colorful square.

The Costa Brava and Beyond

Leaving Besalú follow signs to **Figueras**, the birthplace of surrealistic painter Salvador Dalí (1904–1989). If surrealism interests you, we positively recommend a visit to the bizarre **Teatro Museo Dalí** where numerous (often humorous) paintings and sculptures by the famous artist are displayed.

You will be glad to find there is a freeway connecting Figueras to Gerona and a good highway from there to **S'Agaró** (take the Gerona South exit to San Feliu de Guixols and then the coast road a couple of kilometers north). The **Hostal de La Gavina** (seagull), where we suggest you spend the night, is a premier hotel, just north of the little town. Settle in for a few days of luxurious relaxation overlooking the beautiful Costa Brava.

S'Agaró is a small beach town sandwiched between two larger, more lively resorts—**San Feliu** and **Platja d'Aro**. Both are worth a visit for their chic shops, huge white sand beaches, and animated cafés and restaurants. Also, while staying at the luxurious Hostal de la Gavina, be sure to meander along the path below the hotel that traces the edge of the ocean. This is a marvelous walk that allows you not only to enjoy beautiful vistas of the sea, but also to gaze in wonder at the magnificent private homes lining the waterfront.

If you are in the mood for an excursion return to Figueras on the freeway and head northeast toward **Llansa**. You pass through rather barren country at first and, before you reach Llansa, you see the **Castello de Quermanco** on your right. Watch carefully, because it almost blends into the landscape on the hillside. From Llansa turn south down the **Costa Brava** (Wild Coast)—a lot less brava than it used to be with the appearance every few miles of another little resort settlement filled with white cottages with red-tile roofs and all the support and entertainment services that go with them. But the sea and the rugged coastline are as beautiful as ever. The water is a clear, deep blue and dotted with sail- and fishing boats. Continue south through El Puerto de la Selva, then wind the scenic way to **Cadaques**, a whitewashed and picturesque fishing-town-cum-artist-colony that surrounds the harbor. Take time to stroll along the waterfront and enjoy the play of the light on the colorful fishing boats.

Retrace your steps 5 kilometers and take a left toward Roses, located on a bay of the same name. Once a typical fishing village, **Roses** is fast becoming a holiday resort (as are most "villages" along this coast). Continue to the walled, old market town of **Castello de Ampurias**, turn south across the fruit-tree-dotted Ampurdán plain, turn left near Viladamat and follow the signs leading to the archaeological excavation at **Ampurias**. Scipio landed here in the Second Punic War in 219 B C. The town was founded in the 6th century B.C. as a Greek trading station. Tour the Neapolis, with many ancient walls and original floors. A museum displays the interesting artifacts that have been uncovered. A short freeway journey returns you to S'Agaró and the Hostal de la Gavina.

Other nearby spots to visit are reached by heading up the coast to **Platja d'Aro**, **Palamos**, and **Calella**, a pretty resort town with an impressive botanical garden on a cliff overlooking the sea at Cap Roig, just to the south of town. The beautifully planned garden has a shady walk through flowers and trees and spectacular views over the sea.

If you go south through San Feliu and continue along the coast toward Tossa de Mar and Lloret de Mar, you have a breathtaking and dramatic drive along a winding corniche road carved into the mountainside above the deep-blue sea. The rugged cliffs demonstrate clearly why this is called the wild coast. **Tossa de Mar** is a pretty little beach town with a harbor, and your first sight of it—crowned by a castle and surrounded by 12th-century walls and impressive round towers—is magnificent. **Lloret de Mar** (whose natural beauty is somewhat tempered by high-rise apartments and hotels) has a long golden beach, which makes it exceedingly popular, especially in the summer months (when its population more than triples).

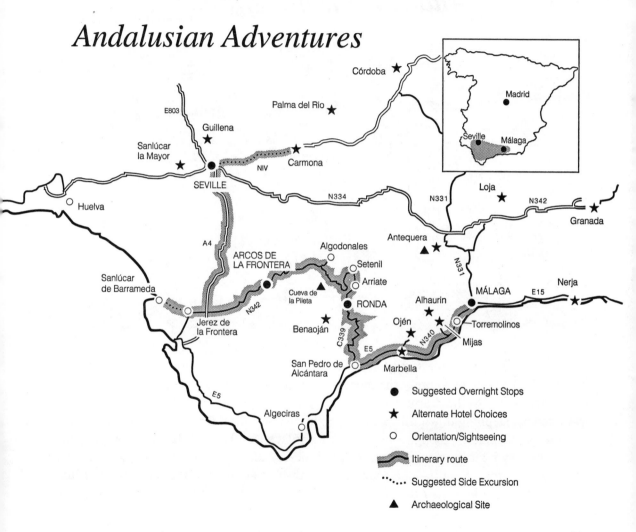

Andalusian Adventures

Córdoba ★

Palma del Rio ★

Madrid ●

Seville
Málaga

E803

Guillena ★

Sanlúcar
la Mayor ★

Carmona ★

NIV

SEVILLE ●

Huelva ○

N334

Loja ★

N331

N342

Granada ★

A4

Antequera ▲ ★

ARCOS DE
LA FRONTERA

Algodonales ○

Setenil ○

Arriate ○

N331

MÁLAGA ●

Nerja ★

E15

Sanlúcar
de Barrameda ○

Cueva de
la Pileta ▲

RONDA ●

Alhaurin ★

N342

Jerez de
la Frontera ○

Benaoján ★

C339

Ojén ★

N340

Torremolinos ○

Mijas

San Pedro de
Alcántara ○

E5

Marbella ★

E5

Algeciras ○

● Suggested Overnight Stops

★ Alternate Hotel Choices

○ Orientation/Sightseeing

〰️ Itinerary route

····· Suggested Side Excursion

▲ Archaeological Site

135

Andalusian Adventures

Antequera

This itinerary features western Andalusia, the area that most foreigners picture when they think of Spain, and surely the most-often visited by tourists. This part of the region is characterized by the warmth of its people as well as its climate. *Pueblos blancos,* white towns, stepping down hillsides topped by the brooding ruins of ancient castles will become a common, though never commonplace, sight. While this is primarily agricultural and cattle-raising country, this itinerary also includes one of Spain's major metropolitan areas, Seville—the country's fourth-largest city and the scene of Don Juan, Bizet's *Carmen*, Mozart's *Figaro,* and glorious 16th-century adventures to and from the exotic New World. It also includes the most tourist-intensive area in the country—the Costa del Sol from Málaga to San Pedro de Alcántara.

This is the part of Spain that extends to within about 15 kilometers of the northern tip of Africa and was the first area conquered by the Moors in 711. Except for the relatively small group of Moslems in Granada, Seville was also the last area reconquered by the Christians in the 13th century, and it is the area that retains the strongest traces of Moorish culture—not necessarily just architecture—to the present day.

The culinary specialties of the area include gazpacho and fried seafood dishes. Due to the warm climate, sangría is also delightfully ubiquitous. And, of course, this is the home of sherry, whose name comes from the English pronunciation of the wine-producing center of Jerez (formerly spelled Xerez, with the *x* pronounced *sh*).

ORIGINATING CITY   MÁLAGA

Málaga had seen occupation by the Romans, Visigoths, and Moors, before being recaptured by the Catholic monarchs in 1487. Today, Málaga lies prey to a new onslaught, as tourists flock from Northern Europe to soak up the sun—an invasion that has somewhat dimmed its old-world charm. However, this seaside town still has much to offer. It is famous for its Málaga dessert and aperitif wines (sweet Pedro Ximenes, and Dulce and Lágrimas muscatel). Early works of Picasso can be found in the **Museo de Bellas Artes** on the Calle San Agustín. Explore the cobbled side streets off the main plaza where you can relax at outdoor cafés, and check out the bustling shopping street, Marquñs de Larios. From the 14th-century ramparts on the nearby **Gibralfaro** (lighthouse hill) are gorgeous gardens with magnificent views of the town and harbor, and just down from there is the 11th-century Alcazaba (Moorish fortress). Also situated on Mount Gibralfaro, high above the sprawling port of Málaga, is the **Parador de Gibralfaro**, a lovely hotel with a sweeping view of the coast.

Ahead is a short drive into some of the most attractive natural landscape in Andalusia. Leave Málaga on N340 along the coast (following the signs for Cadiz, among various other destinations) past touristy **Torremolinos** (which Michener's characters from *The Drifters* would no longer recognize) and Fuengirola before reaching **Marbella**. We suggest you spend some time exploring this chic playground (only about 30 minutes lie between you and your hotel)—this is the most aristocratic of the **Costa del Sol** resorts, with its hidden villas, lavish hotels, long, pebbly beach, and the inevitable remains of a Moorish castle. If you like shopping, you will enjoy the many elegant international shops in the city, where strolling along the main street and side streets is a pleasure. Numerous restaurants of all types and categories are available here, including La Fonda, with a Michelin star, on the Plaza de Santo Cristo. From Marbella, return to the N340 and continue west for a few kilometers west to **Puerto Banus**, where the marina harbors enough yachts to rival Monaco or the French Riviera. Unless your yacht is moored there, you will have to park in the lot just outside the harbor area proper and walk in. Inside are numerous chic shops, bars, and restaurants. This is the center of Spain's jet-set scene.

From Puerto Banus, return to the N340 for just a few kilometers and turn north on C339 towards **Ronda**. For sheer dramatic setting, Ronda takes the prize. Ronda is perched on the edge of the Serranía de Ronda, slashed by 153-meter gorges and cut in two (the old *Ciudad* through which you enter from the south, and the new *Mercadillo*) by the Tajo ravine carved by the Guadalevín river (which explains why every other sentence describing the site must necessarily include the word "view"). We suggest two hotels in Ronda. We fell in love with the **Parador de Ronda** which opened in 1994. This is one of the most dramatic paradors in Spain and also has the advantage of a large parking garage (an extra charge is made for parking, but is well worth it). From the parador there are incredible views of the gorge and sweeping landscape. Just across the plaza is the much

Ronda, Puente Nuevo

smaller **Hotel Don Miguel**. It does not have the pizzazz of the parador, but is less expensive and also has a superb setting overlooking the gorge.

After you have enjoyed a sangría along with the views from the hotel terrace, stroll to the **bullring** with its wrought-iron balconies. One of Spain's oldest (1785), it inspired several works by Goya. Francisco Romero, the father of modern bullfighting (he introduced the cape and numerous so-called classical rules), was born here in 1698. His descendants continued what is still known as the Ronda school of bullfighting. Farther on you discover the spectacular **Puente Nuevo** (the 18th-century bridge that connects the two parts of town and which you crossed on your way in) with its incredible view of the ravine. When you cross it, you are in the Ciudad section with its winding streets and old stone palaces. Visit the Plaza de la Ciudad and its church, **Santa María la Mayor**, whose tower (a former minaret) affords still more picture-perfect views. Some dramatic walking excursions (30 minutes each) can be taken on footpaths leading off the Plaza del Campanillo down to ruined Moorish mills; or look for the footpath to the upper mills that offer spectacular views of a waterfall and the Puente Nuevo. To the left of the Puente Nuevo (near the Puente Romano, or Roman Bridge) is the **Casa del Rey Moro** (note the Moorish azulejo plaque in the façade), a lavishly furnished old mansion with terraced gardens and a flight of 365 stairs cut into the living rock and leading to the river and the Moorish baths. The ancient ambiance is hard to beat and invites you to take your time strolling around the lovely streets and plazas. In the newer Mercadillo section of town, Carrera de Espinel is a picturesque, pedestrian-only shopping street. You find it running east from near the bullring.

DESTINATION II   ARCOS DE LA FRONTERA

Though Ronda encourages you to linger, take comfort in the fact that you are headed to another impressive site. Since today's drive is a short one, take time for a leisurely breakfast on the hotel terrace before heading northeast out of town, following the signs to **Arriate** and **Setenil**. The latter is a classic little white town with one very interesting aspect—at the bottom of the town, in the ravine, the houses are actually built into the cliff itself. All along this route you enjoy numerous spectacular views of the mountainous countryside. Leave Setenil in a westerly direction and follow MA486, then MA449, which seem to be taking you back to Ronda. However, on reaching C339, take a right and you'll be back on the road to Arcos de la Frontera.

Back on C339, after about 6 kilometers, you see a road (MA501) to the left indicating the way to the **Cueva de la Pileta**. Upon arrival in this desolate place, park your car and climb the steep path to the small entrance to the cave, almost hidden amongst the rocks. You need to join a group of other tourists and follow a guide to visit the caves. (Before leaving Ronda, best check with the tourist office or at your hotel to verify what hours the caves are open.) If there are only a small number of tourists when you visit, you may be allowed to see some of the ancient black-and-red animal drawings found here. The paintings are said to predate those in the famous Altamira Caves and apparently indicate that the caves were inhabited 25,000 years ago. The ceramic remains from the caves are claimed to be the oldest known pottery specimens in Europe.

Santa María, Arcos de la Frontera

Wind your way back to C339 and continue west. You are on a road called the **Ruta de los Pueblos Blancos,** or white-town route, and you soon see why as you pass several very picturesque little towns with their whitewashed buildings and red-tile roofs. On the right you'll see **Montecorto** and have a splendid view of the mountains in front of you. A bit farther, the town of **Zahara,** with a ruined castle and Arab bridge, rises to your left. Built on a ridge, it was a stronghold against the kingdom of Granada during the Moorish occupation. If you have time, you might want to stop and savor the atmosphere, but if you must rush, save your time for today's destination—the spell-binding town of **Arcos de la Frontera.**

(You notice on this itinerary several towns with the "de la Frontera" tag on their names. This means "on the border" and alludes to their status during the Reconquest of Spain from the Moors.) As you approach Arcos, you have several marvelous opportunities to capture its incredible setting on film.

Arcos de la Frontera clings impossibly to an outcropping of rock with the Guadalete river at its foot. Navigate carefully up its maze of narrow, one-way alleys or you may (as we did once) find yourself backing down those steep, twisty streets in the face of a big truck with traffic being expertly (sort of) directed by amused locals. Since you are approaching from the north, the route up the hill to the Plaza de España at the heart of the old town on top is fairly easy. Gracing one side of the plaza is a lovely white (of course) mansion, somewhat austere from the outside, but pretty within. It is the **Parador Casa del Corregidor** which is one of our suggestions for where to stay in Arcos. The parador was built in 1966, but manages to reproduce quite handsomely a Renaissance building. On the other side of the parador is nothing but a crowd-stopping view to the plains below, the full impact of which ought to be absorbed with a sherry at sunset from the terrace—a similarly spectacular view is available from the west side of the plaza in front of the hotel. In addition to the parador, we also highly recommend two others hotels in Arcos—the **El Convento** (a delightful, family-run hotel tucked onto a small street behind the parador) and **Cortijo Faín**, a stunning, 17th-century farm nestled in the countryside 3 kilometers southeast of Arcos on the route to Algar.

Although the view here is the main attraction, you will also want to see the **Santa María de la Asunción** church on the plaza and wander through the ancient, romantic, winding streets of the old town, where you get a real feeling that you have stepped into life as it was in the Middle Ages.

The next destination is the centerpiece of romantic Spain and, appropriately, has retained its beauty and ambiance even in this modern age. We hope you have managed to leave enough time to enjoy its unsurpassable attractions. Leave Arcos heading west, still on the white-town route, and you pass rolling hillsides resplendent with sunflowers (if it is summer), numerous typical Andalusian *cortijo,* or ranches, and more dazzling white villages. Then the terrain becomes flatter and the roadside towns less impressive as you approach the famous town of **Jerez de la Frontera.**

The major reason for stopping in Jerez is to visit the bodegas where sherry is made. The traffic in and out of Jerez is exasperating, and we found the town to be dirty so only make this side trip if you are interested in wines. Most of the bodegas are open for visitors only from 9 am to 1 pm, so plan your time accordingly. Unfortunately, due to the ever-increasing number of interested visitors, some bodegas have instituted a reservation policy. To be on the safe side, call ahead as soon as you know when you plan to be in Jerez (ask for assistance from your hotel desk staff). English seamen in the 18th century found sherry wine an agreeable alternative to French wine and it still occupies a place of honor in English bars. The varieties commonly produced here are: *fino* (extra dry, light in color and body), *amontillado* (dry, darker in color and fuller-bodied), *oloroso* (medium, full bodied, and golden), and *dulce* (sweet dessert wine).

The Jerez region is also renowned for quality horse-breeding. The famous Lippizaner horses, still used at the Spanish Riding School of Vienna, originally came from this area. For information on equestrian-related events, check with the local tourist office.

When you are ready to call it a day and discover what **Seville** has in store for you, make your way to the A4 toll road, which takes you there in no time. From the outskirts, follow the signs indicating *centro ciudad*, while keeping your eye on the skyline's most outstanding landmark—the towering golden spire of the Giralda, attached to the magnificent cathedral.

All of the hotels we recommend are within a short walking distance of the **Plaza Virgen de los Reyes,** the large plaza just behind the cathedral. If you prefer a deluxe hotel, the **Hotel Alfonso XIII** is outstanding. For a less expensive place to stay without sacrificing location or old-world ambiance, the **Hotel Doña María** is a real winner. One of our favorites, the reasonably priced **Taberna del Alabardero,** is not only one of the best buys in Spain, but also has charming rooms and a fabulous restaurant.

In order to fully appreciate the many marvels of Seville, turn to page 157 where the itinerary *Seville Highlights* begins.

Hotel Alfonso XIII, Seville

Andalusian Adventures

Madrid and More

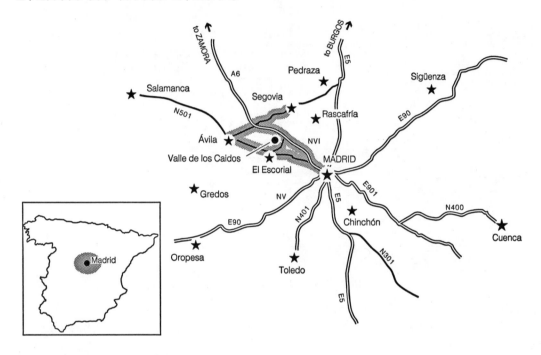

★   Destinations with Hotel Choices

●   Orientation/Sightseeing

〰   Itinerary route

Madrid and More

Parque del Buen Retiro, Madrid

We rediscover Madrid with increasing pleasure each time we visit. Our delight is mingled with increasing astonishment at the "new" face of the city that has emerged since Franco's death in 1975. Madrid (the highest capital in Europe) is a big, vigorous city—comparable in size to other western European capitals—but yet a comfortable one for the first-time visitor. Madrid's attractions will not overwhelm you if you have only a few days to devote to the city, but offer more than enough diversity and stimulation for a longer stay. If you are experiencing Madrid for the first time, a popular method of familiarization is to take one of the numerous city tours available in English (ask at the front desk of your hotel). You will get an idea of the city layout, and can return at your convenience to spend more time in places that pique your interest, or you may prefer to strike out on your own from the start, armed with a detailed sightseeing guide, a good city map (available at any bookstore or newsstand), and your sense of adventure.

A car is more trouble than it is worth in Madrid, which shares the traffic problems common to all large cities. If your visit here is at the outset of your trip, we suggest that you not get your car until you are ready to leave and, if Madrid is your last stop, that you turn your car in the day you get here. Otherwise, leave your car in a protected parking lot for the duration of your stay.

The major things to do and see are often within walking distance of downtown hotels, or readily accessible by "metro," the easily understood and extensive subway system that transports you swiftly and inexpensively to every important intersection in the city. Cabs are also reasonable for trips around town. But walk when you can, because downtown Madrid is made for wandering—with wide, bustling boulevards lined with gracious, old-world buildings and lively outdoor cafés, and narrow old streets winding through colorful neighborhoods and picturesque plazas. Below we mention a few of our favorite sights.

Probably the greatest attraction in the city is the world-class **Prado Museum**, housed in a splendid 18th-century building. Its facilities are constantly being expanded and upgraded, and it boasts one of the finest permanent art collections in Europe, as well as popular and well-presented special exhibitions. Most of the private collections of the Spanish monarchs are here. As with the Louvre in Paris or the Uffizi in Florence, you could spend days here and still not do justice to its treasures. Depending on your knowledge of and interest in the arts, we suggest you either take a tour of the museum's highlights (private if possible), or purchase a guidebook, study the directory, and set out in search of your particular favorites. The best of Goya, Velázquez, El Greco, and Murillo are here and should be seen, if nothing else.

Just a few minutes' walk from the Prado is another rare prize, the **Thyssen Bornemisza Museum**. Here you find a stunning collection of over 800 paintings that span the range of great masters from the 13th century to the present day. This art is the collection of Baron Hans Heinrich Thyssen Bornemisza and before finding its new home in Madrid, was housed in the Villa Favorita Museum near Lugano.

The **Parque del Buen Retiro** across the street is an enormous Central Park-like haven where *madrileños* stroll, bike, boat, and relax at all hours. The park also hosts outdoor concerts and theater (check the local paper or ask at your hotel desk for information).

A short distance south of the Retiro Park, near the Atocha train station on Calle Fuenterrabía, is the fascinating **Royal Tapestry Factory** (Real Fábrica de Tapices) where tapestries are being made as they have been since the 18th century. There are also some original tapestry drawings by Goya.

The neo-classic **Royal Palace**, at the west end of downtown, was conceived by Phillip V, but first occupied by Charles III. Napoleon proclaimed it the equal of Versailles, and it is definitely worth a visit. The extensive grounds and rooms, each a veritable art museum, provide a glimpse of how the Bourbons lived during their heyday in Spain. The beautiful **Plaza de Oriente** (so named because it lies on the east side of the palace) is downtown's largest and is adorned with over 40 statues of Spanish and Visigothic royalty, with an equestrian statue of Phillip IV at its center.

For archaeology buffs, the **Museo Arqueológico** emphasizes Iberian and classical material and includes the famous Dama de Elche.

If you are traveling with children, don't miss a visit to the huge **Casa de Campo** where there is a nice zoo (with one of the first pandas born in captivity), an amusement park, and a lake. The area used to be the royal hunting grounds.

Just southeast of the Royal Palace is the heart of the old city and one of the most monumental squares in the country, the 17th-century **Plaza Mayor**. An excellent place to people-watch from an outdoor café, the old plaza is completely enclosed by tall historic buildings and has a statue of Phillip III in the middle. If you depart from the plaza through the Arco de los Cuchilleros (on the south side), you will discover many typical bars and restaurants, tucked on streets which take you back in time.

Plaza Mayor, Madrid

There is a colorful flea market, called **El Rastro**, a few blocks south of the Plaza Mayor on Ribera de Curtidores street. Though it operates every day, Sunday is the liveliest time to go. Absolutely everything is sold here, both in permanent shops and temporary booths, and *madrileños* and tourists alike shop here in droves. You may even find some genuine antiques at bargain prices, but "buyer beware" is the rule here. Haggling over prices (*regateando*) is appropriate at El Rastro, unlike most other places in Spain.

About halfway between the Royal Palace and the Prado Museum is the huge plaza called **Puerta del Sol**. This is the center of activity in downtown Madrid and, in a sense, the center of Spain because all of the main highways (those designated with an "N") radiate from here. Inlaid into the sidewalk on one side of the plaza you find a plaque marking *Kilometro 0*. Some of the city's best shopping is to be found in the immediate vicinity, including a bustling pedestrian street lined with boutiques.

Shopping for antiques can be fun in Madrid. The largest concentration of antique shops is in the area southeast of the Puerta del Sol, especially on Calle del Prado between the Plaza de Santa Ana and the Plaza de las Cortes.

Madrid's night scene has something for everyone—from elegant dining and highbrow cultural events to colorful hole-in-the-wall tapa bars and pulsating, new-wave discotheques. Progressive and relatively liberal administrations following Franco's death have opened the door to new freedoms (or license, depending on your point of view) not experienced here as little as 20 years ago. The lifting of Franco's severe censorship has

paved the way not only for pornography, fast food, rock music, and divorce, but also for political argument, public gatherings, and displays of affection without fear of retribution; and you will most likely witness all of the above. Spain's recently condoned freedom of expression is nowhere as colorful and varied as in her capital city. Today, those same silent streets that were monitored by civil guards under Franco are not rolled up until dawn in many areas throughout Madrid. One of the liveliest (and safest) late-night spots in the city is located about halfway between the Cibeles fountain and the Columbus monument on the **Paseo de Recoletos**. Here indoor and outdoor cafés hum with the nation's favorite pastime: conversation. Your best sources for information about what is going on in Madrid, day or night, are the local newspapers, one of the numerous activity guides available at street kiosks and often found in hotel rooms, or, better yet, if you do not read Spanish, the concierge at your hotel can make arrangements for you, too—from dinner to bullfights to flamenco shows.

SIDE TRIPS: **El Escorial**, **Ávila**, **Segovia**, and **Pedraza** may be visited in several ways. There are organized bus tours leaving from the Plaza de Oriente early every morning which include visits to El Escorial, Ávila, and Segovia (but not Pedraza) in one day. Your hotel can make the arrangements for you: the price is reasonable and the guides speak English. This method, however, is necessarily a rather quick tour of these wonderful towns and gives you very little flexibility. But, if all you want (or have time for) is a quick look, this is probably your best bet.

A better way to go, in our opinion, is to drive yourself. This allows you to allocate your time as you please. These towns are all close to Madrid and close to each other. If you leave very early in the morning and plan just a short time in each, you could see El Escorial, Ávila, and Segovia then drive on to Pedraza, where you could have dinner. But, if you decide you want to relax and not rush your sightseeing, just see part of the towns mentioned or else stay overnight en route (you will find hotel recommendations for all four towns in the *Hotel Descriptions* section).

Head northwest on A6 from Madrid, turning left about 30 kilometers out of town on C600 to reach the **Monastery of Saint Lawrence the Royal of El Escorial** (Monasterio de San Lorenzo el Real de El Escorial), better known as just **El Escorial** and one of Spain's most impressive edifices. Built by King Phillip II in the late 16th century, the building was designed to house a church, a monastery, a mausoleum, and the palace for the royal family. One of Phillip's main motivations was a promise he had made to dedicate a church to Saint Lawrence on the occasion of an important Spanish victory over France which occurred on the feast day of that saint. A second motive was that his father, Charles V, emperor of the largest empire the world had ever known, had expressed the wish that a proper tomb be erected for him. So when Phillip II moved the capital from Toledo to Madrid in 1559 in order to put the capital in the center of the country, he began construction of El Escorial on the site of the slag heap (*escorial*) of some abandoned iron mines. The construction took place from 1563 to 1584 and resulted in a huge complex that measures 206 x 161 meters and has approximately 1,200 doors and 2,600 windows. Perhaps no other building more faithfully reflects the personality of its owner than this.

Phillip II was a deeply religious man, obsessively so in the opinion of many. (It is perhaps understandable, since he spent most of his life in mourning. Seventeen of his close relatives died during his lifetime, including all of his sons but one, and his four wives.) He thus lavished great sums of money on the decoration of the religious parts of the building, while the palace itself was a simple, even austere affair from which Phillip ruled half the world. Subsequent monarchs added some decorative touches to the apartments or installed additional ones, as in the case of the Bourbon apartments. The Pantheon of the Kings, directly below the high altar of the church, contains the remains of almost all the Spanish monarchs from Charles V on (with the kings on the left, queens on the right). The lavishly decorated library contains some 40,000 volumes, and there and elsewhere in the building you discover examples of the works of all the great painters of the 16th century. El Escorial elicits varied reactions from visitors, some seeing it as a morose pile of rock with 2,600 too-small windows, others as a totally unique royal monument built by a unique monarch. There is certainly no denying its interest as a symbol of some important aspects of 16th-century Spain.

Head back toward A6 via C600 and watch for a turnoff to the left leading to the **Valle de los Caidos** (Valley of the Fallen). This memorial to Spain's Civil War dead is dominated by a 120-meter-high by 46-meter-wide cross (which has an elevator on the north side) and is the final resting place of Generalísimo Francisco Franco, who ruled Spain from 1939–1975.

Return to the A6 freeway and continue northwest to Villacastin, where you exit to reach **Ávila**, traversing pretty countryside of rolling hills. Approached from any direction, Ávila is a dramatic sight, but the most stunning view is when you arrive from the west. Enclosed by stone walls, it stands today as it must have appeared to potential aggressors in the Middle Ages. The 11th-century fortifications (the oldest and best preserved in

Spain) are over 2 kilometers long, 3 meters thick, and average 10 meters in height. They have 9 gates and 88 towers. A stroll along the sentry path atop the walls gives you a close-up view of the many storks' nests perched in the towers and rooftops of the city.

Ávila Wall

Within the medieval city, the fortress-like **cathedral** is a particularly fine one: mostly early Gothic in form, it contains some beautiful stained glass and ironwork. The **Convento de Santa Teresa**, a few blocks southwest of the cathedral, is built on the birthplace of the famous 16th-century mystic writer, who is generally credited with defeating the Reformation in Spain by carrying out reforms of her own. Inside there are relics related to the saint and some fine altars. In the immediate vicinity are some lovely and picturesque 15th-century houses. You will enjoy strolling around this ancient town with its tiny plazas and cobbled streets.

Just outside the walls on the northeast corner is **St. Vincent's Church**, founded in 1307. Noteworthy are the Tomb of the Patron Saints (12th century), a crypt with the stone where Saint Vincent and his sisters were martyred (in the 4th century), and the west entrance with its rich Romanesque sculpture.

Also outside the walls, via the Puerta del Alcázar gate and across the Plaza de Santa María, is **Saint Peter's Church**, with its impressive rose window. To the left is the Calle del Duque de Alba which leads (400 meters) to the **Convento de San José,** the first convent founded by **Santa Teresa**—now home to a museum of mementos about her life.

To reach **Segovia**, return the way you came to the A6 freeway and continue past it on N110. Segovia was an important city even before the Romans came in 80 B.C. It was occupied by the Moors between the 8th and 11th centuries, and was reconquered by the Christians in 1085.

The highlight of Segovia is the 14th-century **Alcázar** castle. Dramatically situated like a ship on the high sea, it is a sight not soon forgotten. This is the castle used in the film *Camelot*, from whose ramparts Lancelot launches into the song *C'est moi* before crossing the English Channel to join King Arthur's knights of the round table. Probably the most-photographed edifice in Spain, it is surprisingly barren inside—the tour is most memorable for its views. In 1474, Castilian King Henry IV's sister, Isabella, was here proclaimed Queen of Castile (which at that time included most of the western half of Spain and Andalusia). Isabella's marriage to Ferdinand, heir of Aragón, laid the groundwork for the creation of the modern nation.

Segovia claims one of the finest **Roman aqueducts** in existence today, and it still functions to bring water from the Riofrío river to the city. Thought to have been built in the 1st or 2nd century A.D., it is constructed, without mortar, of granite from the nearby mountains. It is almost a kilometer long and over 27 meters above the ground at its highest point as it crosses the Plaza de Azoguejo.

A tour around the outside of the city walls to the north affords some excellent perspectives on the setting. Bear left from the aqueduct and you pass the old Moneda (Mint) and the Monasterio del Parral, on the left bank of the Eresma river. After crossing the bridge bear left, then right to the Church of the Vera Cruz, from where you can enjoy

Alcázar Castle, Segovia

a spectacular view of the city. A little farther north is the **Convento de Carmelitas Descalzos,** where the great mystic poet of the 15th century, Saint John of the Cross, is buried. To wind up your sightseeing with more city views, return to town via the Cuesta de los Hoyos.

In the old city are narrow, picturesque streets that deserve a half-day walking tour. The **Church of Saint Stephen** is a lovely Romanesque building from the 13th century. Farther down is the **cathedral,** said to be the last Gothic cathedral built in Spain. East another block is Saint Martin's (12th century), and a couple of blocks farther on is one of the most unique mansions in Segovia, the **Casa de los Picos,** a 15th-century home adorned with diamond-shaped stones. Northwest of there is the Plaza del Conde de Cheste with its numerous palaces. If you head south from here, you find yourself back where the aqueduct crosses the Plaza del Azoguejo.

Continue northeast on N110 for about 25 kilometers and turn left, following the signs for **Pedraza,** which is about 13 kilometers farther. Whereas El Escorial, Ávila, and Segovia are well-known tourist destinations, most people have never heard of Pedraza, a fact that makes it even more fun to visit. This walled, medieval hilltop village is truly a jewel. From the moment you enter through the lower gate, time stands still as you meander through the maze of little streets. There are no major sights to visit, although on the edge of town is a brooding castle where the sons of King François I of France were once held captive. The main attraction here is the town itself. The heart of Pedraza is its picturesque Plaza Mayor faced by houses that date back to the 16th century. The small side streets have many delightful boutiques, restaurants, and two lovely small hotels, **La Posada de Don Mariano** and **Hotel de La Villa** (both are described in the back of this guide in the *Hotel Descriptions* section).

Seville Highlights

The Cathedral and Giralda, Seville

We should preface this section highlighting Seville with a frank admission of prejudice. It is one of our favorite cities, chock-full of fond memories of good times and good friends. Every time we return we fall under Seville's spell—and it won't surprise us a bit if you're enchanted, too. It is not that Seville is totally different from other Spanish cities, it is just that the town and its inhabitants are the quintessence of Spain. We strongly suggest several days in Seville. You need time to see its many sights, as well as time to wander along the orange-tree-lined streets and soak up the special feeling that the city imparts to its guests.

We recommend several places to stay in Seville, the **Hotel Alfonso XIII**, the **Hotel Doña María** , and the **Taberna del Alabardero**. All three are outstanding in their category (look in the *Hotel Descriptions* section for pertinent details) and in the heart of the city within walking distance of sightseeing.

After settling in your hotel, you must first visit the **cathedral**, one of the largest Gothic churches in the world, ranking in size with Saint Peter's in Rome and Saint Paul's in London. It was constructed between 1402 and 1506 on the site of a mosque. In the elaborate Royal Chapel at the east end is buried Alfonso X "The Wise," one of Spain's most brilliant medieval monarchs, who supervised the codification of existing Roman law in the 13th century. When his son Sancho rebelled, Seville remained loyal to Alfonso. Alfonso's gratified statement *No me ha dejado* (It has not deserted me) is the basis for the rebus symbol you are bound to notice painted and carved all over the city: a double knot (called a *madeja*) between the syllables "no" and "do," thus producing *No madeja do* which is pronounced approximately the same as *No me ha dejado*. Ferdinand III, later Saint Ferdinand, who freed Seville from Moorish domination, is buried in a silver shrine in front of the altar. On one side, in an ornate mausoleum, is one of the tombs of Christopher Columbus (the other is in Santo Domingo in the Caribbean—both cities claim to have his real remains).

Just outside the east entrance to the cathedral is the best known of Seville's architectural sights, the **Giralda**. Originally it was the mosque's minaret and was retained when the church was built. Be sure to enter and ascend the ramp up the 70-meter spire (stairs were not used in order to allow horses access). The view of the city is outstanding, especially in the late afternoon. The name *Giralda* means weather vane and refers to the weather vane on the top, which was added in the 16th century.

On the opposite side of the cathedral from the Giralda is an impressive Renaissance building—originally built to be a customs house but later converted into the **Archives of the Indies**—into which were put most of the documents (comprised of some 86,000,000

Alcázar, Seville

pages spanning 400 years) pertaining to the discovery and conquest of America. Students of colonial Spanish American history still come across undocumented material when they make pilgrimages here for a rich feast of research.

On the north side of the cathedral (a pleasant spot to sit and watch Seville go by) there are cafés that are slightly more tranquil than those along Avenida de la Constitución. To the south of the cathedral is the **Alcázar**—not as impressive as the Alhambra in Granada, but a lovely and refreshingly cool spot to spend a hot afternoon. Most of it was restored by King Pedro "The Cruel" (14th century), but he used Moorish architects and thus retained much of its authenticity.

If you leave the Alcázar by way of the southeast corner of the *Patio de las Banderas* (Flag Court), you are in the old Jewish Quarter, the **Barrio de Santa Cruz**. Looking something like a set for an opera, this is a mixture of old, typical whitewashed houses and shops—all, it seems, with flowers tumbling from wrought-iron windows and balconies. The painter Murillo is buried in the Plaza de Santa Cruz and the house where he died is in the nearby Plaza de Alfaro. Southeast of these two plazas, hugging the Alcázar walls, are the lovely **Murillo Gardens** (*Jardines de Murillo*), where painters are often engrossed in capturing the setting on canvas.

North from the cathedral you can stroll a few long blocks down the Avenida de la Constitución to the **Plaza de San Francisco** behind the city hall (*Ayuntamiento*), a center of outdoor events during Holy Week. Running parallel to Sierpes and out of the Plaza Nueva is Calle Tetuán, another major shopping street.

At the north end of Sierpes, turn left on Calle Alfonso XII, after which a few blocks' walk brings you to the **Museo de Bellas Artes** (Fine Arts Museum), housing one of the most important collections in Spain. There are well-presented paintings of El Greco, Zurbarán, Velázquez, and Murillo, among others.

On Calle San Fernando, flanking the handsome Hotel Alfonso XIII, is a golden 18th-century building, once a tobacco factory, where Bizet's beautiful and fiery Carmen worked. This is now the **University of Seville**. Feel free, if it is open, to go in and stroll its wide hallways through the collection of interior patios. Upstairs (to the right of the main entrance) you can find the university bar, where students and faculty convene for a between-class cognac, beer, coffee, or sandwich. A visit here gives you an insight into Spanish academic life.

Behind the university is the entrance to the **Parque de María Luisa** (laid out by a former princess of Spain), a popular local retreat from the summer heat. Here you'll discover the **Plaza de España**, a large semi-circle complete with boat rides and tiled niches representing each of the provinces of Spain, where Spanish families like to have their pictures taken in front of their "home-town" plaque. This plaza was constructed for the International Exposition in Seville in 1929, as were several other buildings in the park and as was the Hotel Alfonso XIII. In the Plaza de América, farther down, is the **Museo Arqueológico** with a very regional collection of Roman antiquities and an arts-

and-crafts museum. If you fancy being covered with doves, there is a spot where a lady sells you some seeds which, when held out in your hand, attract dozens of the white birds to perch greedily on your arms, shoulders, and head—this makes a fun picture to take home. There are also, of course, numerous spots to sit and people-watch.

You must not miss the **Casa Pilatos**, a stunning palace built in 1540 for the Marqués of Tarifa. The name derives from Pontius Pilate's home in Jerusalem (which supposedly the Marqués visited and admired). The palace is a delight—filled with brilliantly colored tiles, sunny courtyards filled with flowers, lacy balustrades, and Roman statues. A bit far off the beaten path (but within walking distance), the Casa Pilatos is usually not brimming with tourists.

The major festivals in Seville are Holy Week and the Feria (Fair) de Sevilla (about the second week after Easter). Although both are absolutely spectacular events, do not dream of securing a hotel reservation unless you plan a year in advance. And be aware that things can get pretty wild during the ten days of the Feria.

If time allows, you can take several good side trips from Seville:

CARMONA: Head northeast out of town on NIV through fertile hills to the ancient town of Carmona (38 kilometers), which still retains some of its ramparts and much of its old-world ambiance. The Puerta de Sevilla, a curious architectural blend of Roman and Moorish, opens onto the old town, where whitewashed alleyways and stone gateways lead to private patios of what were once noble mansions. The plaza is lined with 17th- and 18th-century houses. In the patio of the town hall (Calle San Salvador) there is a large Roman mosaic. Stroll down the nearby Calle Santa María de Gracia to the Puerta de Córdoba (built into the Roman wall in the 17th century diametrically opposite the Puerta de Sevilla) for a lovely view over a golden plain of wheat fields. The **Casa de Carmona** is an excellent place to stay.

The Church at Jerez de la Frontera

ITALICA: Just 10 kilometers out of Seville on N630, a little past the town of Santiponce, is the Roman town of Italica, founded in 205 B.C. by Scipio Africanus and birthplace of emperors Trajan and Hadrian. Still being excavated and restored, its baths, mosaics, and amphitheater are interesting and well worth the short drive (especially if you will not get the chance to visit the incredibly impressive Roman ruins at Mérida). Open-air dramatic performances are occasionally given in the amphitheater here (check with the tourist office on Avenida de la Constitución in Seville for a schedule if you are interested).

JEREZ DE LA FRONTERA: If you have not yet gone sherry-tasting in Jerez, the sherry capital of the world, it is easily visited from Seville, being just a quick 67 kilometers south on the freeway (see the description in the *Andalusian Adventures* itinerary).

Barcelona Highlights

Barcelona

Barcelona is Spain's second-largest city, but its distinct history and regional culture make it anything but a small-scale Madrid. Its personality, architecture, customs, proximity to France, and long-term importance as a Mediterranean seaport make it a sophisticated and cosmopolitan city. The whole region of Catalonia, but especially its capital city of Barcelona, has long resisted absorption by Castile-dominated central authority. Catalans pride themselves on their industriousness and prosperity, both immediately evident to the visitor. Barcelona is a fascinating, bustling, charming city that will enchant you. There is a lot to see and do, so try to budget sufficient time to explore fully the delights the city has to offer.

As in most large, unfamiliar cities, a good way to start your visit is by taking advantage of an organized bus tour, which orients you and gives you a more enlightened idea of how and where to concentrate your time. There is a variety of tours available in English—ask the hotel concierge to arrange one for you.

Street signs (and maps) are often in the Catalan language. In Barcelona, you see *carrer* instead of *calle* for street, *passeig* instead of *paseo* for passage, *avinguda* instead of *avenida* for avenue, and *placa* instead of *plaza* for town square. The nerve center of the city is the large Plaza de Catalonia on the border between the old city and the new. It is singularly impressive, with many fine monuments and sculptures. Beneath it is the hub of the subway system and the shopping arcades along the underground Avenida de las Luces (Lights).

All of the downtown sights are within walking distance of the plaza, including the festive **Ramblas**—a cosmopolitan, stone-paved promenade running generally south from the plaza to the waterfront. Ramblas comes from the Arabic for river bed, which is what this once was. Now it is a chic and shady street, lined with shops and hotels and frequented by anyone and everyone visiting Barcelona. At the plaza end are kiosks selling newspapers and books in many languages; then a bird market takes over and the street is adorned with cages full of colorful birds. Next are lovely flower stalls, then a series of tree-shaded cafés, perfect for people-watching. On the right side of the street (as you walk toward the waterfront), just before you reach the flower stalls you find a busy public market where it is fun to stroll, enjoying the amazing variety of produce and fresh fish that Barcelonans have to choose from.

At the waterfront end of Ramblas is a monument to Christopher Columbus and a re-creation of his famous ship, the *Santa Maria*. King Ferdinand and Queen Isabella were holding court here when Columbus returned from his first voyage and announced the incredible news of his discovery of a route to the Orient (he still thought this is what he had found). Visit the *Santa María* and try to imagine what it would be like to set out into unknown waters on a two-month voyage as Columbus did in this tiny ship in 1492. You can also take boat rides around the harbor from here.

A few blocks east of the Ramblas is the colorful Gothic Quarter (Barrio Gótico), a virtual maze of old buildings, streets, and alleyways. A marvelous 15th-century cathedral dominates the area, which also contains the city hall (*ayuntamiento*), with its lovely sculptures and paintings and beautifully decorated chambers and halls. There is a rich selection of atmospheric *tapa* bars and chic shops, including some interesting antique stores, in this lively area.

Still farther east is the famed Calle Montcada, lined with handsome old mansions. Two of these contain the **Picasso Museum** with an impressive display of virtually every period of the famous painter's work. Although born in Málaga, Picasso spent much of his life (especially during his formative years) in Barcelona. His most famous paintings are not housed here, but the museum does contain many examples of his early work.

Even more intriguing are the works of another famous Barcelona artist, Antonio Gaudí (1852–1926), the avant-garde architect. His **Holy Family (Sagrada Familia) Church** is the city's most famous landmark, its perforated spires visible from various points around the city. You certainly want to take a closer look at this marvelous unfinished building with its intricately carved façades and molten-rock textures (it is best reached by cab). Even more fanciful is the **Guell Park** overlooking the city (Eusebio Guell was a wealthy patron of Gaudí)—also unfinished, but delightful in its conception and whimsical atmosphere. (Many of Gaudí's imaginative creations resemble life-size gingerbread houses.) Numerous examples of his work can be found in the city: the **Casa Batlló, Casa Mila**, and the **Pedrera** are on the Paseo de Gracia, west of the Plaza de Catalunya, and the **Palacio Guell** is just off the Ramblas. They all attest to the apparent rejection of the straight line as a design element in the highly individualistic style of this innovative artist. Because they cannot be moved from Barcelona, they are more an integral part of the city's personality than the paintings of Picasso or Miró which can be seen in art museums all over the world.

Another not-to-be-missed area is the **Parque de Montjuich**, occupying the hill of the same name south of the Plaza de Catalunya. Originally the site of a 17th-century defensive fort (which now contains a military museum), a number of interesting public buildings were erected here for the 1929 exposition. (This is a branch of the same exposition for which a number of buildings in the **Parque de María Luisa** were constructed in Seville. The exposition was divided between the two cities.) The **Museum of Catalan Art** is in the **Palacio Nacional** and it contains fine Gothic and Romanesque sections, featuring wonderful examples of religious art that have been rescued from abandoned churches all over the region. These are magnificently displayed, often as complete church interiors.

Also in Montjuich is the **Pueblo Español** (Spanish town) which is an entire little village, constructed for the 1929 exposition, utilizing the varied architectural styles of Spain. Some of the structures are re-creations of actual buildings, and some simply imitate regional styles. The entrance. for example, is a

Holy Family Church, Barcelona

reconstruction of the towers of the city wall of Ávila. It is an impressive achievement and is now essentially a shopping area featuring *artesanía* (arts and crafts) from the different regions. If you have been to other areas of Spain, you will be struck by the unique juxtaposition of the various architectural styles.

Montjuich is also the setting of one of the most wonderful of all the sights in Barcelona—the beautiful **dancing fountains** (*fuentes*). For a truly unforgettable experience, ask at your hotel for the days of the week and the time at night they are augmented with lights and music. Music from classical to contemporary accompanies the multi-colored, ever-changing spouts in a symphony of sensory experience. If you go an hour early and are prepared to wile away the time watching the Barcelonans stroll around the park, you should be able to secure a seat in front of the palace.

Also in the park is the **Fundación Joan Miró**, with several hundred examples of this native son's bold and colorful paintings, along with works by other contemporary artists— definitely worth a visit if you are a modern art devotee.

Children particularly enjoy the new amusement park on the Montjuich hill, and an older one, reached by funicular railway, on the hill called Tibidabo. Both spots have fine city views. In the **Parque de la Ciudadela** there is a good zoo.

There is ample night life in Barcelona. The best approach is to ask your hotel concierge, since shows change constantly. One permanent offering, however, is the **Scala**, an international, Las Vegas-style review which is very professionally presented and is enjoyable even if you do not have an understanding of the Spanish language. There is a dinner show—the food is only passable—and a later show at midnight without dinner. You need to ask your hotel concierge to make reservations for the Scala, since it is highly popular both with locals and tourists.

Barcelona Highlights

Hotel Descriptions

This spectacular parador crowns the tiny fortified town of Alarcón on the rocky central meseta south of Madrid. Perched on a promontory, this dramatic 8th-century Arab fortress resembles an island surrounded by the deep, natural gorges created by the looping Júcar river below. The imposing castle-hotel is superbly preserved and retains a considerable portion of its original construction, including crenellated towers, ramparts, and the vigilant castle keep, featuring a guestroom on each floor. The main lounge off the entry patio is awe-inspiring: its towering stone- and wood-beamed ceiling arches over gigantic tapestries, suits of armor, and a corner fireplace—you can all but hear the rattling of swords borne by the Knights of the Order of Saint James who readied themselves here to combat the Moors during the Reconquest. There are few guestrooms, and each is unique, though they all feature traditional Castilian wood furnishings, high ceilings, breathtaking views beyond thick walls, and a mini-bar. Room 103 has windows so high that steps are carved to reach them. Room 105 is also special with a vaulted ceiling and balcony. Take a turn around the ramparts—it will make you realize why the Moors chose it as a stronghold and wonder how the Christians ever wrested it from them.

PARADOR "MARQUÉS DE VILLENA"
Manager: Joaquin Gutierrez López
Avenida Amigos de Los Castillos, s/n
16213 Alarcón (Cuenca), Spain
Tel: (69) 33.03.15, Fax: (69) 33.03.03
13 rooms, Double: Pts 19,000*
*IVA not included, breakfast Pts 1,300
Open all year, Credit cards: all major
Restaurant open daily
170 km W of Valencia, 85 km S of Cuenca
Michelin Map 444, Region: Castilla-La Mancha

The Parador de la Mancha is located in the flat countryside just outside Albacete, a city well known for its Archaeological Museum. The hotel (of fairly recent construction) is not a historic monument, but it has the appealing ambiance of a Spanish hacienda. The whitewashed building, accented by wrought-iron lamps and a terra cotta roof, is built around a large central courtyard, wrapped on four sides by a window-enclosed, wide hallway with a red-tiled floor. In this cheery corridor colorful plates and old prints accent the walls and green plants, nurtured by the sunny exposure, abound. A few antiques, such as handsome carved chests and saddles, lend a nice old-world touch. Behind the hotel, set in a grassy lawn, is a large swimming pool which offers a restful respite on a hot summer day. There are also two tennis courts for sports enthusiasts. The guestrooms and bathrooms are especially spacious. Although when we visited the paint on the doors was a bit chipped, the furnishings were very pleasant and in keeping with the mood of the building—headboards of black wrought-iron trimmed with brass, red-tiled floors, rustic wooden furniture, and windows enclosed by heavy shutters. There is a guest lounge with brown leather sofas, game tables, and a large fireplace. The dining room, appointed with simple wooden tables and chairs, serves La Mancha specialties.

PARADOR DE LA MANCHA
Manager: Carmelo Martinez Grande
02000 Albacete (Albacete), Spain
Tel: (67) 24.53.21, Fax: (67) 24.32.71
70 rooms, Double: Pts 15,000*
*IVA not included, breakfast Pts 1,300
Open all year, Credit cards: all major
Restaurant open daily, pool
180 km SE of Valencia, 4 km SE of Albacete
Michelin Map 444, Region: Castilla-La Mancha

On the top of a hill, dominating the town of Alcañiz and the beautifully fertile Maestrazgo valley, the Parador de la Concordia is installed in a majestic 18th-century Aragonese palace, once a 12th-century castle. Its double rooms have extensive views framed by thick castle walls and wooden windows (some windows set so high that steps have been built in to reach them), lovely rustic wood furnishings, pale-blue bedspreads and burnished red-tile floors highlighted by colorfully patterned rugs. All of the rooms have air conditioning, television, and mini-bar. Due to the spaciousness of the beamed hallways, sitting areas, beautiful, high-ceilinged dining room, and handsome lounge, the palace has deceptively few rooms to accommodate guests. Room 1 (a large corner bedroom with sweeping views in two directions) is especially outstanding. Your visit here will be a trip back through time. A 12th-century tower which was constructed when the Knights of the Order of Calatrava were based here is found on the grounds, and a small cloister and the remains of walls dating from the 12th through the 15th centuries share the hotel's dramatic hilltop setting. Medieval Alcañiz and its parador offer a lovely and tranquil stop for the traveler.

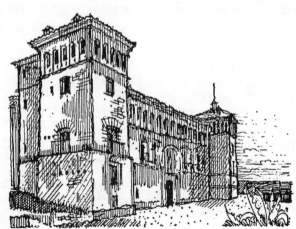

PARADOR DE LA CONCORDIA
Manager: Miguel Cruz Sanchez
Castillo de Calatravos, s/n
44600 Alcañiz (Teruel), Spain
Tel: (78) 83.04.00, Fax: (78) 83.03.66
12 rooms, Double: Pts 17,000*
*IVA not included, breakfast Pts 1,300
Open Feb to mid-Dec, Credit cards: all major
Restaurant open daily
105 km SE of Zaragoza. Road N-232
Michelin Map 443, Region: Aragon

In the verdant Andalusian hills, ten minutes from Mijas and less than an hour from the bustle of Málaga and the beaches of the Costa del Sol, a 300-year-old farmhouse has been restored by Arun Narang, an American, and his British wife, Jean. The rambling, red-roofed building is surrounded by orchards, a grass-edged swimming pool, and grazing horses. Arun is the chef and creates an interesting, international menu (including many Indian specialties and barbecue). Except in winter, meals are served on a shady terrace near the pool. Throughout there is a mood of easy-going informality—a "get to know the other guests," bed-and-breakfast atmosphere prevails. Enclosed within whitewashed walls are several garden patios and a sitting-room lined with books and enhanced with a cozy fireplace. The billiard room (where the former owner once housed lions) has been converted into a honeymoon suite complete with four-poster bed. The rather small guestrooms are decorated simply with dark-wood furniture, fresh white bedspreads, and floral fabrics (brought by Jean's mother from England) for the curtains. One of my favorites, the Panther room, has twin four-poster beds. With its pool, horse riding, and mini-golf, for a budget getaway (but not too far), the finca provides a relaxed, family-oriented, friendly atmosphere. Note: Finca La Mota is not in the town of Alhaurín, but about 4 kilometers south on the road marked to Mijas.

FINCA LA MOTA
Owners: Jean & Arun Narang
Carretera de Mijas
29120 Alhaurín El Grande (Málaga), Spain
Tel: (5) 24.90.901, Fax: (5) 25.94.120
13 rooms, Double: Pts 7,000 (shared bathroom)–9,000*
*IVA & breakfast included
Open all year, Credit cards: all major
Restaurant open daily, pool
30 km NW of Málaga
Michelin Map 446, Region: Andalucia

For a rustic hideaway, tucked off the beaten path in the beautiful mountains of Asturias, La Tahona is an exceptional find. Besnes (La Tahona's official address) is so tiny that it rarely appears on any map—the closest town is Alles. The location is what makes this inn so remarkable: that in a beautiful, remote area you could possibly find such a Shangri-La. Please do not misunderstand: La Tahona is not a fancy hotel in any way, nor does it pretend to be, but it shines in its simplicity. From the C6312 (which runs between Cangas and Panes), you take a small road north toward Alles. In less than a kilometer, you take an even less significant lane on the left to Besnes and La Tahona. Then, in just a few minutes, you come to an appealing, two-story stone building with a red-tiled roof deep in the woods beside a small stream. The rustic charm continues when you step inside where there is a reception desk to the right and a fireplace nook to the left. Beyond is a charming dining room, surrounded with windows on three sides, looking out to the forest and a babbling brook. The tables, set with checkered cloths, lend to the country ambiance. A staircase lined with antique farm implements leads down to a guest lounge. There are thirteen rooms in this building which in days of yore was a bakery. Just down the lane is an old mill where six more guestrooms are located. All the bedrooms are appropriately decorated in a simple, rustic motif.

LA TAHONA
Manager: Lorenzo Nilsson
33578 Alles-Besnes (Asturias), Spain
Tel: (85) 41 57 49, Fax: (42) 72 24 02 or (85) 41 57 49
www.karenbrown.com/spaininns/latahona.html
13 rooms, Double: Pts 8,400–8,700*
*IVA not included, breakfast Pts 750
Open all year, Credit cards: all major
Restaurant open daily
12 km W of Panes, 45 km E of Cangas
Michelin Map 442, Region: Cantabria

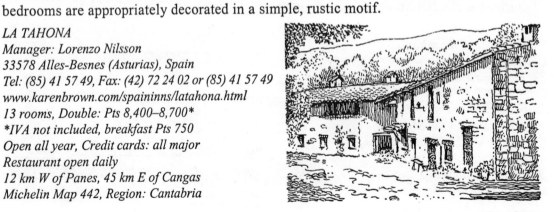

Surprisingly, this parador is not a bona fide restoration of the 16th-century original, but was in fact built in 1979, and principally the entry and attached church are all that remain of the former 1596 convent. However, the newness is hard to detect and you will marvel at the attention to detail. Everything from the bricks to the windows to the rough stones used for the floor were custom made. Elegant antiques abound in the public rooms. Cozy, quiet sitting areas, often with fireplaces, are located on each floor and 16 lovely patios are spaced invitingly around the premises. The bedrooms are impressive, with ancient-looking windows and quaint wooden beds surrounded by pretty ceramic-tiled walls instead of headboards. The other furnishings are harmonious in style and color, contrasting delightfully with the whitewashed walls. The bar is similarly enchanting: built in the style of an old wine cellar, it holds giant clay vats which extend from the lower sitting area through the floor above. Surrounding the vats are rough wooden tables which complete the ancient bodega atmosphere.

PARADOR DE ALMAGRO
Manager: José M. López Santos
Ronda de San Francisco
13270 Almagro (Ciudad Real), Spain
Tel: (26) 86.01.00, Fax: (26) 86.01.50
55 rooms, Double: Pts 17,500*
*IVA not included, breakfast Pts 1,300
Open all year, Credit cards: all major
Restaurant open daily, pool
218 km S of Madrid, 22 km SE of Ciudad Real
Michelin Map 444, Region: Castilla-La Mancha

This 1980's addition to the parador chain is of modern, whitewashed construction, built on a high point in town and overlooking the green sea of the Antequera plain. Just an hour from Málaga and two from Granada, it offers a restful, rural alternative to city sounds and pace, in a town with no less than thirty-eight churches and three remarkable prehistoric dolmens. The dining room and vast lounge are on split levels, complemented by a blonde-wood cathedral ceiling, Oriental carpets, and contemporary furniture. Wall-to-wall windows afford expansive countryside views from both. An immaculate green-and-white hallway leads past a tiny, sunlit interior patio to the guestrooms, all identical, with good-size white-tile baths, brick-red terra cotta floors with beige-weave rugs, pastel-print bedspreads, and wood and leather furnishings. All the rooms have lovely views, though if you request *una habitación en la segunda planta con vista de la vega* you'll get the best orientation. If you make a rest stop here, don't fail to visit nearby El Torcal, an incredible natural display of rock formations.

PARADOR DE ANTEQUERA
Manager: Eugenio Sos Roy
Paseo García de Olmo
29200 Antequera (Málaga), Spain
Tel: (52) 84.09.01, Fax: (52) 84.13.12
55 rooms, Double: Pts 13,500*
*IVA not included, breakfast Pts 1,200
Open all year, Credit cards: all major
Restaurant open daily, pool
58 km N of Málaga
Michelin Map 446, Region: Andalucia

If you wish, while driving through Andalusia, that you could spend the night in one of the beautiful estates you see snuggled in the countryside, then the Cortijo Faín will fulfill your dream. I can think of no other place to stay in Spain that exceeds the rustic authenticity of this marvelous old cortijo. From the moment you enter through the gate into the walled courtyard, you step back into a world long past—there is not a hint of modern commercialism. The discreet reception desk is in the old stables where harnesses hang from the walls and saddles stand ready for the day's ride. Across the cobbled courtyard with its old well stands a large, picturesque, tiled-roofed manor, whose thick, whitewashed walls are draped with bougainvillea. Inside is a spacious entry hall with steps winding up to a galleried upper level where most of the bedrooms are located. Antiques abound throughout. All but two of the rooms are suites. Of these, number 5 is especially enticing with a large terrace where you can look out over a grove of olive trees with huge trunks gnarled with age to the swimming pool. An air of faded elegance pervades the old cortijo–expect the family dogs to be present at dinner, do not expect decorator perfection or a staff that speaks English.

CORTIJO FAÍN
Owner: Sra. Soledad Gil de Zalba
Carretera de Algar, Km 3
11630 Arcos de la Frontera (Cádiz), Spain
Tel & fax: (56) 23.13.96
8 rooms, Double: Pts 10,700–16, 050*
*IVA not included, breakfast Pts 1,000
Open all year, Credit cards: all major
Set dinner Pts 4,500 per person, pool
108 km SE of Seville, 3 km SE of Arcos, road to Algar
Michelin Map 446, Region: Andalusia

The popular government parador in Arcos de La Frontera is frequently filled, but do not despair. Just behind the parador is an intimate, family-run inn that offers personalized service and wonderful prices. As you might guess from the name, this small hotel was originally a convent, dating back to the 17th century. Each of the guestrooms has individual charm and is named for a famous person, such as a poet or journalist. Adorning the walls of the rooms are photos and press releases spotlighting the person for whom the room is named. Although small, all but one of the bedrooms are graced by a terrace or balcony and number 7, a double-bedded room, has an especially enchanting view. There is no public lounge—instead guests relax on an interior patio. The hotel's restaurant is located just down the street in a beautiful 16th-century mansion. Like the hotel, the restaurant (which specializes in authentic local cooking) oozes charm and hospitality. El Convento was opened in 1987 after extensive renovations by the Roldán family. They obviously have excellent taste because their hotel, although simple, offers a wealth of charm. The family also owns a second hotel in Arcos, Los Olivos, composed of several houses facing onto a small courtyard. Although not as centrally located, Los Olivos is a nicely decorated hotel that is recommended if a room at El Convento is not available.

HOTEL "EL CONVENTO"
Manager: María Moreno
Maldonado, 2
11630 Arcos de la Frontera (Cádiz), Spain
Tel & fax: (56) 70.23.33
www.karenbrown.com/spaininns/hotelelconvento.html
8 rooms, Double: Pts 10,700*
*IVA not included, breakfast Pts 700
Open all year, Credit cards: all major
Restaurant open daily
105 km SE of Seville
Michelin Map 446, Region: Andalusia

This wonderfully situated inn was built in 1966 on the site of an old mansion on the Plaza de España in the center of the hilltop white town of Arcos. With the attention to authenticity characteristic of the parador architects, this parador was restored and reopened in 1985 and appears as a mansion several centuries old. The lobby and lounges are accented with antiques and enlivened with ceramic-tile pictures. The hallways are elegant with either open-beamed or lovely vaulted ceilings. Off the dining room is an enclosed garden patio that features an old tiled, stone well—a delightful spot for refreshment. The patio faces stiff competition from the terrace off the pretty little bar, which offers an endlessly dramatic view over the vast plains far below. The spacious bedrooms are extremely attractive, appointed with dark, carved-wood beds and deep-dred drapes and bedspreads which contrast beautifully with the stark white walls. Some rooms overlook the town's picturesque main square, or, for a small surcharge, you can request a room with its own terrace overlooking the valley.

PARADOR CASA DEL CORREGIDOR
Manager: Máximo Pérez
Plaza de España, 5
11630 Arcos de la Frontera (Cádiz), Spain
Tel: (56) 70.05.00, Fax: (56) 70.11.16
24 rooms, Double: Pts 17,500*
*IVA not included, breakfast Pts 1,300
Open all year, Credit cards: all major
Restaurant open daily
105 km SE of Seville
Michelin Map 446, Region: Andalucia

The Áran Valley, located in the high Pyrenees, is such a favorite target for skiers and sports enthusiasts that many of its once-picturesque villages are now buried behind giant condominium complexes. Happily, the tiny hamlet of Artíes, with stone houses lining its narrow winding streets, still retains much of its old-world charm. Driving into town, you cannot miss the parador—it faces directly onto the main road. The hotel has a cheerful, friendly look with honey-colored stone walls and a steeply pitched gray-tile 'roof, accented by two rows of whimsical gables. The original parador, which had only a few rooms, was built into the *Casa de Portolá*, the house of Don Gaspar de Portolá (a famous Spanish captain of the Dragoons who in the 18th century explored California, founded the Mission of San Diego, and went on to become the first Governor of San Francisco). In recent years, the parador has been greatly expanded. However a small chapel and the medieval core of the original mansion are still incorporated into one wing of the hotel. The decor is predominantly modern with dark-gray slate floors, contemporary chairs and sofas, and some abstract paintings. Relieving the newness of the decor are concessions to the inn's heritage such as an antique grandfather clock, heavy, wrought-iron chandeliers, and a beamed ceiling in the spacious dining room.

PARADOR DON GASPAR DE PORTOLÁ
Manager: Manuel Español
25599 Artíes (Lleida), Spain
Tel: (73) 64.08.01, Fax: (73) 64.10.01
57 rooms, Double: Pts 14,500–16,900*
*IVA not included, breakfast Pts 1,300
Open all year, Credit cards: all major
Restaurant open daily
170 km N of Lleida, 338 km NW of Barcelona
Michelin Map 443, Region: Catalonia

From the 14th until the 18th centuries, one of the most influential families in the ancient walled town of Ávila lived next to the cathedral in the mansion which is today the Gran Hotel Palacio Valderrábanos. Their escutcheons (family crests) can still be seen above the magnificent stone entryway, which today leads into a large marble-floored reception area accented with genuine suits of armor. Antiques are generously distributed throughout the grand, high-ceilinged public rooms. The bedrooms are comfortably furnished with occasional antiques, hand-woven rugs, and original art. Of the three suites, number 229 is most impressive: on two levels, it has vaulted ceilings and a view across the rooftops to the cathedral. Some front doubles also look onto the cathedral square, but they are noisier than the interior rooms. Breakfast is served in the cozy English-pub-style bar. The restaurant is quite good, although somewhat lacking in ambiance. The hotel is a fine choice in the ancient walled town of Ávila, both for its location and creative maintenance of its historic situation.

GRAN HOTEL PALACIO VALDERRÁBANOS
Manager: José del Caz Gomez
Plaza de la Catedral, 9
05005 Ávila, Spain
Tel: (20) 21.10.23, Fax: (20) 25.16.91
73 rooms, Double: Pts 14,000*
*IVA not included, breakfast Pts 1,000
Open all year, Credit cards: all major
Restaurant open daily
113 km NW of Madrid
Michelin Maps 444, Region: Castilla y León

If you enjoy cozy, family-run hotels brimming with warmth and charm, the Hostería de Bracamonte will surely win your heart. This beige, stone mansion with wrought-iron balconies is typical of the many 16th-century homes that line the narrow streets in the spectacular walled city of Ávila. As soon as you step into the large reception room you also step back in time. You see to your left under an arched doorway a picture-perfect dining room with rustic charm—just a cluster of small wooden tables, dressed with fresh flowers and soft lighting, set against exposed stone walls. Also off the reception lounge is a sunny enclosed courtyard with greenery lacing the walls, an old well, stone oven, and wooden farm implements. The hotel also has an appealing bar plus a second beautiful dining room. A maze of immaculately kept narrow hallways lined with tapestries, antique chests, old clocks, and baskets of flowers lead to the guestrooms. Some bedrooms have genuine antiques, but all the furniture, even if new, blends with the old style. Each bedroom has its own tiled bathroom, usually with a small bathtub. There are several suites with two bedrooms, but unless you are traveling with a family, the regular doubles are certainly satisfactory. One of my favorites, room 108, has a double four-poster bed. If you prefer twin beds, room 114, decorated in tones of beiges and whites, is very pretty.

HOSTERÍA DE BRACAMONTE
Owner: Family Costa
Bracamonte 6
05001 Ávila, Spain
Tel: (20) 25.12.80 & (20) 25.38.38, No fax
20 rooms, Double: Pts 8,000–10,000*
*IVA not included, breakfast Pts 400
Open all year, Credit cards: MC, VS
Restaurant closed Tuesdays
113 km NW of Madrid
Michelin Map 444, Region: Castilla y León

The Parador de Ávila is tucked within the walls of Ávila, the first fortified Romanesque city in Europe. Partially installed within the 15th-century noble home of Piedras Albas, both the renovated palace and its new addition are in keeping with the original architectural style. The massive granite, limestone, and wrought-iron staircase off the lobby testifies to the success of this intention. The gracefully columned interior patio's focus is on its stone bull—a traditional symbol of nobility in the ancient Iberian past. In the bar are Arabic tiles salvaged from the original patio of the palace. After being closed for complete renovation, the parador reopened in 1996. We have not had the opportunity to see the hotel since its facelift, but if it follows the pattern of other paradors that have been rejuvenated, it should be more outstanding than ever. With Spain's top-notch decorators redoing the interior, you can expect the decor to be lovely. Note: While staying at the parador, be sure to stroll in the evening along the city ramparts.

PARADOR DE ÁVILA
Manager: Sr. Juan de la Torre
Calle Marqués Canales de Chozas, 2
05001 Ávila, Spain
Tel: (20) 21.13.40, Fax: (20) 22.61.66
61 rooms, Double: Pts 15,000*
*IVA not included, breakfast Pts 1,300
Open all year, Credit cards: all major
Restaurant open daily
113 km NW of Madrid
Michelin Map 444, Region: Castilla y León

The Colón is a stately hotel with some elegant touches, built in 1951 right in the middle of the enchanting Gothic Quarter (*Barrio Gótico*) of Barcelona. The lobby is entered up a broad, cream-carpeted stairway which passes through an impressive, square stone arch. The decor here, as throughout the hotel's public rooms, is perfectly lovely and makes you want to linger to watch the passersby in front of the massive cathedral across the street. On certain days local folklore buffs gather here for a session of the regional dance, the *sardanya* (ask at the hotel desk for the current schedule). Some 34 of its rooms overlook the city's famous cathedral—a few have terraces. When making reservations request a room with a terrace, preferably a quieter location on one of the upper floors, and, if the budget allows, a suite or double room with a sitting area, for more money, but also more space. All of the rooms have wonderful high ceilings and are accented with old-world touches which lend an intimate feeling to this fairly big hotel. The Colón is a good, not-too-expensive hotel which enjoys an incomparable location.

HOTEL COLÓN
Manager: Eliseo Gretz Badia
Avenida de la Catedral, 7
08002 Barcelona, Spain
Tel: (3) 30.11.404, Fax: (3) 31.72.915
147 rooms, Double: Pts 23,000*
*IVA not included, breakfast Pts 1,600
Open all year, Credit cards: all major
Restaurant open daily
Across from cathedral in Gothic Quarter
Michelin Map 443, Region: Catalonia

Built in 1899 as an elegant mansion, Duques de Bergara still maintains the ambiance of a private home. From the outside, the hotel has an art-deco feel, created by a design of windows and balconies. In the center of the building there are four strips of balconies, each strip having six windows which are divided by stone columns, and to each side are single, iron-railed balconies. To enter, ornate front doors swing open to reveal an extraordinary floor with a harlequin design of black-, white-, and rose-colored marble. Enhancing the drama, a white marble staircase leads to the upper floors. Tucked under the stairs is a modern reception desk. Another architectural feature that adds to the richness of the interior is a charming stained-glass skylight. The bedrooms do not continue the old-world ambiance—they look like modern-day guestrooms seen in good hotels all over the world, with built-in headboards, good reading lights, TVs, mini-bars, and desks. Like the bedrooms, the bathrooms are almost identical, with handsome gray-and-white-grained marble walls and sinks. The Duques de Bergara has a large dining room with modern chairs. For warm days, there is a small balcony where breakfast can be enjoyed outside. The Duques de Bergara is a good choice for a well-located hotel that is not too expensive.

DUQUES DE BERGARA
Manager: Mireia Jane
Bergara, 11
08002 Barcelona , Spain
Tel: (3) 426.26.00, Fax: (3) 426 04 00
150 rooms, Double: Pts 16,900*
*IVA not included, breakfast Pts 1,200
Open all year, Credit cards: all major
Restaurant open daily
In heart of Barcelona near Plaza Cataluña
Michelin Map 443, Region: Catalonia

Although not in the old quarter of Barcelona, the Gallery Hotel is close to very good shopping and within walking distance to most points of interest. A brochure available at the front desk outlines five tours you can take on foot from the hotel and what to see along the way. From the exterior, the Gallery Hotel does not have much to distinguish it from many other modern hotels—it has an unadorned stone façade with identical rows of windows facing the tree-lined street. However, once you are through the front door, there is an exceptionally cheerful, inviting ambiance. Large windows face onto the street, so the room is filled with sunlight during the day. A hand-loomed carpet adds accent to the creamy marble floor—a pretty color that is repeated on the walls. Dark-brown leather sofas, oil paintings, and potted plants give an ambiance that is neither modern nor antique, but just one of timeless good taste. Just beyond the reception area, a few steps lead up to the Café de Gallery, a pleasant dining room with one wall of glass which opens onto one of the hotel's nicest features—a courtyard where dark-green wrought-iron chairs and tables are romantically enclosed by a high wall draped in ivy. The guestrooms are similar in decor, with dark wooden headboards, built-in writing desks, and exceptionally nice bathrooms completely tiled in marble.

GALLERY HOTEL
Manager: Armando Rojas Aleix
Rosellón 245, 08008 Barcelona, Spain.
Tel: (3) 415 99 11, Fax: (3) 415 91 84
115 rooms, Double: Pts 27,500*
*IVA not included, breakfast Pts 2,100
Open all year, Credit cards: all major
Restaurant open daily, gym
Off Paseo de Gracia, near Avenida Diagonal
Michelin Map 443, Region: Catalonia

The Hotel Mesón Castilla is a simple two-star hotel, but for those who prefer to watch their pesetas, it is not only moderately priced, but also well located and offers an old-world ambiance. It is on a small side street, just off the Plaza Cataluña and steps from Barcelona's popular Las Ramblas street. The mood is set when you enter into the reception lounge which is paneled (walls and ceiling) with a dark wood. Torch-like wall lamps give the room an almost mock-medieval look. A larger guest lounge and breakfast room are located one level up where the mood of days gone by continues. Here you find colorful antique wooden chairs with gilt trim, large wall murals, and stained-glass windows. A lighter note appears in arched windows which open off the breakfast room to a small inner garden courtyard. The bedrooms display the same style: each is individual in decor, but with similar furnishings of ornate painted headboards and coordinating chairs and chests. Some of these pieces of richly painted furniture are exceptionally handsome antiques, while others seem to be reproductions. Although this is a "budget" hotel, the bathrooms are newly remodeled and the rooms all have air conditioning, TVs, and direct-dial telephones. Just 50 meters from the hotel is the new museum of contemporary art (MACBA). Another bonus–there's a parking garage next door.

HOTEL MESÓN CASTILLA
Manager: Maria Quinto
Valldoncella Street, 5
08001 Barcelona, Spain
Tel: (3) 318 21 82, Fax: (3) 412 40 20
www.karenbrown.com/spaininns/hotelmesoncastilla.html
56 rooms, Double: Pts 11,750–2,000*
*IVA not included, breakfast Pts 800
Open all year, Credit cards: all major
No restaurant, breakfast only
In heart of city next to Plaza Cataluña
Michelin Map 443, Region: Catalonia

The Montecarlo, originally a private palace, has one of the prettiest hotel façades in Barcelona. Facing directly onto one of Barcelona's most colorful streets, La Rambla (affectionately known as "Las Ramblas"), the hotel looks like an ornate wedding cake with tiers of fancy frosting. The four-room-wide, cream-colored building rises six stories high—each floor a fantasy of ornate balconies and baroque stucco designs. The opulence of the exterior is not reflected in the decor of the reception area, or beyond in the lounge, bar, and breakfast room. Here you find a very contemporary look with white marble floors, leather couches, glass-topped coffee tables, and white wooden columns. Oil paintings accenting white walls add a more traditional touch. One floor up, the mood changes dramatically in the sumptuous lounge where the original architectural features have been meticulously restored, including a handsome, wood-paneled ceiling, crystal chandeliers, ornate fireplace, fancy wall sconces, gilt mirrors, and ornate windows. The traditionally furnished, air-conditioned bedrooms are all similar in decor and have good reading lamps, writing desks, mini-bars, TVs, and safe deposit boxes. There is no restaurant but the hotel has an extensive menu from which guests can order room service. The Montecarlo offers exceptional value for a friendly hotel with quality at a moderate price. Note: The hotel has a parking garage at pts 2,000 per day.

HOTEL MONTECARLO
Manager: Carlos Sanchez-Azor
La Rambla, 124
08002 Barcelona, Spain
Tel: (3) 41.20.404, Fax: (3) 31.87.323
76 rooms, Double: Pts 15,000*
*IVA not included, breakfast Pts 1,200
Open all year, Credit cards: all major
No restaurant, breakfast only
In heart of Barcelona on "Las Ramblas"
Michelin Map 443, Region: Catalonia

"Palace" denotes luxury and this lovely old lady (formerly known as the Ritz) lives up to her name. The 1919 hotel has recently undergone extensive remodeling and the old rooms have only gained in ambiance. The walls are painted in soft colors and climb to ceilings that are at least 4 meters high. The bedrooms are immense by modern hotel standards, and furnished handsomely in old-world style—what the Spanish call *al gran estilo*. Salvador Dali's favorite room, and ours, is number 110, with a sunken Roman bath and its bed tucked into an alcove. The renovation of the Palace Hotel's public rooms is masterful, and the resulting lobby, central hall, lounges, and excellent restaurants are elegant without being intimidating. Gleaming marble floors, shiny, solid brass fixtures, stunning crystal chandeliers, gilded mirrors, bathtubs you sink into, subdued piano music, finest quality linens, turn-down service at night—all add up to a nostalgic, old-fashioned luxury and refined grace. The service is nothing short of perfection, and the English-speaking concierges go out of their way to anticipate your needs—a real asset in this city with so much to offer. You will feel pampered at the Palace and that is a feeling hard to come by in large city hotels these days.

PALACE HOTEL
Manager: José Luis Torres
Gran Via de les Corts Catalanes, 668
08010 Barcelona, Spain
Tel: (3) 31.85.200, Fax:(3) 31.80.148
156 rooms, Double: Pts 35,000–43,000*
*IVA & breakfast not included
Open all year, Credit cards: all major
Restaurant open daily
In the center of Barcelona
Michelin Map 443, Region: Catalonia

This fortress parador on the sea is undoubtedly one of the most remarkable in Spain. Isolated on a tiny, craggy peninsula just southwest of the little fishing village of Bayona, it is encircled by the ramparts of the former fortress of Monte Real, which protect it on three sides from the wild, crashing sea. The bedrooms, with wooden floors and ceilings, are large and charmingly furnished. Request well in advance a room with a view to the sea to fully appreciate the beauty of this popular spot. Room 102—with its circular corner balcony, private sitting room, and four-poster canopy beds—is spectacular and worth the splurge. Lovely antiques are as at home here and throughout the hotel as the comfortable, traditional wood and leather Spanish furniture. With its massive stone stairway and original stone, domed ceiling, the lobby is stunning and an interior patio with its fountain is delightful. An elegant dining room is found off the lobby and a more informal tavern, *La Pinta*, is located on the grounds overlooking the sea. Several days could easily be enjoyed in this romantic, luxurious hotel with its dramatic backdrop of the clear Atlantic Ocean. Note: As we go to press, the Parador de Gondomar is closed for renovations, but is planning to reopen in mid-April, 1997.

PARADOR CONDE DE GONDOMAR
Manager: Rafael Vázquez
36300 Bayona (Pontevedra), Spain
Tel: (86) 35.50.00, Fax: (86) 35.50.76
128 rooms, Double: Pts 20,000*
*IVA not included, breakfast Pts 1,400
Open all year, Credit cards: all major
Restaurant open daily, pool
114 km SW of Santiago de Compostela
21 km SW of Vigo
Michelin Map 441, Region: Galicia

BEGUR–Aiguablava   HOTEL AIGUA BLAVA   Map: 3b

The Hotel Aigua Blava (located on Spain's most dramatic stretch of coast, the beautiful Costa Brava) has a prime position on a promontory overlooking an incredibly blue inlet dotted with boats and rocky beaches. The Capella family converted their home into a small hotel in 1940 after it was returned to them following the disastrous Civil War. The original owner, the much-loved Xiquet Sabater who warmly welcomed all the guests, died in 1996, but his nephew, Juan (who worked with Xiquet for 46 years), has taken over the management and continues to run the hotel in the same friendly manner as his uncle. Now a fairly large hotel, the Aigua Blava retains the atmosphere of several homes jumbled together around flowered terraces and *rinconcitos* (little corners). Decorated by family members, each room is unique—from simple to elaborate—and many have sea views and terraces (for a surcharge). Set under a slanted ceiling, the Chez Xiquet room (containing family memorabilia) looks out to a large terrace and a fantastic view. For any room, however, reservations should be made well in advance during high season, as many guests return here year after year for their week or two in the sun. For a relaxing sojourn in an enchanting seaside spot with a family atmosphere, you can't go wrong at the Aigua Blava.

HOTEL AIGUA BLAVA   0034
Manager: Juan Gispert
Playa de Fornells
17255 Begur-Aiguablava (Gerona), Spain
Tel: (72) 62.20.59, Fax: (72) 62.21.12
90 rooms, Double: Pts 10,700–17,600*
*IVA not included, breakfast Pts 1,500
Open: Mar to mid-Nov, Credit cards: all major
Restaurant open daily, pool
116 km NE of Barcelona
Michelin Map 443, Region: Catalonia (Costa Brava)

On the high, isolated, tree-covered point of Esmuts, overlooking the open sea on one side and a turquoise bay on the other, sits the Parador "Costa Brava"—a modern, secluded hideaway for the visitor seeking every comfort on the Wild Coast. Unlike most paradors, this one does not strive for an antique ambiance. The attractive public rooms are airy and open, accented in bright spring colors, and the bedrooms are spacious and bright with red-tiled floors and terraces with lovely views of either the ocean or the bay. There are six extra-large special rooms (*habitaciones especiales*), with large round bathtubs, separate, sunken showers, and exercise areas featuring exercycles and weights. For our money, these are special enough to merit the surprisingly few additional pesetas. There is in addition, a public exercise/game room downstairs with saunas. Guests here are two minutes by a footpath from the beach on the bay or can save the effort and choose to lounge around the lovely fresh-water pool overlooking the ocean. For a short or long stay, this contemporary parador above the idyllic white town of Aiguablava is an excellent choice.

PARADOR "COSTA BRAVA"
Manager: Jaime Sebastian Sánchez
Playa de Aiguablava
17255 Begur-Aiguablava (Gerona), Spain
Tel: (72) 62.21.62 Fax (72) 62.21.66
87 rooms, Double: Pts 16,500*
*IVA not included, breakfast Pts 1,300
Open all year, Credit cards: all major
Restaurant open daily, pool
116 km NE of Barcelona
Michelin Map 443, Region: Catalonia (Costa Brava)

Deep in the countryside of almond and olive groves, yet only a 15-minute drive from Ronda, Molino del Santo makes the perfect hub from which to venture out each day to explore the many wonders of Andalusia. Quite truthfully, you might forget all thoughts of sightseeing because the Molino del Santo is such a gem you won't want to leave. Originally an old grain and olive mill, the property was bought in 1987 by Pauline Elkin and Andy Chapell (formerly schoolteachers in England) who converted the mill into an outstanding small inn. The charming old water mill now houses the reception area, lounge, bar, and dining room. Sparkling white-walled guestrooms in cozy cottages, most with their own terrace, have been added over the years. Everything is faultless. The guestrooms are simply but tastefully decorated. Each has tiled floors, comfortable beds with good reading lights, attractive, wooden carved chairs, and handsome fabrics with a hand-loomed look at the windows. Every detail is well thought out by owners who obviously care. The solar-heated pool and the immaculately kept gardens display the same touch of perfection. In the morning, guests linger over breakfast on the flower-bedecked terrace listening to the gurgling mill stream as it meanders below. If you enjoy casual informality, for both price and ambiance, Molino del Santo is absolute perfection.

MOLINO DEL SANTO
Owners: Pauline Elkin & Andy Chapell
Bda. Estacion s/n
29370 Benaoján (Málaga), Spain
Tel: (5) 21.67.151, Fax: (5) 21.67.327
www.karenbrown.com/spaininns/molinodelsanto.html
14 rooms, Double: Pts 7,500–11,300
*IVA not included, breakfast Pts 950
Open Feb to Dec, Credit cards: all major
Restaurant open daily, pool
12 km SW of Ronda
Michelin Map 446, Region: Andalusia

This 12th-century palace on the edge of a sleepy village was practically devastated by the French in 1808, but was rescued and restored by the government as a historical monument. The royal family of Ferdinand and Isabella stayed at this delightful hotel on their pilgrimage to Santiago. Of the original castle, there remains only the **Torreón**, which can be visited on Friday afternoons. The tower bar, located in the cellar and remarkably reconstructed from the original foundation, is reached down a narrow stone stairway whose thick stone walls are draped with colorful tapestries, and whose vaulted, painted, 11-meter-high wooden ceiling has massive beams which support a huge, antique iron chandelier. Another highlight is the fabulous Mudéjar ceiling in the Salón Artesonado, brought here from the town of San Román del Valle in León and lovingly reassembled. The spacious bedrooms flank long, whitewashed hallways lined with antique benches and have a rustic, almost "western" ambiance, with tile floors and leather furnishings. They have lovely views of the town and countryside, and those on the upper floor have terraces.

PARADOR REY FERNANDO II DE LEÓN
Manager: Maria Concepcion Lechuga
49600 Benavente (Zamora), Spain
Tel: (88) 63.03.00, Fax: (88) 63.03.03
30 rooms, Double: Pts 16,500*
*IVA not included, breakfast Pts 1,300
Open all year, Credit cards: all major
Restaurant open daily
71 km S of León, 60 km N of Zamora
Michelin Maps 441 & 442, Region: Castilla y León

The setting of the Parador Monte Perdido is nothing less than sensational. From Bielsa, the road weaves down a beautiful, narrow valley, following the River Cinca for 14 kilometers, until the way is blocked by granite walls of some of the highest mountains in the Pyrenees. The hotel is perched on the side of the hill, looking across the rushing stream and idyllic meadow to a glacial backdrop of mountains laced with waterfalls. The gray stone building (of relatively new construction) blends well with the rugged landscape. The interior also blends in perfectly—the ambiance is that of a rustic mountain lodge. Throughout the hotel good taste prevails in every detail. The polished pine floors are accented by hand-woven carpets, the light fixtures are of heavy, black wrought-iron, the ceilings are supported by thick beams, the antique wood-paneled walls are accented by handsome oil paintings and framed prints. Green plants flourish in their window settings and comfortable brown leather sofas and chairs form cozy areas for friends to gather before the massive fireplace. The guestrooms have wood-paneled headboards, wrought-iron reading lamps, and sturdy wooden desks and chairs. Ask for the third floor—room 205 promises an unforgettable view!

PARADOR MONTE PERDIDO
Manager: Sra. Alicia Pierrette Bardin
Valle de Pineta
22350 Bielsa (Huesca), Spain
Tel: (74) 50.10.11, Fax: (74) 50.11.88
24 rooms, Double: Pts 15,000–16,500*
*IVA not included, breakfast Pts 1,300
Closed mid-Jan to mid-Mar
Credit cards: all major
Restaurant open daily
14 km NW of Bielsa, 184 km N of Lleida
Michelin Map 443, Region: Aragon

For those who want to overnight in Cáceres, the Parador de Cáceres is the choice place to stay. It is difficult to weave your way through the not-too-attractive new section of the city, but be patient and follow the parador signs. The quaint, walled old quarter of Cáceres (named as a national monument) is almost hidden within the new city. However, once through one of the medieval gates, you are suddenly immersed into a well-preserved city which in its heyday was home to many wealthy Spaniards who made their fortunes in the "New World." The 14th-century Parador de Cáceres, just off the Plaza de San Mateo, was built by Don Diego García de Ulloa. Like most of the mansions in town, it has a façade of cut stone with ornamental wrought-iron balconies stretching over the narrow street. Once through the massive doors and up a few steps, you enter an open courtyard and then the lobby. One of the nicest features of the hotel is its several interior gardens and courtyards. My favorite courtyard has whitewashed walls laced with bougainvillea and wicker chairs where you can enjoy the quiet. The guestrooms are large and attractive with tiled floors, white walls, and wooden furniture.

PARADOR DE CÁCERES
Manager: Enrique Comino Aguilar
Calle Ancha, 6
10003 Cáceres, Spain
Tel: (27) 21.17.59, Fax: (27) 21.17.29
31 rooms, Double: Pts 17,500*
*IVA not included, breakfast Pts 1,300
Open all year, Credit cards: all major
Restaurant open daily
265 km N of Seville, 217 km SW of Salamanca
Michelin Map 444, Region: Extremadura

One of the most dramatic paradors in the country, the Duques de Cardona has dominated the fortified town of Cardona for centuries from its 460-meter-high hilltop setting. This site was chosen as a home by the Duke in the 10th century and, although much of the construction is recent, the period flavor and authentic nature of the original building have been maintained. Behind the hotel are a unique 2nd-century tower and 11th-century church along with a beautiful Roman patio from which you can get a "bird's eye" view of the unusual salt hills, the pueblo, and the Pyrenees. All the bedrooms have been totally renovated during 1996. The restaurant is spectacularly situated in a forever-long, dramatic, vaulted-ceilinged room. The ochre-toned walls create a warm glow in the evening, making dinner a special occasion. Although out of the way, this parador offers a memorable night's stay in a carefully renovated historic setting with all the modern comforts of home.

PARADOR DUQUES DE CARDONA
Manager: Francisco Contreras
Castillo s/n
08261 Cardona (Barcelona), Spain
Tel: (3) 86.91.275, Fax: (3) 86.91.636
54 rooms, Double: Pts 16,500–18,000*
*IVA not included, breakfast Pts 1,300
Open all year
Credit cards: all major
Restaurant open daily
99 km NE of Barcelona
Michelin Map 443, Region: Catalonia

The exquisite Casa de Carmona, a noble 15th-century palace located in the picturesque town of Carmona, had fallen into sad disrepair when purchased by Sra. Medina. It took five years plus many pesetas, patience, and love to restore this masterpiece to its original grandeur. No expense was spared to bring every modern amenity, yet retain the authentic character of days gone by. From the moment you step through the massive wooden door into an inner courtyard, the magic begins. Wander through the maze of secluded "secret" patios—your heart will be captivated. Potted fruit trees, marble colonnades, fragrant flowers, the singing of birds, and the gentle gurgling of fountains are entrancing. A romantic walled patio with an exquisite formal garden features a picture-perfect swimming pool fed by five fountains. Doña Marta Medina personally oversaw the interior design and each room is outstanding. On the ground floor is a series of secluded lounges, each with elegant, English-style fabrics and superb antiques. Each guestroom has its own personality, yet maintains a similar look of refined elegance. One of my favorites, room 23, has a romantic view of the rooftops of old Carmona studded by many church steeples. As an added bonus, the Casa de Carmona has the personal touch of a manager who truly cares—Doña Marta Medina's personable son, Felipe.

CASA DE CARMONA
Manager: Felipe Guardiola Medina
Plaza de Lasso 1
41410 Carmona in Andalusia (Seville), Spain
Tel: (5) 41.43.300, Fax: (5) 41.43.752
www.karenbrown.com/spaininns/casadecarmona.html
30 rooms, Double: Pts 18,000–34,000*
*IVA not included, breakfast Pts 2,000
Open all year, Credit cards: all major
Restaurant open daily, pool
44 km E of Seville
Michelin Map 446, Region: Andalusia

Part of the magic of Spain is its surprises. Who could expect to find a restaurant, recommended by Michelin with two red forks, located far off the tourist path in the beautiful, unspoiled countryside of Cantabria? As you drive through this unpopulated area, you will think you are certainly on the wrong road. But, sure enough, in the tiny hamlet of Carmona on a small knoll overlooking a cluster of charming pinkish-stone farmhouses, you find the Venta de Carmona. This nobleman's home, built in 1719 by Don Francisco Díaz, is lovely in its simplicity—a cut-stone, two-story house flanked by twin square towers. The hotel faces an idyllic view of rolling, lush green pastures stretching to wooded hills. The reception area has arched doorways that have been glassed in, allowing the sunlight to brighten the room. Beyond the entry with the reception desk a hallway leads to what makes this hotel so well known—the restaurant. Here you find a very simple dining room with wooden tables and chairs. There is nothing modern to jar the senses. Here country-style meals are served, with regional dishes always featured on the menu. Stairs lead up to the eight guestrooms. These are very basic in decor—just two strips of wood to form the headboards, wooden and leather chairs, and simple bedspreads. Although without an air of sophistication, everything is spotlessly clean and the bathrooms are modern.

VENTA DE CARMONA
Manager: Teresa Martínez Gutiérrez
39014 Carmona (Cantabria), Spain
Tel: (42) 72.80.57, Fax: (42) 32.30.58
9 rooms, Double: Pts 7,000–8,000*
*IVA not included, breakfast Pts 500
Closed Jan to mid-Mar, Credit cards: VS
Restaurant open daily
69 km SW of Santander, 162 km E of Oviedo
Michelin Map 442, Region: Cantabria

The Parador "El Adelantado" is definitely off the beaten path—do not plan to stay here just as a convenient overnight stop, but rather as a sightseeing experience in itself. The address reads Cazorla, but it is actually 25 kilometers away in the Cazorla Sierra nature reserve. Upon reaching Cazorla, follow the signs to the park—the road climbs up from the valley and into the hills. Once beyond the barricade and into the park, it is about 15 kilometers farther to "El Adelantado." The road is well signposted, but be sure to go in daylight or you might get lost. The setting on a small plateau with a sweeping vista of pine-covered mountains is beautiful. On the grassy terrace in front of the hotel there is a large swimming pool that captures the same lovely view. The newly built hotel has a traditional look (which is supposed to resemble an Andalusian farmhouse) with a white stucco façade and red-tiled roof. Inside, the ambiance is appropriately simple. The lounge has leather sofas, an enormous fireplace to warm the room on chilly days, and a spectacular antique oil painting of a hunting scene that almost covers one wall. The dining room has high-backed upholstered chairs, wrought-iron chandeliers, and French doors leading to a terrace. The bedrooms are spacious and nicely decorated with simple wood and leather furniture. Ask for a room with a view (number 1—an enormous room with a balcony—is the very best).

PARADOR "EL ADELANTADO"
Manager: Carmela Doña Diaz
23470 Cazorla (Jaén), Spain
Tel: (53) 72.10.75, Fax: (53) 72.13.03
33 rooms, Double: Pts 13,500–15,000*
*IVA not included, breakfast Pts 1,200
Closed mid-Dec 15 to mid-Feb
Credit cards: all major
Restaurant open daily, pool
46 km E of Ubeda
Michelin Maps 444 & 446, Region: Andalusia

Imaginatively and extensively renovated, this relatively recent addition to the parador chain is a member of the select group that merits four stars. It is located just off the main plaza in the charming, historic town of Chinchón (justifiably famous for its anise liqueur). The plaza, with its many overhanging wood balconies, is very picturesque. The parador is installed in a 17th-century Augustinian monastery, and fountains, hanging and terraced gardens, reflecting pools, and worn stone patios soothe the secular guest here with the same tranquillity once treasured by its previous religious residents. The pale-brick-paved central cloister features a glass-enclosed colonnade, lined with antiques and hung with tapestries. The guestrooms are simple and lovely, floored in red tile, with whitewashed walls and colorful wooden beds topped with cream-colored spreads. The rooms in *la parte vieja* overlooking the garden are particularly attractive, and room 8, with a private sitting room and balcony, is superior for not too many more pesetas. The cheerful dining room is accented with colorful *azulejos* (tiles) and offers an interesting variety of dishes. Try to fit in a visit to the historic restaurant Mesón Cuevas de Vino at the top of town, well known locally for its traditional grills and sangría. Note: The central plaza in Chinchón magically transforms into a bullring in summer.

PARADOR DE CHINCHÓN
Manager: José Menguiano Corbacho
Avenida Generalísimo, 1
28370 Chinchón, Spain
Tel: (1) 89.40.836, Fax: (1) 89.40.908
38 rooms, Double: Pts 17,500*
*IVA not included, breakfast Pts 1,200
Open all year, Credit cards: all major
Restaurant open daily, pool
53 km SE of Madrid
Michelin Map 444, Region: Madrid

Spain has so many lovely old cities that some gems almost go unnoticed. Such is the case with Ciudad Rodrigo, a most convenient overnight stop if you are on your way to Portugal. This walled town perched on a gentle hill is charming and delightfully lacking the hustle and bustle of tourists. Happily, the Parador de Ciudad Rodrigo offers excellent accommodations. The hotel is tucked beside the old stone walls, just a few blocks from the Plaza Mayor. The long, low, ivy-covered stone building is dramatized by a tall stone crenelated tower that rises just behind. Although the building is very old, it has been completely remodeled and some of the original old-world ambiance has been lost with the refinement of new construction. The decor, however, is much more tasteful than that found in many of the paradors and the overall look is warm and cheerful. The bedrooms are attractive. Room 26 (overlooking the back garden) is especially appealing, with hand-carved headboards, rustic wood furniture, and colorful striped, hand-loomed draperies and spreads. The lounge has leather sofas and chairs that stand out nicely against the parquet floor. The dining room is handsome with beamed ceiling and leather and wood chairs. One of the nicest features of this parador is its exquisite terraced rear garden, embraced on two sides by the city walls.

PARADOR DE CIUDAD RODRIGO
Manager: Angel Aliste López
Plaza del Castillo, 1
37500 Ciudad Rodrigo (Salamanca), Spain
Tel: (23) 46.01.50, Fax: (23) 46.04.04
27 rooms, Double: Pts 15,000*
*IVA not included, breakfast Pts 1,200
Open all year, Credit cards: all major
Restaurant open daily
294 km W of Madrid, 89 km SW of Salamanca
Michelin Map 441, Region: Castilla y León

The Hotel Albucasis is a welcome oasis of tranquillity in the bustling tourist center of Córdoba, just a short walk to the colorful mosque and other points of cultural interest. Although centrally located in the Old Jewish Quarter (*Barrio de la Judería*) with its maze of narrow, twisting streets, whitewashed houses, pots of colorful flowers, and romantic wrought-iron balconies, the hotel is quiet. Reflecting the Arabic and Roman style, the Albucasis faces onto its own small courtyard with fresh white walls laced with greenery and potted plants. From the courtyard you enter into the reception area that also serves as a bar and breakfast lounge. Light streams in through a wall of French windows, making the room especially cheerful. The decor is simple and uncluttered with white walls, terra cotta floors, and round tables with wooden chairs. There are nine double and six single rooms—all similar in decor with wooden headboards and matching desk and chair. Although not large, the rooms are of ample size so that you do not feel cramped, and the tiled bathroom are spacious. Best of all, this small hotel is spotless and the high standard of management is apparent throughout. There are many larger, more deluxe hotels in Córdoba, but we think this small, simple hotel offers some of the best quality in town. Note: The Albucasis is difficult to find. The best bet is to park your car, and with a detailed map, first find the hotel on foot (then a parking garage is available for Pts 1,900).

HOTEL ALBUCASIS
Owner: Alfonso Salas Camacho
Buen Pastor, 11
14003 Córdoba, Spain
Tel & fax: (57) 47.86.25
15 rooms, Double: Pts 9,500*
*IVA included, breakfast Pts 850
Closed Jul, Credit cards: MC, VS
No restaurant, breakfast only
143 km NE of Seville
Michelin Maps 444 & 446, Region: Andalusia

The grounds of this parador include acres of grassy hillside, a huge blue swimming pool overlooking the city, and tree-shaded areas ideal for cool walks on hot days—very inviting for travelers who simply want to relax and spend time in the sun. Being of the modern persuasion, this parador does not have the usual antique ambiance—that is certainly not to say that it is not attractive, however. The public rooms seem to cover almost as many acres as the lawn and command spectacular views of the valley and the city. Appointments are equally modern, with occasional tapestries and old-style chandeliers to remind you of the past. The spacious bedrooms are similarly furnished in contemporary Spanish style, and for a ten percent surcharge you can procure a room with the same gorgeous view you see from the lobby and dining room—over the lawn and trees to the city below. The vista is especially attractive at night. All this natural (and man-made) air-conditioned luxury is still only 15 minutes by car or taxi from the Mezquita and the fascinating and colorful old Jewish Quarter.

PARADOR DE LA ARRUZAFA
Manager: Manuel Vietes Rodriguez
Carretera de El Brillante
Avenida de la Arruzafa, s/n
14012 Córdoba, Spain
Tel: (57) 27.59.00, Fax: (57) 57.28.04.09
94 rooms, Double: Pts 15,000–17,500*
*IVA not included, breakfast Pts 1,300
Open all year, Credit cards: all major
Restaurant open daily, pool
143 km NE of Seville
Michelin Maps 444 & 446, Region: Andalusia

Can Fabrica is a charming 17th-century stone farmhouse, only a little over an hour's drive from Barcelona yet blissfully set in the Catalan countryside. In every direction all you see are rolling fields dotted with woodlands and the Pyrenees rising in the distance. This is a simple place to stay—definitely not for those seeking sophisticated luxury, but if you are traveling on a budget, the ambiance, the amenities, the cooking, and the warmth of welcome far exceed what you would expect for such a modest price. (There is even a large swimming pool tucked on the terrace above the inn.) There are six moderate-sized bedrooms, each with a private bath, sweetly decorated by Marta, your enchanting hostess who speaks good English. All of the rooms are tastefully decorated with pieces of furniture either handed down as family heirlooms or found at antique shops and restored by Marta herself. One of my favorites is a corner room with pastel-blue walls, beamed ceiling, an antique queen-sized bed, and an old-fashioned washstand. The dining room, where simple, very good, home-cooked meals are served, exudes a rustic charm. Marta's husband, Ramón, is also very involved in the operation of Can Fabrica and gladly helps guests plan excursions to explore this lovely niche of Spain. Note: The hotel is tucked out in the countryside—ask for a brochure with directions.

CAN FABRICA
Owner: Marta Casanovas-Bohigas
Sta. Llogaia del Terri
17844 Cornellà del Terri (Girona), Spain
Tel & fax: (72) 59.46.29
6 rooms, Double: Pts 7,200*
*IVA & breakfast included
Open from Easter–Christmas, Credit cards: none
Restaurant open daily (hotel guests only), pool
112 km NE of Barcelona, 14 km N of Girona
Michelin Map 443, Region: Catalonia

Have you ever wished you had friends in Spain who owned a romantic hideaway where you could spend your holiday? Wish no more. While staying at Finca Listonero, you will feel like a pampered guest in a private home—and indeed you are. Finca Listonero is the home of Graeme Gibson (originally from Australia) and David Rice (originally from Ireland), who for many years owned an extremely popular restaurant on the Costa del Sol, followed by an equally successful restaurant in Sydney. Now they are back in Spain where they found their dream—a 300-year-old farmhouse tucked up in the hills, not far from the quaint Moorish coastal town of Mojacar. Graeme is an interior designer, and David a talented chef—a perfect combination for their latest venture. The farmhouse, painted a deep rosy-pink, enhanced by bright-green shutters, laced with vines, and accented by a profusion of potted plants, is a happy sight to behold. Inside, the ever-so-cheerful use of color continues: deep rose and green remain the predominant theme, but other colors are used boldly throughout. The eclectic decor reflects Graeme's and David's years of travel. Art Nouveau, European, and Oriental antiques; English fabrics; Spanish tiles; and hand-loomed carpets are cleverly combined to create a welcoming ambiance. Each of the pretty bedrooms has its own color scheme—the Blue Room, featuring pretty English floral fabric, is especially inviting. Note: Plan to dine here—David's meals are truly memorable.

FINCA LISTONERO
Owners: Graeme Gibson & David Rice
Cortijo Grande
04639 Turre (Almería), Spain
Tel & fax: (50) 47.90.94
6 rooms, Double: Pts 10,000–12,000*
*IVA & breakfast included
Closed Aug, Credit cards: MC, VS
Restaurant open daily
288 km E of Málaga
Michelin Map 446, Region: Andalusia

You cannot help falling in love with the Hotel del Oso, superbly located in the glorious mountain range called Picos de Europa. Although it is officially rated two stars, many deluxe hotels could take lessons from this gem. Rarely do you find such a combination of warmth of welcome, faultless housekeeping, superb cuisine, and beautiful displays of flowers. Undoubtedly this degree of excellence is the work of the Rivas family. Sr. Rivas designed the hotel which, although of new construction, maintains a traditional air, blending in with the other beige stone buildings in the region. His charming, friendly wife is the talented chef, and people come from afar to sample her fabulous food (specialties are regional dishes). However, the greatest asset is what few other hotels can offer—four wonderful, talented daughters (Ana, Irene, Teresa, and Cari) who assist in every aspect of the running of the hotel. Their sparkle and genuine hospitality would be difficult to duplicate. On the ground floor there is a wood-paneled reception room, a large dining room, and a cozy bar which opens up to a terrace where tables overlook a crystal-clear stream. The guestrooms are located on two upper floors (each level has its own sitting room). Each of the bedrooms has the same furniture—only the matching fabrics used on the spreads, the curtains, and the cushions vary. Ask for one of the rooms numbered 209 to 213—these have some of the best mountain views.

HOTEL DEL OSO

Manager: Ana Rivas Gonzalez
39539 Cosgaya-Potes (Cantabria), Spain
Tel: (42) 73.30.18, Fax: (42) 73.30.36
www.karenbrown.com/spaininns/hoteldeloso.html
36 rooms, Double: Pts 8,800–9,800*
*IVA not included, breakfast Pts 575
Closed Jan to mid-Feb, Credit cards: MC, VS
Restaurant open daily
129 km SW of Santander, 18 km SW of Potes
Michelin Map 442, Region: Cantabria

Each research trip to Spain reveals a few surprises—such as Covarrubias, an untouristy village tucked into a pocket of rolling hills southeast of Burgos. The town is not top on the list of tourist attractions that one must include on an itinerary, so retains its simple charm, untainted by an onslaught of shops selling souvenirs. You come into the town via a gate that tunnels through a lovely, medieval, honey-colored stone building bearing a coat of arms above the entrance. Almost immediately you are in the main square, the Plaza Mayor, surrounded by interesting buildings, quite different from those you are used to seeing in Spain. Many of the houses in Covarrubias look more Norman than Spanish—timbered buildings with wooden balconies enhanced by cascading geraniums. One of the buildings facing the main square is the Hotel Arlanza whose entrance is sheltered by an arcade formed by massive stone columns. Inside, there is a reception area that opens on the left to a small bar where tables and benches are actually built into the medieval kitchen underneath what in days of yore was the giant flue of the fireplace. There is also an attractive restaurant in the hotel that exudes a rustic charm, with wooden tables surrounded by chairs with rush seats. Like everything in the hotel, the guestrooms are simple and spotlessly clean. I especially liked room 202 with a pretty view over the square.

HOTEL ARLANZA
Manager: Mercedes Miguel Briones
Plaza Mayor 11
09346 Covarrubias (Burgos), Spain
Tel: (47) 40.64.41, Fax: (47) 40.63.59
40 rooms, Double: Pts 10,000*
*IVA not included, breakfast Pts 650
Open mid-Mar mid-Dec, Credit cards: AX, VS
Restaurant open daily
39 km SE of Burgos, 228 km N of Madrid
Michelin Map 442, Region: Castilla y León

One of the latest stars to be added to the Spanish parador group is set in the spectacular 16th-century Convento de San Pablo. The hotel, crowning a rocky promontory, faces across the gorge to Cuenca, a breathtaking town hewn out of the rocks. When staying at the Convento de San Pablo, you can leave your car parked at the parador and take the long footbridge that spans the gorge between two giant outcrops of rock. The interior has been restored with skill to preserve the authentic soul of the old convent. The cloister still remains as the garden in the core of the hotel. The colonnaded walkway (which wraps around the cloister on four sides) now serves as a lounge area for guests, and is furnished with brown wicker furniture accented with cushions in tones of rust and green. The bar, entered through an ornately decorated portal, has dark-green wicker chairs with cushions in green and terra cotta, repeating the color in the potted palms and tiled floor. The vaulted ceiling is elaborately frescoed. In one of the wings there is a beautifully restored, tiny chapel. The dining room is dramatic, with a row of tiered chandeliers highlighting the intricately paneled ceiling. The guestrooms are decorated with reproduction painted headboards and floral-patterned draperies which are color-coordinated with bedspreads and chair coverings.

PARADOR CONVENTO DE SAN PABLO
Manager: José Navio Serrano
Paseo Hoz del Huécar, s/n
16001 Cuenca, Spain
Tel: (69) 23.23.20, Fax: (69) 23.25.34
63 rooms, Double: Pts 17,500–18,500*
*IVA not included, breakfast Pts 1,200
Open all year, Credit cards: all major
Restaurant open daily, pool
164 km SE of Madrid, 209 km NW of Valencia
Michelin Maps 444 & 445, Region: Castilla-La Mancha

The Posada de San José, located in the heart of the walled city of Cuenca, is truly a gem. The inn is tucked onto a tiny cobbled lane behind the church on the Plaza Mayor in this fascinating old city. The entrance is easy to miss—just an antique doorway with a niche alcove above it featuring a charming statue of San José holding the infant Christ. Although not decorator-perfect, the uncontrived ambiance is one of a family-owned hotel that is striving (successfully) on a limited budget to stay true to the authentic, old-world charm of this 16th-century home with its thick stuccoed walls, beamed ceilings, and fabulous old tiled floors. The owners are always on the premises to assure that guests are well taken care of. Jennifer Morter (raised in Canada) speaks perfect English and is especially adept at lending a helping hand when language seems to be a barrier. There is no restaurant, but an ever-so-cozy bar offers light suppers and snacks. The hotel terraces down the hillside, providing most of the guestrooms with stunning views across the Huecar river gorge to the Convento de San Pablo, which is romantically illuminated at night. All of the rooms are pleasant: my favorites are room 33, an incredibly lovely corner room with two balconies, and room 24 with a small alcove with French windows opening to a glorious view. For value and charm, the Posada de San José is a real winner.

POSADA DE SAN JOSÉ
Owners: Jennifer Morter & Antonio Cortinas
Julian Romero 4
16001 Cuenca, Spain
Tel: (69) 21.13.00, Fax: (69) 23.03.65
www.karenbrown.com/spaininns/posadadesanjose.html
30 rooms, Double: Pts 8,400*
*IVA not included, breakfast Pts 500
Open all year, Credit cards: all major
Bar serving light meals closed Mondays
164 km SE of Madrid, 209 km NW of Valencia
Michelin Maps 444 & 445, Region: Castilla-La Mancha

The stately Hotel Victoria Palace, with its English-country-manor flavor, is located a stone's throw from one of the most popular tourist attractions in Spain, yet offers a quiet and luxurious refuge from El Escorial's day trippers and the fast-lane pace of Madrid. To see the whole monastery-cum-palace properly, you will need two visits, and this hotel will make that a pleasant prospect. A welcoming garden café in front (seemingly created for the turn-of-the-century tea-drinking crowd) entices you into the marble-floored lobby and up a graceful, brass-railed double stairway to a spacious lounge with cozy brocade chairs, rich wood paneling, and corner fireplace. Upstairs, past wide landings dappled with sunlight streaming through stained glass, are tastefully appointed bedrooms with lofty ceilings, polished wood floors, and large windows overlooking the gardens. The service, though a bit formal, is correct and knowledgeable. By contrast, the warmly intimate, pub-style bar is charming and friendly. This impressive hotel, with its unique spired roof, will enhance a trip to Phillip II's palace.

HOTEL VICTORIA PALACE
Owner/Manager: J. Miguel Rico
Juan de Toledo, 4
28200 San Lorenzo de El (Madrid), Spain
Tel: (1) 89.01.511, Fax: (1) 89.01.248
87 rooms, Double: Pts 14,500–15,700*
*IVA not included, breakfast Pts 1,100
Open all year, Credit cards: all major
Restaurant open daily, pool
55 km NW of Madrid
Michelin Map 444, Region: Madrid

The restaurant at San Roman de Escalante has three red forks for charm plus a Michelin star for its cuisine. This well-known dining room is in the former stable—a long, low building which is full of character. After dinner, guests can walk across the courtyard to eight guestrooms which are incorporated into a two-story, light-tan-stone, 17th-century farmhouse. As you step through the arched portal into the sunny reception area, a mood of antique elegance is tempered with a modern, avant-garde flair. A large modern chandelier of lavender blown glass sets a color scheme that continues with wicker chairs and sofa with cushions in lavender fabric. Beyond the reception area, a short flight of steps leads to a comfortable guest lounge. Here accents of antiques complement comfortable groupings of chairs and sofas upholstered in blue fabric, blue-and-white-striped draperies, and modern paintings on stark white walls. Throughout the hotel there are many modern paintings and works of art, all of which are for sale. Each of the bedrooms is individually decorated, but all are attractive and have a liberal use of antiques. After a good night's sleep and a hearty breakfast, guests enjoy relaxing in the garden which is surrounded by a large park. Across the small road from the hotel is a beautiful 12th-century chapel also called San Roman de Escalante.

SAN ROMAN DE ESCALANTE
Manager: Juan Melis
39795 Escalante (Cantabria), Spain
Tel: (42) 67.77.45, Fax: (42) 67.76.43
10 rooms, Double: from Pts 13,000–18,000*
*IVA not included, breakfast Pts 1,250
Closed last week Dec, Credit cards: all major
Restaurant open daily
1.5 km from Escalante, on road to Castillo
35 km E of Santander, 68 km NW of Bilbao
Michelin Map 442, Region: Cantabria

This parador has a distinctly different flavor from most of the other paradors in Spain. Instead of presenting an old-world look, there is an unpretentious, rather masculine, nautical ambiance—a most appropriate theme for its waterfront position. The square, three-story building (painted white with stone trim around the windows) is not very old, but definitely has a traditional feel. The setting (particularly if you are interested in ships) is very interesting: the hotel sits on a high embankment overlooking Ferrol's long row of naval yards, and beyond to the commercial docks. A wide terrace in front of the hotel has benches, rose gardens, a gigantic anchor, and several antique canons—poised guarding the harbor. To the right of the lobby (which has a handsome floor with a harlequin pattern of alternating large dark-gray and beige marble tiles) is a large lounge which looks a bit like a men's club with dark-red leather chairs and sofas, potted palms, fresh flowers, nautical prints on the walls, and a marvelous antique oil painting of two ships in the midst of battle. A sunny dining room with bentwood chairs set around small tables and two entire walls of windows overlooks the harbor. The guestrooms are spacious and traditional in decor. Number 25, a corner room, is especially large and has a great view of the harbor.

PARADOR DE FERROL
Manager: Amando Baños
Plaza Eduardo Pondal
15401 Ferrol (La Coruña), Spain
Tel & fax: (81) 35.67.20
39 rooms, Double: Pts 13,500–15,000*
*IVA not included, breakfast Pts 1,200
Open all year, Credit cards: all major
Restaurant open daily
104 km NE of Santiago de Compostela
Michelin Map 441, Region: Galicia

Granada's Parador San Francisco is the most popular parador in Spain—snaring a room is well nigh impossible in the high season unless reservations are made months in advance. An excellent alternate choice is the Hotel Alhambra Palace, a deluxe, well-located hotel with splendid views. From here you can gaze out from your room over the Alhambra, the cathedral, and the historic city through Moorish arched windows. The Hotel Alhambra Palace is on the road that weaves up through the wooded parklike grounds to the gate where you buy your tickets to visit the Alhambra. From the hotel it is a pleasant walk to this entrance. Opened in 1910, the Hotel Alhambra Palace has long been a mainstay of the Alhambra hotels. Andrés Segovia, the famous Spanish guitarist, played his first concert here, and it remains a favorite hotel choice in Granada for most visiting dignitaries. The sumptuous decor of the public rooms is enchantingly, almost overwhelmingly, Moorish—from the intricately carved ceilings, unusual decorative touches, to the symmetrically placed arched doorways and colorful tiled walls. The bedrooms are large and comfortable (the Andrés Segovia suite is magnificent). The hotel is air conditioned—a blessing in Granada's hot summer months. Savor one of the best views in Spain from the expansive bar area or the outdoor terrace.

HOTEL ALHAMBRA PALACE
Manager: Francisco Hernandez
Peña Partida, 2
18009 Granada, Spain
Tel: (58) 22.14.68, Fax: (58) 22.64.04
145 rooms, Double: Pts 20,500*
*IVA not included, breakfast Pts 1,300
Open all year, Credit cards: all major
Restaurant open daily
127 km NE of Málaga
Michelin Map 446, Region: Andalusia

Although officially holding just a one-star rating, the Hotel America is in our estimation far superior in many ways to some so-called "superior" class hotels. Its most outstanding feature is its location. No matter what you pay, you cannot be any closer to the portion of the Alhambra reserved for paying sightseers—the Hotel America is on the citadel grounds, just steps away from the entrance. But the America has more than location. The hotel is a pretty, cream-colored stucco, three-story building with red-tiled roof, enhanced by lacy vines and black wrought-iron light fixtures. To the left of the reception area is a sitting area with a cozy clutter of old-fashioned furniture. When days are balmy, guests' favorite place to congregate is the inner courtyard—an inviting small oasis enhanced by blue-and-white-tile tables and an overhead leafy trellis. My favorite room of all is the hotel's romantic little dining room, a real gem with beautiful antique paneling and walls decorated by oil paintings, handsome mirrors, and colorful plates. There are only eight tables, surrounded by pretty, country-style chairs with rush seats. The meals are reasonably priced and excellent. Remember that this is a simple hotel, so if you are fussy and like everything just perfect, this is not the place for you, but the Hotel America makes an excellent choice for a cozy, family-run hotel with an unbeatable location.

HOTEL AMERICA
Manager: Maribel Alconchel
53, Real de La Alhambra
18009 Granada, Spain
Tel: (58) 22.74.71, Fax: (58) 22.74.70
13 rooms, Double: Pts 14,460*
*IVA & breakfast included
Open Mar to Nov 9, Credit cards: all major
Restaurant open daily
127 km NE of Málaga
Michelin Map 446, Region: Andalusia

This is Spain's most famous and popular parador, and as a result reservations must be secured at least six to eight months in advance. Installed in a 15th-century convent, restoration has been carried out so as to retain much of the original structure, including the chapel where Queen Isabella was first buried before being moved to the cathedral downtown. Outside, lovely Alhambra-style gardens and walks blend well with the neighboring marvel. Inside, the decor is a mixture of Moorish and Christian. The former shows up in wonderful ceilings, carved doors, ceramic tile, and the graceful arches in the beautiful interior patio. The public rooms are rich in antique religious art objects— paintings, sculpture, and colorful tapestries. The guestrooms are comfortably unostentatious, with period accents and views varying from excellent to ordinary. The dining room is in a style apart—its walls are lined with handsome contemporary abstract paintings. An outstanding feature of the parador is its secluded location within the Alhambra—an oasis of calm in the usually bustling tourist area.

PARADOR SAN FRANCISCO
Manager: Juan Antonio Gianello Louro
Real de La Alhambra s/n
18009 Granada, Spain
Tel: (58) 22.14.40, Fax: (58) 22.22.64
38 rooms, Double: Pts 33,000*
*IVA not included, breakfast Pts 1,300
Open all year, Credit cards: all major
Restaurant open daily
127 km NE of Málaga
Michelin Map 446, Region: Andalusia

The Parador de Gredos, built in 1926 as a hunting lodge for King Alfonso XIII, was the very first in what has grown to be a large network of government-sponsored hotels. Surrounded by pine forests, mountains, large rock formations, green meadows, and rushing streams, the hotel is a favorite weekend getaway for residents of Madrid. The parador's charm is not immediately apparent: at first glance, it appears as a large, rather sterile, gray stone building with a French gray-tile mansard roof. Once you are inside, the charm of the hotel emerges. The decor is most appealing: nothing is cute or contrived—just a simple, hunting-lodge ambiance. The floors are wood-planked, the ceilings timbered, the furniture mostly leather. The white walls are decorated with hunting scenes, prints of wild animals found in the area, and hunting trophies. Wrought-iron chandeliers hang from beamed ceilings and fresh green plants are strategically placed throughout the immaculately kept rooms. The emphasis is not on antiques, but there are many hand-carved chests, authentic high-backed benches, fine writing desks, clocks, and rustic-style tables. The guestrooms continue the simple hunting-lodge look with wooden furniture, hand-woven-look drapes and spreads, and pretty scatter rugs on hardwood floors. There is a large play yard with gym sets and slides for young guests on a terrace behind the hotel.

PARADOR DE GREDOS
Manager: Fernando Alonso Almeida
05635 Sierra de Gredos (Ávila), Spain
Tel: (20) 34.80.48, Fax: (20) 34.82.05
77 rooms, Double: Pts 11,500–12,500*
*IVA not included, breakfast Pts 1,300
Open all year, Credit cards: all major
Restaurant open daily
170 km W of Madrid, 60 km SW of Ávila
Michelin Map 444, Region: Castilla y León

Shadowed by the famous monastery's towers, this inn was a Hieronymite hospital and pharmacy in the 16th century, but since the days of Ferdinand and Isabella has sheltered those who came to worship. Until 1960 visitors exchanged a daily donation of a mere 50 pesetas for accommodation. Still today, for value received and atmosphere, follow the footsteps of the faithful to this inn, as there is nothing comparable in Guadalupe, or anywhere else. Sharing and managing the edifice is an active Franciscan religious order, whose guides regularly conduct an insider's tour of their monastery, museum, and cathedral—a crazy and wonderful mixture of Mudéjar and Gothic architecture. The hotel rooms overlook the original stone-arched and paved hospital patio. Their decor varies wildly—some incredible, but all adequate and all with baths. To stay here is to live and breathe the history of Spain. Request a room on the gallery: number 120 is especially nice—given to visiting religious notables; the second-floor corner suite (number 108) is baroquely elegant and many third-floor rooms boast original Mudéjar ceilings. Delicious fare and homemade wine are served under a high wooden ceiling in a richly paneled dining room.

HOSPEDERÍA EL REAL MONASTERIO
Manager: Juan Barrerra
Plaza S.M. Juan Carlos I
10140 Guadalupe (Cáceres), Spain
Tel: (27) 36.70.00, Fax: (27) 36.71.77
47 rooms, Double: Pts 7,250*
*IVA not included, breakfast Pts 800
Closed mid-Jan to mid-Feb, Credit cards: MC, VS
Restaurant open daily
225 km SW of Madrid, 129 km NE of Mérida
Michelin Map 444, Region: Extremadura

Built in the 14th century as a hospital to shelter and minister to pilgrims who came to venerate the famous Black Virgin of Guadalupe, this parador now provides admirably for the needs of the modern-day visitor. It is located directly across the street from the Franciscan monastery in a village from which the Catholic monarchs granted permission for Columbus's ships to depart for the New World. Whitewashed, with red roof tiles, the Zurbarán invites you to enjoy its cool, Moorish gardens sheltering a sparkling turquoise pool, and to dine on its outdoor terrace overlooking a tiled, Mudéjar fountain. Thanks to the local craftsmen, colorful tile is found throughout the hotel: the interior patio is especially lovely. When remodeled, the parador added 20 new rooms, all with garden-view terraces, which maintain the period ambiance faithfully. However, the old rooms with low, stone doorways are still the favorites—some have canopied beds, fireplaces, and balconies (ask for *una habitación antigua con terraza*). But, no matter the room, this is a special inn in a tranquil and picturesque locale.

PARADOR DE GUADALUPE
Manager: José Manuel Piña
Marqués de la Romana, 12
10140 Guadalupe (Cáceres), Spain
Tel: (27) 36.70.75, Fax: (27) 36.70.76
40 rooms, Double: Pts 13,500–15,000*
*IVA not included, breakfast 1,300
Open all year, Credit cards: all major
Restaurant open daily, pool
225 km SW of Madrid, 129 km NE of Mérida
Michelin Map 444, Region: Extremadura

Just after you enter into the walled medieval town of Hondarribia by way of the Santa María gate, a small "Hotel Obispo" sign indicates that you turn right and go around the corner. Here you find wrought-iron gates leading into a completely enclosed courtyard, embraced on one side by the 14th-century ramparts of the town. The lush green lawn studded with colorful beds of well tended flowers is set off to perfection by the austerity of the cut-stone façade. A wide stone staircase leads up from the courtyard to the reception lounge where you might be greeted by the owner, Bihor Alza, who takes a very personal interest in the running of his intimate hotel. Throughout the hotel there are a few antiques plus some reproductions which are enhanced by lovely traditional fabrics. Each of the guestrooms has its own personality, with a color scheme set by the painted walls (in pink, blue, green, or yellow). My favorite, 202, is a most attractive room with walls painted a soft yellow, black wrought-iron headboard, a blue-and-off-white bedspread, and two small French-style carved wooden chairs with cushions in blue and cream striped fabric. There is a 14-person cozy dining room with exposed stone walls which is open in the summer, but one of my favorite rooms is the cheerful breakfast room, walled on one side with windows opening onto the lovely garden.

HOTEL OBISPO
Owner: Bihor Alza
Obispo Square, 1
20280 Hondarribia (Guipúzcoa), Spain
Tel: (43) 34 64.54.00, Fax: (43) 34 64.23.86
17 rooms, Double: Pts 11,500–15,200*
*IVA not included, breakfast Pts 1,000
Open all year, Credit cards: all major
Restaurant open daily
18 km E of Sebastián
Michelin Map 442, Region: Pays Basque

As you enter through the Santa María gate of Hondarribia and head up toward the main square (Plaza de Armas), the Hotel Pampinot is located on the right side of the Calle Mayor in the shadow of the beautiful parish church of Santa Maria de Asunción. From the outside, the austere stone façade looks similar to the other 16th- and 17th-century gray stone mansions that line the narrow street—just a small hotel sign indicates you have found the proper house. Inside, a surprise awaits: the stern exterior does not hint at the opulence within. The reception is a spacious area with a massive stone floor and exposed stone walls which set off to perfection two large altar pieces, intricately and colorfully painted, which dominate facing walls. Beyond the entrance lobby is one of my favorite rooms, a delightful little bar tucked into what was once the fireplace. A huge antique chest set below the mantle serves as the "bar" and the entire space above the mantle is filled with a collection of brightly painted antique plates. A wide staircase with iron railings topped by a polished brass banister leads up to the guestrooms. There are only eight—four on each level—each individually decorated. One of my favorites, room 103, has whimsical clouds and birds painted on the ceiling. Pampinot is filled with history: in its days of glory it even housed María Theresa while on her journey to marry Louis XIV of France.

HOTEL PAMPINOT
Owner/Manager: Olga Alvarez
Calle Mayor 5
20280 Hondarribia (Guipúzcoa), Spain
Tel: (43) 64.06.00, Fax: (43) 64.51.28
8 rooms, Double: Pts 12,500*
*IVA not included, breakfast Pts 1,100
Open all year, Credit cards: all major
No restaurant, breakfast only
18 km E of Sebastián
Michelin Map 442, Region: Pays Basque

Parador El Emperador is located on the border of the Basque country, in the picturesque medieval walled town of Hondarribia (also called Fuenterrabía). Installed in a 12th-century castle, overlooking a beautiful square lined by brightly colored houses, the imposing stone castle has been occupied by Ferdinand and Isabella and also their grandson Charles V. The building's incredible 3-meter-thick walls have withstood countless assaults over the centuries. An outstanding feature of the Emperador is its stone-paved lobby, featuring lances, cannon, suits of armor, tapestries, and a remarkable, soaring 15-meter ceiling, overlooked through stone arches by a cozy lounge with a beamed ceiling. The interior glass-enclosed, flower-filled courtyard has comfortable wicker chairs where guests can relax. (One side of the courtyard retains the original stone wall.) Beyond the inner courtyard is a grand outdoor terrace with a sweeping view of the blue bay dotted with colorful boats. Not only are the setting and structure of this parador outstanding, but the interior (filled with astounding antiques) is stunning—rivaling the finest hotels in Spain. There is absolutely nothing to fault in this incredible parador. But be sure to book far in advance since it is very popular.

PARADOR EL EMPERADOR
Manager: Pilar de Miguel
Plaza de Armas, 14
20280 Hondarribia (Guipúzcoa), Spain
Tel: (43) 64.55.00, Fax: (43) 64.21.53
36 rooms, Double: Pts 18,000–19,000*
*IVA not included, breakfast Pts 1,300
Open all year, Credit cards: all major
No restaurant, breakfast only
18 km E of Sebastián
Michelin Map 442, Region: Pays Basque

Pikes (pronounced *Peekays*) has its own special personality. Not your "run-of-the-mill" hotel at all, this intimate inn is a favorite hideaway of the world's rich and famous and it is not at all surprising they flock here. Pikes offers 24 guestrooms, each decorated with a dramatic flair worthy of a stage setting. They are discreetly housed in a cluster of honey-beige-toned cottages that offer privacy. However, most of the guests I saw did not seem to be seeking seclusion, but were sunning by the swimming pool, playing tennis, taking advantage of the exercise room, or laughing with friends at the bar. An air of unpretentious informality prevails, conducive to guests becoming friends. Pathways crisscross through the beautifully tended gardens which include walls of cascading bougainvillea, roses, hibiscus, geraniums, daisies, carnations, and fragrant lavender. The heart of the property is a 300-year-old finca (farmhouse) where the stunning dining room and bar offer authentic rustic charm. The thick stone walls, arched doorways, low, beamed ceilings, and old olive press create a romantic atmosphere for tables set with pretty linens, fresh flowers, and softly glowing candles. And, best of all, the food is outstanding. If you can tear yourself away from this oasis tucked into the low hills outside of San Antoni, there are beaches, golf, and sights to see nearby.

HOTEL PIKES
Owner: Anthony J. Pike
Calle Sa Vurera
07820 San Antoni de Portmany, Ibiza
Balearic Islands, Spain
Tel: (71) 34.22.22, Fax: (71) 34.23.12
24 rooms, Double: Pts 27,000–36,000*
*IVA not included, breakfast Pts 1,200
Open all year, Credit cards: all major
Restaurant open daily, pool
1.5 km E of San Antoni de Portmany
Michelin Map 443, Region: Balearic Islands

Words cannot prepare you for the magical setting of the Hotel Hacienda. As you approach, the road gradually climbs through a gentle forest of pines to a sparkling white building. When you check in, the Hacienda seems lovely, but not so different from other luxury hotels: it is only when you open the door into your bedroom that the absolute splendor of the Hacienda unfolds. The hotel is built into the hillside and what appears at first to be a one-story structure actually cascades down the hill with six floors of guestrooms—each with a view "to die for." Views just don't get any better. Spread before you are giant cliffs of granite that plunge into the sea, forming idyllic, small coves where the blue sea dances in the sunlight. All of the bedrooms have either a terrace or a balcony. The superior rooms and suites have large Jacuzzi tubs in front of picture windows. If your heart is not set on relaxing in your bath while soaking in the view, the standard rooms offer the same amenities, but, instead of a Jacuzzi, have a larger balcony. The public areas combine the feel of Ibiza with a touch of Andalusia, reflected in two inner courtyards, one with palm trees, the other with a covered pool. There are two more swimming pools, one romantically perched on the cliff overlooking the sea.

HOTEL HACIENDA
Owner: Sr Lipszyc
Xamena, 07815 San Miguel
Ibiza, Balearic Islands, Spain
(Mailing address: Apartado 423, 07800, Ibiza)
Tel: (71) 33.45.00, Fax: (71) 33.45.14
www.karenbrown.com/spaininns/hotelhacienda.html
63 rooms, Double: Pts 37,300–45,100*
*IVA not included, breakfast Pts 2,100
Open mid-Apr to Nov, Credit cards: all major
Restaurant open daily, pools
6 km N of San Miguel
Michelin Map 443, Region: Balearic Islands

For many years Ellen Trauffer came from Switzerland to Ibiza on holiday. In 1987 she purchased a whitewashed, centuries-old finca (farmhouse)—one of only a few that still exist on the island—and opened it as a hotel. You enter into a large living room exuding a fresh and pretty rustic charm. In the corner is a fireplace with a cozy grouping of white slip-covered chairs, and a blue-and-white-striped sofa. The blue-and-white color scheme continues in the cheerful dining room which has a flagstone floor and windows on three sides. The chef (who is co-owner of the property) prepares excellent meals using fresh produce from the island. All of the individually decorated bedrooms are attractive. Number 14 (with a four-poster canopy bed and a view of the garden) is a special favorite. Ibiza has many moderately priced hotels, but most from the same cookie cutter—modern white high-rises. In comparison, La Colina is truly a gem. Although not on the sea, it has a large swimming pool and makes a good base from which to venture out each day to explore Ibiza's many enchanting small beaches and coves. It is not by chance that this remarkably inexpensive hotel offers such quality since Ellen is no novice: she also has a hotel in Switzerland. Guests come back year after year.

LA COLINA
Owner: Ellen Trauffer
Carretera Ibiza a Santa Eulalia
07840 Santa Eulalia del Río
Balearic Islands, Spain
Tel & fax: (71) 33.27.67
www.karenbrown.com/spain/santaeulaliadelrio.html
16 rooms, Double: Pts 10,800–13,600*
*IVA & breakfast included
Open all year, Credit cards: all major
Restaurant open daily, pool
5 km SW of Santa Eulalia on PM 810 to Ibiza
Michelin Map 443, Region: Balearic Islands

This engaging Parador Castillo de Santa Catalina crowns the ridge of Cerro (hill) de Santa Catalina, the patron saint of Jaén, and flanks the 13th-century Arabic fortress after which it is named and whose architecture it imitates. It is immediately apparent that much imaginative effort went into the construction of this "copycat" castle-hotel. The public rooms feature cavernous fireplaces, recessed windows, and tapestry-hung stone-brick walls which soar to carved-wood or granite ceilings. The drawing room is especially dramatic with 20-meter-tall crossed arches. The high-ceilinged guestrooms are spacious and bright, with rough-hewn brick floors trimmed in green tile, leather and wood furniture, cheery spreads and throw-rugs, and shiny green-and-white-tiled baths. Each has a roomy terrace commanding panoramic vistas over the city, the fertile Guadalquivir river valley, and an endless expanse of undulating hills studded with the olive groves for which this region is renowned. Tranquil will define your stay here, which should be combined with a visit to the Arab baths and the *barrio de Magdalena* in Jaén, which spreads out in the valley below the hotel.

PARADOR CASTILLO DE SANTA
CATALINA
Manager: Antonio Romero Huete
23001 Jaén, Spain
Tel: (53) 23.00.00, Fax: (53) 23.09.30
45 rooms, Double: Pts 17,500*
*IVA not included, breakfast Pts 1,300
Open all year, Credit cards: all major
Restaurant open daily, pool
90 km N of Granada
Michelin Map 446, Region: Andalusia

In the 15th century, the Counts of Oropesa built a fortress surrounded by gardens on the hillside above the fertile, tobacco-growing Tiétar Valley. Their noble home is now the Carlos V, beautifully preserved, with odd-shaped towers, ramparts, and a drawbridge completing the late-medieval picture. As you might guess from the name, Carlos V once briefly resided here, and the dramatic large fireplace in the lounge was added at his request since he found the castle chilly in winter. The wooded grounds surrounding the parador are beautifully tended and just beckon you to stroll around. Tucked into the gardens are a pretty swimming pool, a tennis court, and a children's play yard. The cool, stone-paved inner courtyard has ivy-covered walls and a placid central pool, overlooked by a terraced second-floor lounge with fireplace and lovely antiques. There are 16 guestrooms in the original building and an additional 37 in a modern annex. The parador has been redecorated by one of the best decorators in Spain and has as emerged as one of the "smartest" in the chain. The manager is "keen on cleanliness" and it certainly shows. The spacious high ceilings, rich wood floors, and antique furnishings of the castle chambers lend an atmosphere impossible to duplicate. The addition of a swimming pool and tennis facilities have only enhanced this charming hilltop hideaway.

PARADOR CARLOS V
Manager: Susana de la Rubia Gómez-Morán
Carretera de Plasencia
10450 Jarandilla de la Vera (Cáceres), Spain
Tel: (27) 56.01.17, Fax: (27) 56.00.88
53 rooms, Double: Pts 16,500–17,500*
*IVA not included, breakfast Pts 1,300
Open all year, Credit cards: all major
Restaurant open daily, pool
213 km SW of Madrid
Michelin Map 444, Region: Extremadura

Whereas many of the beach towns on Spain's popular Costa Blanca are dominated by towering hotels and condominium projects, somehow Javea has managed to keep a low profile. There is a small, pretty curve of sandy beach, rimmed by shops and restaurants. Embracing one end of the crescent of sand is a tiny peninsula that is home to the Parador Costa Blanca. The front of the modern hotel—a white stucco, five-story building—looks like a typical beach hotel but on the inside, the true merits of the hotel emerge. The spacious reception area opens onto the lounge with a wall of windows looking out to the terrace and garden. The decor is simple but pleasing, with Spanish hand-loomed rugs accenting cream-colored marble floors, comfortable brown-leather sofas, large paintings on the walls, and a profusion of green plants. Next to the hotel there is a terrace framed by colorful flowers in ceramic pots and beyond that is an expanse of meticulously tended lawn (dotted by large palm trees and rose beds) which stretches out to the sea. The garden is definitely the highlight of this hotel. There are even a few Roman ruins in the garden, attesting to the fact that the Romans, too, thought this a prime location. The bedrooms are spacious, furnished with contemporary, built-in furniture, and all but five have a balcony and view of the sea.

PARADOR COSTA BLANCA
Manager: Victor Teodisio Tirado
Playa del Arenal, 2
03730 Javea (Alicante), Spain
Tel: (6) 57.90.200, Fax: (6) 57.90.308
65 rooms, Double: Pts 18,500–19,500*
*IVA not included, breakfast Pts 1,300
Open all year, Credit cards: all major
Restaurant open daily, pool
110 km SE of Valencia
Michelin Map 445, Region: Valencia (Costa Blanca)

The San Marcos is elegantly installed in what was originally an elaborate stone monastery commissioned by Ferdinand (the Catholic king) at the beginning of the 16th century. Before its conversion to a hotel in 1965, it was used as a military prison and stable which saw lots of activity during the Civil War. Its immense façade is deceptive, as there are only 35 rooms in the historic part of the edifice (referred to as the *zona noble*). The rest of the space is occupied by an exquisite stone patio peopled with statues of saints, an archaeological museum, a chapel, spacious lounges and hallways lavishly furnished with antiques, and a modern restaurant offering a delectable menu (the scallops, or *vieiras*, are superb). The old rooms are discovered off a maze of creaky, worn hallways and are large and comfortable, with high ceilings, old-world ambiance and antique furnishings. The suites overlooking the entrance are a treat: enormous and secured behind walls now centuries old. The rooms in the new addition will not disappoint; they are quiet, maintain a traditional Spanish flavor, and overlook a lovely interior garden. The San Marcos is steeped in history and has a gracious staff.

HOSTAL SAN MARCOS
Manager: Manuel Miguelez
Plaza San Marcos, 7
24001 León, Spain
Tel: (87) 23.73.00, Fax: (87) 23.34.58
35 rooms, Double: Pts 21,500*
*IVA not included, breakfast Pts 1400
Open all year, Credit cards: all major
Restaurant open daily
194 km W of Burgos; 88 km S of Oviedo
Michelin Maps 441 & 442, Region: Castilla y León

This select hotel is an experience unto itself, spectacularly situated on over 1,000 acres of scenic countryside. No detail has been overlooked to offer every convenience in a distinctive atmosphere combining characteristic Andalusian style with contemporary elegance. Graceful Moorish arches, carved-wood ceilings, tiled patios, grilled terraces, marble fountains, and blossoming gardens surround the pampered guest in this intimate hideaway. A sampling of the services that come with the pricey accommodation here is: fitness equipment and programs, saunas, Jacuzzi, tennis, fishing (nearby), horseback riding, climbing, indoor and magnificent outdoor pools, concerts, and a staff that outnumbers the clientele. Each spacious guestroom is unique, richly and imaginatively decorated in soft colors, with a large bathroom (featuring both bath and shower), and either a balcony or garden patio from which you can enjoy the tranquil landscape. The orientation of rooms 1 to 6 (suites) and 7 and 10 (doubles) provides them with particularly ample upstairs terraces. In addition, you have your choice of two dining spots, one of which, La Finca, has gained justifiable regional renown. Note: La Bobadilla is not in Loja, but located north of Salinas (between Granada and Antequera) on C334.

HOTEL LA BOBADILLA
Manager: José E. Sanz SampedroFinca La
Bobadilla
18300 Loja (Granada), Spain
Tel: (58) 32.18.61, Fax: (58) 32.18.10
60 rooms, Double: Pts 36,540–45,900*
*IVA not included, breakfast included
Open all year, Credit cards: all major
Restaurant open daily, pools
72 km W of Granada, 71 km NE of Málaga
A-95 at Km. 175, 72 Kms. far from Granada
Michelin Map 446, Region: Andalucia

The good-value-for-money Hotel Arosa is in a large building in the heart of Madrid. The only part of the hotel at street level is the small lobby (serviced by a doorman)—the actual hotel is on the upper levels. Two elevators go to the different floors. The quaint one on the right—a tiny, five-sided affair—is unique, obviously having been constructed to fit the precise space available. Found on the third floor (Spanish second) is a pleasant reception, lobby, and restaurant area whose decorative style could be called intense: pseudo-French with antique accents. But it is spacious, attractive, and comfortable, and a veritable oasis in the heart of the noisy town. The bedrooms, each different in shape and size, are individually decorated. Some have a modern feel while others (such as 509, a pretty corner room with sprigged floral design on the walls) have a more traditional ambiance. An especially nice feature is that you can request a non-smoking room. The air-conditioning is not .he best so you often have to have your window open which lets in a cacophony of traffic noise. Although you might see some "women of the night" a few blocks away, the location is very good: a few minutes by foot to the chic Puerta del Sol (a shopper's paradise) and the Plaza Mayor with its charming cafés. The Arosa remains one of Madrid's best buys

HOTEL AROSA
Owner: Fernando de Leon
Calle Salud, 21
28013 Madrid, Spain
Tel: (1) 53.21.600, Fax: (1) 53.13.127
www.karenbrown.com/spaininns/hotelarosa.html
139 rooms, Double: Pts 18,745–22,732*
*IVA included, breakfast Pts 1,300
Open all year, Credit cards: all major
Restaurant open daily
Michelin Map 444, Region: Madrid

The Hotel Villa Real, facing a tiny plaza just off the beautiful tree-lined Paseo de la Castellana, is a rare jewel—a tranquil oasis of refined elegance. The location, in the heart of Madrid's famous triangle (formed by the Thyssen Bornemisza Museum, the Prado Museum, and the Reina Sofia Museum) is absolute perfection. Although a deluxe hotel, there is nothing intimidating nor stuffy about the Hotel Villa Real. Every one of the well-trained staff (from the receptionist to the maid who turns down your bed at night) is gracious and seems to take personal pride in making you feel welcome. From the moment you enter, there is a home-like ambiance—subdued lighting, rich wood paneling, fine mirrors, marble floors, and antique French chairs on fine Oriental carpets. Refreshingly lacking is the commercial hurly-burly usually associated with city hotels. The guestrooms are really special. Even the "standard" rooms are mini-suites: the beds are on one level and three steps lead down to a cozy sitting area with comfortable sofa, upholstered chairs, writing desk, and, of course, television. Most of the rooms even have a small balcony where you can step outside to enjoy the magic of Madrid. One of our favorites (room 315) overlooks the tiny Plaza de las Cortes. The Hotel Villa Real's goal "to ensure that whoever visits us will find a family atmosphere in which they can feel truly at home" is without a doubt fulfilled.

Hotel Villa Real
Manager: Félix García Hernán
Plaza de Las Cortes, 10
28014 Madrid, Spain
Tel: (1) 42.03.767, Fax: (1) 42.02.547
115 rooms, Double: Pts 18,000–33,000*
*IVA not included, breakfast Pts 1,800
Open all year, Credit cards: all major
Restaurant open daily
Michelin Map 444, Region: Madrid

Frequently referred to as one of the world's top ten hotels, The Ritz, across the street from the Prado Museum, is all one could ask for in a world-class hotel. The opulent old-world decor has been restored and creates a *Belle Époque* ambiance. The restoration is based on considerable research to ensure that the decor re-creates exactly its 1910 glory. A statue of Diana that had graced the upper hall bar was retrieved, restored, and replaced where it had stood for the first 40 years of the hotel's existence. The expanse of lobby and grand hall behind it are magnificent. The restaurant, which features regional specialties, is hung with dramatic tapestries that were refurbished by the original makers, the Royal Tapestry Factory. There is a delightful outdoor garden, an oasis of greenery, where guests relax on old-fashioned white wicker chairs. The bedrooms are spectacular in their decor and the same glorious hand-woven carpet that adorns the rest of the hotel has been custom-woven to fit each one. Everything, from the striking gold bathroom fixtures to the tasteful and handsome furnishings, will make you feel pampered. There is also a fitness center with sauna and massage. The Ritz successfully combines the luxury of the contemporary world with turn-of-the-century elegance. It is able to provide the comfort and facilities all guests could desire, whether they are royalty, diplomats, movie stars, or tourists who desire the finest accommodations.

THE RITZ
Manager: Alfonso Jordán
Plaza de la Lealtad, 5
28014 Madrid, Spain
Tel: (1) 52.12.857, Fax: (1) 53.28.776
158 rooms, Double: Pts 52,000–64,000*
*IVA not included, breakfast Pts 2,950
Open all year, Credit cards: all major
Restaurant open daily
Michelin Map 444, Region: Madrid

The Parador de Málaga de Golf is not actually in Málaga, but well located just a short drive west of town. It is easy to find, with a "Parador" sign marking the exit from the N340, which is also the airport exit. A pretty tree- and flower-lined lane leads to the hotel which, although of new construction, happily mimics the delightful Andalusian style, with white-stuccoed exterior, wrought-iron accents, and the typical red-tiled roof. You enter into a one-story-wing where the reception area, dining room, lounges, and game rooms are located. The guestrooms are found in two wings stretching out from these public areas, forming a U. In the center is a large lawn accented by flowerbeds, palm trees, and a swimming pool. The open end of the U faces the sea where a long, sandy beach beckons to be explored. All of the spacious guestrooms are attractively decorated with rattan furniture which is enhanced by very attractive, color-coordinated fabrics on the chairs, bedspreads, and drapes. As an added bonus, all the bedrooms have either a balcony or patio facing the gardens and pool. As the name might suggest, the emphasis of this parador is on golf and many guests come to play the course that surrounds the hotel. In winter (from November to the end of February) guests may use the golf course free of charge.

PARADOR DE MÁLAGA DE GOLF
Manager: Juan Garcia Alonso
Autovía-Málaga-Algeciras
29080 Málaga, Spain
Tel: (5) 23.81.255, Fax: (5) 23.82.141
60 rooms, Double: Pts 17,500*
*IVA not included, breakfast Pts 1,300
Open all year, Credit cards: all major
Restaurant open daily, pool
8 km W of Málaga, Airport-Coin exit off N340
Michelin Map 446, Region: Andalusia

Situated on Mount Gibralfaro, high above the sprawling port of Málaga, this premier parador commands a stunning view. Installed in an old stone mansion with wrought-iron grilles and arcaded wrap-around galleries, the hotel is surrounded by hillside greenery and located within easy walking distance of a ruined Moorish fortress that once guarded this proud town. This popular parador was closed for a lengthy renovation but reopened in the summer of 1995. Now, once again, if you want to stay along the Costa del Sol, this marvelous parador is truly choice for excellence of accommodation, ambiance, and, above all, the incredible setting. What had been a simple, 12-room hotel has grown in size and quality. In addition to the new bedrooms that have been added to meet the demand for accommodations, a small rooftop swimming pool with a view has also been built. The dramatic panorama is also available from the restaurant, making it an extremely appealing dining spot during warm weather (as evidenced by the number of locals who make the trip up the steep hill to dine). This newly enhanced parador is very popular, so be sure to book well in advance during the high season.

PARADOR DE MÁLAGA GIBRALFARO
Manager: Juan Garcia Alonso
Camino del Castillo de Gibralfaro
29016 Málaga, Spain
Tel: (5) 22.21.902, Fax: (5) 22.21.904
38 rooms, Double: Pts 18,000–20,000*
*IVA not included, breakfast Pts 1,300
Open all year, Credit cards: all major
Restaurant open daily, pool
On Mount Gibralfaro, E side of Málaga
Michelin Map 446, Region: Andalusia

Hotel Mar i Vent is without doubt one of the best values in Mallorca. For less than you pay for a room in most hotels, you also have breakfast and dinner included in the rate. This superbly run, small hotel has been in the Vives family for three generations. Originally it was owned by the grandfather of Francesc Vives, who is now manager. As was customary, his grandfather had to own a house before he could marry his sweetheart, so he went to America and saved enough money for a simple stone house in the small village of Banyalbufar, high in the hills above the sea. There were no cars or roads in those days, but travelers sometimes happened by who needed a place to spend the night. With a kind heart, grandfather Vives took them in and his wife fed them. The village priest suggested that they open their home as a wayside inn and today the same genuine hospitality exists. Francesc's pretty wife, Juana María, helps at the reception; his father, Tony, makes all guests feel special; his mother, Francisca, prepares the home-cooked meals; and aunt Juanita helps, too! Although this hotel is inexpensive, a high quality of service and accommodation exists. Each room is nicely decorated and has a terrace or balcony with a view over the terraced fields to the sea. The hotel is built into the hillside and on the lowest level is a large pool cantilevered over the cliffs with a panoramic view.

HOTEL MAR I VENT
Owners: Family Vives
Calle Major 49, 07191 Banyalbufar, Mallorca
Balearic Islands, Spain
Tel: (71) 61.80.00, Fax: (71) 61.82.01
23 rooms, Double: Pts 11,000*
*IVA included, breakfast Pts, 1,100
Open Feb to Dec, Credit cards: MC, VS
Restaurant closed Sunday night, pool
28 km NW of Palma
Michelin Map 443, Region: Balearic Islands

Finca es Palmer has been in Francisca Juan's family since the time of her great-grandparents. With farming less profitable, the house (located only 5 kilometers from the finest beach on Mallorca) was falling into ruins but it was rescued by Francisca, your charming young English-speaking hostess, and her husband, Pedro. With a labor of love and total devotion to their heritage, they have transformed the simple stone farmhouse, built in the typical Mallorcan style around a courtyard, into a very special small hotel. Dinner is served by candlelight in a garden-like dining room (covered by a glass roof in winter) using glasses and ceramic plates handmade in Mallorca. Almost all the food served comes from the garden where everything is grown as in days of yore, without the use of preservatives. In the picture-perfect kitchen, shelves are filled with row upon row of colorful jars of homemade marmalades, vegetables, and fruits. There are ten guestrooms, all decorated with artistic flair and rustic simplicity, using fabric woven in Mallorca, handpainted Mallorcan tiles, and family antiques. All have satellite television, mini-bar, shampoo, perfume, and even bathrobes. One of my favorites is a spacious corner room in the windmill. Since our original visit, a swimming pool has been constructed near the palm tree terrace.

FINCA ES PALMER
Owner: Francisca Juan
Carretera Campos-Colonia Sant Jordi, km 6.4
07638 Colonia de Sant Jordi, Mallorca
Balearic Islands, Spain
Tel: (71) 18.12.65, Fax: (71) 18 10 63
10 rooms, Double: Pts 16,000–18,500*
*IVA & breakfast included
Closed Dec, Credit cards: all major
Restaurant open daily (for guests only), pool
6.4 km S of Campos on road to Colonia de Sant Jordi
Michelin Map 443, Region: Balearic Islands

La Residencia, perched high in the hills with views to the sea yet just steps from the quaint village of Deia, is a faultless hideaway. This gem of a hotel, nestled in 34 acres, is imaginatively created from two 17th-century farmhouses built of the golden-tan stone of the region. In keeping with its past, the decor is elegantly simple with white walls accented by beautiful antiques and bouquets of fresh flowers. Even the reception is exceptional. Check-in is handled quietly and without fuss at an antique desk. Nearby are intimate lounges and bars where guests can sit quietly with friends as if in a private home. However, most guests "live" outdoors—the hotel has its own private club by the sea, serviced by a shuttle bus. For those who don't want to leave the property, the manicured gardens offer an exquisite retreat, with secluded shady nooks where guests can relax with only the fragrance of flowers and the song of birds for company. The hotel is built on a hillside with two swimming pools tucked onto terraces. Adjacent to the lower pool is a bar where guests can order lunch or have dinner if they want to dine casually. For those who want to dine elegantly, in the room where the olives were pressed, there is a gourmet restaurant, El Olivo, which holds a Michelin star for excellence. The bedrooms are all fabulously furnished. The suites are stunning, but even the standard doubles (such as number 9, overlooking the garden) are outstanding.

LA RESIDENCIA
07179 Deia, Mallorca
Balearic Islands, Spain
Tel: (71) 63.90.11, Fax: (71) 63.93.70
www.karenbrown.com/spaininns/laresidencia.html
65 rooms, Double: Pts 35,000–38,000*
*IVA not included, breakfast included
Open all year, Credit cards: all major
Restaurant open daily, pools
27 km N of Palma de Mallorca
Michelin Map 443, Region: Balearic Islands

Vistamar is perfection—a stunning country manor offering genuine warmth of hospitality and an ambiance of understated elegance without a hint of ostentation. You approach through an orchard of 900-year-old olive trees to massive, double wooden doors that open into the central courtyard where the old well still stands. When the wealthy landowner came to the mountains in the summer to escape the heat of Palma, he stayed with his family on the upper floor while the ground level of the home was the farmer's quarters. The farmer's living space has been converted into several intimate lounges, each tastefully decorated with chairs and sofas slip-covered with handsome Mallorcan fabrics. On the walls are original paintings (predominantly modern art) which nicely complement the handsome antiques. You dine in a glass-enclosed sunroom that looks out to a terrace embraced by a semi-circle of enormous palm trees. Beyond are towering pines through which you get a glimpse of the sea. Some of the guestrooms are in the main house, others in the old stables. Room 8 (formerly the homeowner's dining room) is fabulous, with beautiful, antique spool beds and an enormous balcony. But don't worry which room you get: each is superbly decorated. As an added bonus, there is a magnificent swimming pool on a terrace with a view to the sea.

VISTAMAR DE VALLDEMOSA
Owner: Pedro Coll Pastor
Cra Valldemosa-Andraitx, km 2.5
07170 Valldemosa, Mallorca
Balearic Islands, Spain
Tel: (71) 61.23.00, Fax: (71) 61.25.83
18 rooms, Double: Pts 25,000–30,000*
*IVA not included, breakfast Pts 1,500
Open Feb to Oct, Credit cards: AX, VS
Restaurant closed lunch Mondays, pool
2.5 km W of Valldemosa on road to Andraitx
Michelin Map 443, Region: Balearic Islands

If your heart is set on a posh resort along the Costa del Sol, you can do no better than the Marbella Club Hotel. At one time this property was even more exclusive—it was the residence of Prince Alfonso von Hohenlohe who in 1954 began to take in paying guests. Of course, not just any guests—only such celebrities as Cristina Onassis, David Niven, Ava Gardner, the Duke of Windsor, and Grace Kelly were on the invitation list. The rich and famous still frequent the resort which blends nicely the formality of a staff in tuxedos with the relaxed atmosphere of a beach resort. Whereas most hotels along the Costa del Sol are high-rises, the Marbella Club is blessed with a large piece of land allowing for low-rise clusters of bougainvillea-draped, whitewashed, Andalusian-style buildings and cottages which house the suites and guestrooms. There is a swimming pool tucked in the garden and another facing the long stretch of excellent beach. Except for a new, deluxe complex of ultra-luxurious suites next to the beach club, the rooms do not have a sea view, but all have either a terrace or balcony looking out to the gardens. All the rooms are extremely spacious and include a large sitting area. The decorator-perfect decor is the same in all the doubles, with beautiful fabrics that vary only by color scheme.

MARBELLA CLUB HOTEL
Manager: Erik Jansen
Boulevard Prince Alfonso von Hohenlohe, s/n
29600 Marbella (Málaga), Spain
Tel: (5) 28.22.211, Fax: (5) 28.29.884
129 rooms, Double: Pts 16,000–52,000*
*IVA not included, breakfast Pts 2,500
Open all year, Credit cards: all major
Restaurant open daily, pool
3 km S of Marbella on the coastal road
Michelin Map 443, Region: Andalusia

Finca Buenvino was built by the Chestertons (Jeannie is Scottish and Sam is Irish) in the 1980s on a hilltop, snuggled in a wooded haven of chestnut and cork trees. The Buenvino is like an Italian villa—painted a soft pink and accented by green trim. Climbing roses lace the building and flowers abound, giving the home a cheerful ambiance. Inside, the happy mood continues with a sitting room with comfy sofas and chairs grouped around a large fireplace. Beyond is an inviting, glassed-in sun porch with a stunning view of wooded, rolling hills. The bedrooms are individually decorated, reflecting a homey feeling. My favorite is a twin with an en-suite bathroom: it is prettily decorated with pink floral curtains at a small window framing a view of the hills. Breakfast and dinner are included in the rate of the room, and, to put the icing on the cake, Jeannie is a cordon bleu cook. A path through the woods takes you up to a Hollywood-like swimming pool perched on a terrace overlooking an incredible view of the rolling hills. The Finca Buenvino is more like a bed and breakfast than a hotel—the Chestertons live here with their three children, welcoming guests like family and a feeling of casual informality prevails. For a home-like stay surrounded by natural beauty and genuine hospitality, Finca Buenvino is a winner. In 1997 the Chestertons added a small, rustic 2-bedroom cottage which they let for self-catering on a weekly basis.

FINCA BUENVINO
Owners: Jeannie & Sam Chesterton
21293 Los Marines (Huelva), Spain
Tel & fax: (59) 12.40.34
5 rooms & 1 cottage, Double: Pts 26,000*,
Cottage Pts90,000 per week
*IVA not included, breakfast & dinner included
Closed mid-Dec to mid-Jan, Credit cards: MC, VS
Meals taken with family, pool
1.5 km W of Los Marines, 95 km NW of Seville on CN 433
Michelin Map 446, Region: Andalusia

Tucked high in a mountain valley, Meranges is one of the few remaining unspoiled Catalan villages in the Pyrenees. Clinging to the hillside are only a cluster of charming old gray-stone buildings weighted down with heavy slate roofs. As a child, Martha Sole Forn spent her summers in this remote valley with her grandparents—in the same farmhouse where her grandfather was born. She and her husband, Antonio, love this idyllic hamlet, and have bought a 200-year-old farmhouse that offers a few rooms and a charming small restaurant. The bedrooms are all simple, but extremely appealing and in absolute keeping with the nature of the building. Happily, nothing is contrived or too cute. The walls are painted a fresh white, the floors are of pine, the ceilings have natural beams. The only decoration on the walls are beautiful black-and-white photographs of the region, all taken by a local priest (now well up in his years) whose hobby was capturing on film the animals, people, and landscape he knows so well. Along with the lovely mountain setting, it is the restaurant (featuring Catalan country-style cooking) that draws guests. What in days-gone-by was the sheep stable, has been transformed into a cozy restaurant where stone walls, and a low, beamed ceiling, set a romantic stage.

HOTEL CAN BORRELL
Owners: Martha Sole & Antonio Forn
C/ Retorn, 3
17539 Meranges (Gerona), Spain
Tel: (72) 88.00.33, Fax:(72) 88.01.44
www.karenbrown.com/spaininns/hotelcanborrell.html
8 rooms, Double: Pts 7,000–9,000*
*IVA not included, breakfast Pts 650
Open all year (Jan to Mar weekends only)
Credit cards: all major
Restaurant closed Monday nights & Tuesdays
185 km NW of Barcelona, 50 km NE of Seo de Urgel
Michelin Map 443, Region: Catalonia

The Vía de la Plata (named after a Roman road) is installed in a historic church-cum-convent-cum-hospital-cum-jail dating back to the 17th century. There is, in addition, strong archaeological evidence pointing to the conclusion that this was originally the site of the Concordia Temple of Augustus during the Roman occupation of Mérida. There are ancient artifacts scattered throughout the large, whitewashed hotel—all discovered nearby. The architecture is a crazy mix: for example, in the gorgeous, Andalusian interior patio you will discover elegant Mudéjar-style pillars with Roman and Visigothic stones, and the stunning front sitting room was the convent chapel. The Vía de la Plata was recently renovated to include an overall face-lift, additional rooms, and underground parking. The whitewashed rooms with dark Spanish furniture are very pleasant, and many have domed ceilings and colorful rugs brightening the red-tile floors. The doubles in back have balconies and overlook the delightful Moorish gardens. All in all this is a charming, unusual parador.

PARADOR VÍA DE LA PLATA
Manager: Victor Teodosio Tirado
Plaza de la Constitución, 3
06850 Mérida (Badajoz), Spain
Tel: (24) 31.38.00, Fax: (24) 31.92.08
82 rooms, Double: Pts 17,000–18,000*
*IVA not included, breakfast Pts 1,200
Open all year, Credit cards: all major
Restaurant open daily
195 km N of Seville
Michelin Map 444, Region: Extremadura

Nestled in the peaceful hills, slightly inland from Marbella, is a hotel we prefer to many of the modern resorts on the coast. Ascend the mountain into the picturesque, whitewashed town of Mijas. The hotel is easy to spot—it is marked by colorful flags. Although of new construction, the sparkling white, Andalusian-style complex belies its age, blending unobtrusively with the other authentically old buildings in town. The lobby, a stunning mixture of white marble floors softened by deep-red Oriental carpets, beautiful antiques, and elegant regional furniture, features the backdrop of expansive views of Fuengirola and the Mediterranean. Although not small, the hotel is very personal and intimate, and even when completely booked, does not seem crowded. Your room will please you as much as the warmth of management, especially if you pay the slightly higher price for one with a view of the sea. Enhancing the view is the tasteful, muted, Andalusian decor of the rooms that await your arrival. If just sitting on the terrace and gazing at the sea beyond the green hills is not active enough for you, there are two outdoor pools, an exercise area with a Jacuzzi and sauna, bowling, and tennis courts at the hotel, and golf and horseback riding nearby.

HOTEL MIJAS
Manager: Antonio Martinez Molero
Urbanizacion Tamisa, 2
29650 Mijas (Málaga), Spain
Tel: (5) 24.85.800, Fax: (5) 24.85.825
*IVA not included, breakfast Pts 1,350
100 rooms, Double: Pts 14,000–16,000*
Open all year, Credit cards: all major
Restaurant open daily, pools
32 km NW of Málaga
Michelin Map 446, Region: Andalucia

Perched at the edge of a 30-meter cliff overlooking the blue Mediterranean, the Parador de Nerja is a modern hotel. As you first see it from the road, the hotel seems unexceptional, but the interior (though it looks a little tired) is a definite improvement. Featuring just a few antique touches in the halls and public rooms, it offers an attractive alternative to the posh and expensive Costa del Sol resorts, and is a good choice for those who want to include in their trip a few days at the beach. The extremely spacious public areas are Spanish-contemporary in decor, and make extensive use of glass to capitalize on the marvelous view. The Andalusian-style central patio is quite pretty, with plants, flowers, and a typical little fountain—the result is a colorful and relaxed atmosphere. The hotel's best feature is the park-like terrace on the edge of the cliff at the back of the property where guests lounge around the large pool. At the corner of the terrace, just a few pesetas buys an elevator ride down to a beautiful, expansive beach with ample bars and restaurants, and boat rental facilities. After a day in the sun, you can return to an air-conditioned, spacious room commanding the same view as the public rooms.

PARADOR DE NERJA
Manager: Antonio Embiz Fabregas
Avenida. Rodríguez Acosta, s/n
29780 Nerja (Málaga), Spain
Tel: (52) 52.00.50, Fax: (52) 52.19.97
73 rooms, Double: Pts 18,500–19,500*
*IVA not included, breakfast Pts 1,400
Open all year, Credit cards: all major
Restaurant open daily, pool
52 km E of Málaga
Michelin Map 446, Region: Andalucia (Costa del Sol)

hidden among the steep mountains of the *Sistema Ibérico*, a beautiful natural ·falls, lakes, gorges, and stone grottos. In the center of this magical setting sits the Hotel Monasterio de Piedra, originally a monastery established by Cistercian monks in 1194 and active until 1835, when it was abandoned and tragically ransacked. General Prim came into possession of this spectacular piece of property and his descendants own it to this day. Curiously, because of the monastery's uninhabited period, neighboring villages can claim parts of it, too, as evidenced by some fabulous works of art (such as choir stalls, altars, furniture—even wine vats) that grace their otherwise relatively humble holy places. The site is large and rich in history, having fine architectural examples from the Gothic through the baroque periods. Wander at will, exploring every exciting corner, then enter the hotel from the beautiful cloisters. The antique-lined, arched-ceilinged marble hallways must be 6 meters wide and 10 meters high, through which it seems the slightest sound echoes endlessly, and the incredible windows that appear to be covered with parchment are actually made of alabaster. The wood-floored bedrooms are, not surprisingly, the original monks' cells, and therefore simply but nicely furnished, and overlook a natural park, an interior patio, or the cloister. Your stay here is guaranteed to be unforgettable.

HOTEL MONASTERIO DE PIEDRA
Manager: José Maria Montaner
50210 Nuévalos (Zaragoza), Spain
Tel: (76) 84.90.11, Fax: (76) 84.90.54
61 rooms, Double: Pts 9,500–11,000*
*IVA not included, breakfast Pts 575
Open all year, Credit cards: all major
Restaurant open daily, pool
118 km SW of Zaragoza
Michelin Map 444, Region: Aragon

Hotel Descriptions

The Refugio de Juanar used to be part of the parador chain, but was ceded to the regional government of Andalusia. Its somewhat isolated location 16 kilometers from Marbella provides a delightful contrast to the cosmopolitan coastal area and is obviously a destination for travelers with a car. Everything here says relax and settle in for a few days. In keeping with its hunting-lodge origin, the decor is comfortably rustic, with the emphasis on heavy wood furnishings. There are several lounges, one especially attractive with a fireplace and numerous trophies. The restaurant specializes in excellent game dishes, which makes it popular with locals in Marbella. The rooms are simple and offer every comfort, including large modern bathrooms. If you plan to be here between late fall and early spring, you might request rooms 3, 15, or 16 since each has its own little fireplace. But the stellar attraction of this hotel is its natural setting—a pine forest loaded with peace and quiet and, in the summer, a cool, shady terrace where you can breakfast to the scent of pine. Tennis is offered and there is also a small pool, made all the more pleasant by its surrounding towering pine trees. Note: From Marbella drive north on the A355 and look for a sign to the hotel. Turn left and drive about 5 kilometers farther.

REFUGIO DE JUANAR
Manager: José Gómez Ávila
Sierra Blanca, s/n
29610 Ojén (Málaga), Spain
Tel: (52) 88.10.00, Fax: (52) 88.10.01
23 rooms, Double: Pts 12,200*
*IVA not included, breakfast included
Open all year, Credit cards: all major
Restaurant open daily, pool
65 km SW of Málaga
Michelin Map 446, Region: Andalucia

Olite was the medieval capital of the Kingdom of Navarre, and Charles III made this castle fortress his summer residence in the early 15th century. Part of the extensive original dwelling has been incorporated into a charming parador (named after the young prince who spent his childhood here) which offers the modern-day resident unique lodging in this ancient walled town. Situated next to a tiny, elaborate church on a tranquil, tree-lined plaza, the inn has an impressive, almost intimidating, stone façade but, once inside, you will be delighted with the warm red-tile floors, stained glass, antiques, suits of armor, and intimate bar and dining room. Only 16 of its bedrooms are in the historic building, and they are wonderful, with canopied beds and wood floors; some are still sheltered by crude exterior walls dating back hundreds of years, and two (rooms 106 and 107) with massive stone fireplaces. The "new" rooms are also lovely (and larger), decorated in subtle earth colors, with traditional Spanish wood furniture and floors. If you prefer to stay in the old section, be sure you request *la parte vieja* when making your reservation.

PARADOR PRINCIPE DE VIANA
Manager: Antonio Bertolin Blasco
Plaza de los Teobaldos, 2
31390 Olite (Navarra), Spain
Tel: (48) 74.00.00, Fax: (48) 74.02.01
43 rooms, Double: Pts 14,500–17,500*
*IVA not included, breakfast Pts 1,300
Open all year, Credit cards: all major
Restaurant open daily
140 km NW of Zaragoza, 123 S of San Sebastian
Michelin Map 443, Region: Navarra

In the 14th century King Henry granted the medieval town of Oropesa, with its ancient castle, to Don García Alvarez de Toledo, who gradually restored the castle and added to it, as did his descendants. Converted to a parador in 1930, the hotel has handsome bedrooms with thick beige rugs on red-and-blue-tiled floors, beige bedspreads, rich wood furniture, ceramic and iron fixtures, and cavernous, dazzling-white bathrooms. All but a few overlook the fertile Sierra de Gredos Valley: the others look over the interior patio (originally a bullring), a 15th-century Jesuit church, and the remains of the ancient castle. This parador is home to an international cooking school and the cuisine exceeds usual parador standards, as does the dining room itself, laid out on two levels, with skylights, painted-wood ceiling, and large picture windows. In the lounge areas, cozy leather furniture and exquisite antiques cluster around big stone fireplaces. In the basement is a tiny cell where Saint Peter of Alcántara chose to stay when he visited here—it is intriguing, but he might have chosen differently could he have seen the accommodations available now.

PARADOR DE OROPESA Manager: Secundino
Fuertes Alvarez
Plaza del Palacio, 1
45560 Oropesa (Toledo), Spain
Tel: (25) 43.00.00, Fax: (25) 43.07.77
48 rooms, Double: Pts 15,000*
*IVA not included, breakfast Pts 1,300
Open all year, Credit cards: all major
Restaurant open daily, pool
155 km SW of Madrid, 122 km SW of Ávila
Michelin Map 444, Region: Castilla-La Mancha

The Hotel de la Reconquista, located just a block away from Oviedo's beautiful central park, is a real classic. From the first glance you will know this is not an ordinary hotel. The exterior is stunning—a superb 18th-century masterpiece (justifiably designated a national monument). The front of the two-story building is made of pretty ochre-colored stone. Wrought-iron balconies adorn the formal line of windows and a magnificent crest is mounted above the entrance. Inside the splendor continues: the entrance hall opens to an enormous arcaded courtyard (with a patterned red carpet and blue velvet chairs and sofas) roofed in glass to create a lounge that is protected from the sun and rain. This is where guests gather for a cup of tea or an aperitif before dinner, surrounded by an old-fashioned, understated elegance of a bygone era. Beyond the first courtyard, there is a second garden courtyard, and beyond, even a third. Throughout, the decor reflects a formal grandeur with gorgeous large mirrors, beautiful antique chests, fine oil paintings, grandfather clocks, fresh flowers, and green plants. The walls and hallways to the guestrooms are covered in a rich red fabric. The bedrooms are tastefully decorated in a traditional style, many with antique accents.

HOTEL DE LA RECONQUISTA
Manager: Ramón Felip
Gil de Jaz, 16
33004 Oviedo (Asturias), Spain
Tel: (8) 52.41.100, Fax: (8) 52.41.166
www.karenbrown.com/spaininns/hoteldelareconquista.html
142 rooms, Double: Pts 24,970–31,075*
*IVA not included, breakfast Pts 1,900
Open all year, Credit cards: all major
Restaurant open daily
445 km NW of Madrid, 121 km N of León
Michelin Map 441, Region: Asturias

This hospitable hideaway midway between Seville and Córdoba was a Franciscan monastery from the 16th to the 19th centuries, sheltering and educating monks on their way to missions in the New World, including the recently canonized Fray Junípero Serra, famous evangelizer of California. In 1828, when church property was being confiscated by the state all over Spain, the monastery passed into private hands—and subsequent ruin. It was eventually inherited by the Moreno family who, with care and attention to original historical detail, restored it over a three-year period, opening the tiny hotel to the public in 1987. (The family also raises fighting bulls, and the manager will happily arrange a visit to their ranch, if you're interested.) Tucked behind whitewashed walls in the heart of the typical Andalusian town of Palma del Río, you'll discover a superlative restaurant and cozy bar with artesonado ceilings, gardens, and orchards, and a beautiful cloistered patio supporting a gallery around which the guestrooms are situated. The twin-bedded, air-conditioned rooms are simple and comfortable, decorated in earth tones with dark-wood furniture and trim. They have modern, colorfully tiled baths and small sitting areas. Rooms 5 to 8 are particularly spacious and original. The Hospedería offers unique, economical accommodation not far off the beaten track.

HOSPEDERÍA DE SAN FRANCISCO
Manager: Iñagui Martinez
Avenida Pío XII, s/n
14700 Palma del Río (Córdoba), Spain
Tel & fax: (57) 71.01.83
22 rooms, Double: Pts 9,500–10,000*
*IVA not included, breakfast Pts 650
Open all year, Credit cards: VS, MC
Restaurant closed Sundays
82 km NE of Seville
Michelin Map 446, Region: Andalusia

In the picture-perfect hilltop village of Pedraza de la Sierra (only a short drive north of Madrid), Martin Arcones owns one of the most charming restaurants in town, the El Soportal on the Plaza Mayor. In addition, he runs an excellent restaurant in his Hotel de la Villa, located on an attractive side street lined with pretty boutiques. As you walk into the 17th-century, honey-tone stone building, the spacious lounge (painted a deep peach) with its modern chairs and sofas has a clean, contemporary look which is softened by a few antiques. Beyond the reception area and lounge, there is a large dining room opening onto an attractive inner patio. The guestrooms are located on the upper two floors. Each one has its own personality, but a stylish, traditional ambiance prevails with the use of coordinating fine fabrics, beautiful wallpapers, and some antiques. Suite 113, with a large bedroom and separate sitting room, is not only an excellent value (it costs only a little more than the superior doubles), but is also exceptionally pretty. It is decorated with tasteful wallpaper in tones of cream and beige and has exquisite, four-poster twin beds with white canopies. Another favorite is 216, a romantic room on the top floor, tucked under the sloping beamed ceiling. Its color scheme is extremely attractive—the walls and fabrics are color-coordinated in soft tones of green and cream.

EL HOTEL DE LA VILLA
Owner: Martin Arcones
Calzada, 5
40172 Pedraza de la Sierra (Segovia), Spain
Tel: (21) 50.86.51, Fax: (21) 50.86.53
26 rooms, Double: Pts11,000–13,100*
*IVA not included, breakfast Pts 1,100
Open all year, Credit cards: all major
Restaurant open daily
126 km N of Madrid, 37 km NE of Segovia
Michelin Map 444, Region: Castilla y León

La Posada de Don Mariano is absolute perfection. To have such a jewel of a small hotel to complement one of Spain's most beautiful villages is almost too good to be true. The two-story, ochre-colored stone house is enriched by black wrought-iron lamps and balconies brimming with colorful pots of flowers. The reception area is small and simple. Probably one of the family members will be at the front desk to greet you since this is a family-owned and -run hotel. Steps lead to an upper level where there is a courtyard filled with flowers. About half of the bedrooms have balconies that overlook this pretty garden, while the others have views of the village and surrounding hills. Each of the bedrooms is individual in decor, but decorator-perfect in every way—the drapes match the fabric on the bedspreads and chairs and even coordinate with the shower curtains. Every detail shows the attention of owners who truly care. Some of the guestrooms are small, but all have an appealing simplicity with country-style antiques and English-style fabrics. You cannot go wrong with any of the bedrooms. One favorite is number 110 which has twin iron beds draped in a pretty peach-and-cream-colored fabric. Another winner is room 101 which has a canopy bed and is decorated in tones of white—even including white petunias on the balcony. This is not a luxury hotel, but very special. You will love it.

LA POSADA DE DON MARIANO
Manager: Mariano Pascual
Calle Mayor 14
40172 Pedraza de la Sierra (Segovia), Spain
Tel & fax: (21) 50.98.86
18 rooms, Double: Pts 11,000–19,000*
*IVA not included, breakfast Pts 950
Open all year, Credit cards: all major
Restaurant open daily
126 km N of Madrid, 37 km NE of Segovia
Michelin Map 444, Region: Castilla y León

Peratallada, a tiny village tucked in the countryside east of Barcelona, is designated as a historical monument. At one time completely surrounded by a moat, the village today still preserves its romantic medieval character. Boutiques, art galleries, and restaurants have been opened in the stone buildings that line the narrow cobbled lanes. One of these restaurants, the well-known Castell de Peratallada, is built within the walls of the old castle. It has several stunning dining rooms where tables set with fine linens and illuminated by candlelight look especially beautiful in the massive rooms with their vaulted stone ceilings. Most guests come just for the dining, but there are six bedrooms for those who wish to spend the night. These all have a somewhat dark, medieval ambiance with antique furnishings used throughout. Four of the rooms are in the house where the owner lived while restoring the property and there are two suites located in the same building as the restaurants. The suites are exceptionally large rooms with priceless antiques—staying here is a bit like living in a museum. Incorporated into the hotel is an inner garden courtyard, exclusively for the use of overnight guests. Part of the tower wall enclosing this garden dates back to the 9th century. Note: The prices listed below are for most of the year. In high season, which is the first two weeks in August, the prices go much higher.

CASTELL DE PERATALLADA
Manager: Josep Güell
Plaça del Castell, 1
17113 Peratallada (Girona), Spain
Tel: (72) 63.40.21, Fax: (72) 63.40.11
6 rooms, Double: Pts 20,000–25,000*
*IVA not included, breakfast Pts1,400
Open all year, Credit cards: all major
Restaurant open daily in summer
130 km NE of Barcelona
Michelin Map 443, Region: Catalonia

Tucked in the shadows of the snowcapped Guadarrama mountain range, surrounded by pine forest, and within hailing distance of the ski area of Navacerrada, is the serene retreat of Santa María de El Paular. Less than one hour from Madrid, and located just outside the attractive village of Rascafría, the hotel is ensconced in the former living quarters of a monastery dating from the 14th century (and abandoned in the 19th)—in fact, the attached monastery is still active. It has been carefully restored and remodeled, and the most has been made of its marvelous original stone patios, columns, and stairways. Don't miss the small, barren chapel just left of the arch leading to the entry patio (complete with fountain, and outdoor tables in warm weather). In it you'll discover a striking figure of the black virgin Nuestra Señora de Montserrat. Inside the hotel, you'll appreciate the handsome public rooms with beamed ceilings supporting iron chandeliers, wood and red-tile floors, and capacious and cozy Castilian-style furnishings. The guestrooms—all offering tranquil vistas—are roomy, simple, and handsome, with provincial wood furniture, hardwood floors, and woven, earth-tone bedspreads and drapes. To top it all off, the dining room provides above-average cuisine, and the management arranges horseback excursions.

HOTEL SANTA MARÍA DE EL PAULAR
Manager:Manuel Irvela
28741 Rascafría (Madrid), Spain
Tel: (1) 86.91.011, Fax: (1) 86.91.006
58 rooms, Double: Pts 15,000–18,500*
*IVA & breakfast not included
Open all year, Credit cards: all major
Restaurant open daily, pool
78 km NW of Madrid
Michelin Map 444, Region: Madrid

Facing the same plaza as the Parador de Ronda (where it is sometimes difficult to find a room), the Hotel Don Miguel has an equally outstanding setting overlooking the New Bridge and the dramatic gorge that slices the town of Ronda. This hotel is incorporated into what was once the home of the jailer who was in charge of the prison that was housed in the New Bridge. There is an entrance to the hotel's popular restaurant from the Plaza de España, but you need to go around the corner to discover the door that leads to the hotel's small reception area. Although the restaurant and the hotel have separate entrances, you can go directly to the restaurant without leaving the hotel. For a reasonably priced place to stay, the guestrooms are very pleasant. They are all similar in decor with wooden headboards, wooden desks and chairs, tiled floors, and attractive, off-white matching bedspreads and drapes. When making reservations, be sure to request a room overlooking the gorge. The location of this simple hotel is fabulous and the setting gives it another bonus—a restaurant with incredible views. If the day is warm, dine outside on the terrace and watch the old stone bridge change colors in the glow of the sunset. The food is excellent and the setting unsurpassed. One level below the restaurant is a pretty guest breakfast room where you can eat either inside or, if the weather is warm, outside on the terrace. Note: Plans are under way to add more rooms and a pool.

HOTEL DON MIGUEL
Owner: Miguel Coronel
Plaza de España, 3
29400 Ronda (Málaga), Spain
Tel: (5) 28.77.722, Fax: (5) 28.78.377
19 rooms, Double: from Pts 9,000*
*IVA not included, breakfast Pts 450
Closed mid-Dec mid-Jan, Credit cards: all major
Restaurant open daily
120 km NW of Málaga, 102 km NE of Algeciras
Michelin Map 446, Region: Andalusia

In 1994 a new pearl was added to Spain's parador chain, its new construction following the architectural style of Ronda's old town hall and market that previously occupied the site. Even if the romantic town of Ronda were not worth a detour in its own right, this dramatic hotel would warrant one. The hotel is built onto the cliff above the "Tajo," the gorge that splits Ronda, and from either inside or on the terrace by the swimming pool, you have views of the soaring arched bridge that miraculously crosses the impressive, 120-meter cleft formed by the Guadalevin river. You enter the honey-colored stone building into a sky-lit atrium where the reception desk is located. Beyond is a large seating area with comfortable sofas and chairs in tones of blue and yellow. The walls are a beige-colored brick and the floors white marble. The most attractive color scheme of blues, beiges, and yellows is continued throughout the hotel. There is no effort made to create an artificial antique ambiance. Rather, the furnishings are traditional in style with beautiful fabrics of excellent quality used on the sofas, chairs, and drapes in the public rooms and guestrooms. Each of the attractive bedrooms has a balcony. All the views are lovely, but for a truly memorable experience, ask for one of the corner rooms (such as 219) with two balconies that capture the sweeping view.

PARADOR DE RONDA
Manager: Jose Maria Ronda Arauzo
Plaza España s/n
29400 Ronda (Málaga), Spain
Tel: (5) 28.77.500, Fax: (5) 28.78.188
78 rooms, Double: Pts 18,500*
*IVA not included, breakfast Pts 1,300
Open all year, Credit cards: all major
Restaurant open daily, pool
120 km NW of Málaga, 102 km NE of Algeciras
Michelin Map 446, Region: Andalusia

5d

uxurious "hostal" opened in the tiny fishing village of S'Agaró with just six
Gavina (seagull) and the resort town have come a long way since then, but
remained in the Ensesa family, which is personally responsible for the
extraordinary collection of antiques found throughout the premises. Everything you
see—rugs, tapestries, tile, furnishings—is genuine; not a single reproduction blemishes
the scene. Nor does a single room reproduce another: each is unique, and all are
wonderful, spacious, and bright. Careful attention has been given to the tiniest detail in
every corner of every room (a man is employed full-time to do nothing but polish the
wood). This is a hotel of a style and quality of a bygone era, as we are certain such
previous guests as Frank Sinatra, Sylvester Stallone, and Orson Welles would agree. The
hotel is surrounded by lovely gardens and has a divine pool overlooking the ocean which
features fine pool-side dining in one of its three restaurants. You are a mere five-minute
walk from the beach that draws a jet-set crowd in the summer. The Hostal de La Gavina
is very popular. Do not fail to reserve well in advance during the high season.

HOSTAL DE LA GAVINA
Manager: Anna Requena
17248 S'Agaró (Gerona), Spain
Tel: (72) 32.11.00, Fax: (72) 32.15.73
72 rooms, Double: Pts 23,000–41,500*
*IVA not included, breakfast 2,100
Open mid-Apr to mid-Oct, Credit cards: all major
Restaurants open daily, pool
103 km NE of Barcelona
Michelin Map 443, Region: Catalonia (Costa Brava)

If you are looking for a reasonably priced, superbly located hotel in Salamanca, you can do no better than the Hotel Don Juan, just steps from the Plaza Mayor. This is a simple, two-star hotel, but you are truly not compromising. In my estimation, the Don Juan is better than many of Salamanca's "luxury" hotels which cost almost twice as much, but are not as meticulously maintained. The four-story, cut-stone building, accented by black wrought-iron balconies, has two doors. The one on the left goes into the café/bar while the door on the right opens onto an intimate lobby with a pretty, green-marble floor and carved reception desk where you will be warmly welcomed. The two rooms have an interconnecting door that is convenient since breakfast is served in the bar. There is no lounge, but with the many wonders of Salamanca just steps away, I cannot imagine wasting time in a formal sitting area. From the lobby, both an elevator and a staircase lead to the rooms on the upper floors. All the rooms are identical in decor, with a pretty, soft, rose color scheme used throughout in the carpets, bedspreads, and draperies. There are light-wood, built-in headboards with good reading lights, pretty prints above the comfortable beds, satellite TV, and modern marble bathrooms. My favorite bedrooms are those on the top floor: ask for 402 or 404—both have exceptional views.

HOTEL DON JUAN
Manager: David Berrocal
Quintana, 6
37001 Salamanca, Spain
Tel: (23) 26.14.73, Fax: (23) 26.24.75
www.karenbrown.com/spaininns/hoteldonjuan.html
16 rooms, Double: Pts 9,000*
*IVA not included, beakfast Pts 550
Open all year, Credit cards: MC, VS
Bar with snacks, breakfast only
Half a block from Plaza Mayor
Michelin Maps 441 & 444, Region: Castilla y León

The Hotel Rector, located at the edge of the ancient walls of Salamanca, is one of Spain's finest small hotels with a special enhancement—gracious owners who oversee every detail. Although built in the 1940s, it definitely looks several centuries old. The handsome, three-story, beige-stone building (with beautiful sculpted designs over the windows and doors, and black wrought-iron balconies) blends in perfectly with the typical old houses of Salamanca. It is just a short stroll from the hotel to Salamanca's breathtaking cathedrals or an easy, seven-minute walk to the incredible Plaza Mayor. Whereas so many hotels seem to over-strive for the dark Spanish look, the Hotel Rector is refreshingly different. The decor throughout is one of tasteful, traditional ambiance. The colors are mostly pastel, with accents of deep rose. A whimsical touch, just as you enter, are two large arched windows with a colorful "Tiffany" glass effect. The reception area opens on one side to an intimate sitting area and on the other to a small bar with cane-backed chairs. Nothing is on a grand scale—instead, there is a refined, understated elegance. The guestrooms are lovely, with the finest quality, traditional-style furnishings and color-coordinating fabrics on the bedspreads and draperies. They all have large marble bathrooms. Breakfast is served in a pretty little dining room.

HOTEL RECTOR
Manager: Eduardo Ferrán Riba
Rector Esperabé, 10
37008 Salamanca, Spain
Tel: (23) 21.84.82, Fax: (23) 21.40.08
www.karenbrown.com/spaininns/hotelrector.html
14 rooms, Double: Pts 17,000*
*IVA not included, breakfast Pts 1,000
Open all year, Credit cards: all major
No restaurant, breakfast only
205 km NW of Madrid
Michelin Maps 441 & 444, Region: Castilla y León

If you love to be on the sea, yet off the beaten path, the Hotel San José (on the Costa de Almería) is sure to be your cup of tea. San José, a small village located about a 30-kilometer drive from the highway through an arid landscape, has miraculously escaped developers' bulldozers. It is a small, forgotten village with some whitewashed houses, a boat harbor, a smattering of shops, a few restaurants, and discreet clusters of holiday houses. Near the center of town on the slope of a small hill, the Hotel San José (a pretty white building with light-blue trim) offers a simple, yet delightful charm. The reception lounge has a fireplace, wicker sofas with white cushions, and a wall of windows overlooking the sea. The restaurant is extremely attractive, with dark-green chairs, fresh flowers on the tables, and a lovely view. Beyond the dining room is the hotel guest lounge, a cozy hideaway with chairs and sofas slip-covered in deep blue, green plants in large terra cotta pots, colorful ceramic plates on white walls, and antique accent pieces. In back of the hotel is a sunny terrace and a stone staircase leading down to a sandy beach. The bedrooms are all similar in decor (request one with a view of the ocean). Note: While staying in San José, be sure to explore the nearby secluded beaches backed by giant sand dunes.

HOTEL SAN JOSÉ
Manager: Eduardo Zarate
Calle Correo, s/n
04118 San José (Almería), Spain
Tel: (50) 38.01.16, Fax: (50) 38.00.02
8 rooms, Double: Pts 12,500–15,000*
*IVA not included, breakfast Pts 700
Open mid-Mar to Nov, Credit cards: MC, VS
Restaurant open daily, beach
240 km E of Málaga, 40 km SE of Almería
Michelin Map 466, Region: Andalusia (Costa Almería)

The Reyes Católicos, one of the most magnificent inns in Spain, is without a doubt one of the pearls of the parador chain. In the 15th century the building housed a pilgrims' hospice, which nurtured the sick and sheltered the humble who journeyed from all parts of Europe to visit the tomb of Saint James. The "hostal" has four interior patios (Matthew, Mark, Luke, and John) overlooked by enclosed third-floor gallery-lounge areas lined with antiques. The fabulous central court (where a music festival is held every August) has a 15-meter ceiling and beautiful stained-glass windows. Each room, hallway, ceiling, and floor is something special. In addition to its rich history, the Reyes Católicos offers truly sumptuous accommodation for the modern pilgrim. No two rooms are exactly alike, and the attention to detail is unsurpassed, resulting in harmonious old-world decor. The green-marble bathrooms are immense, featuring separate bath and shower and heated towel racks. In a city that must be visited, this is a hotel than cannot be missed, even if you merely take a tour (it is the second most popular tourist attraction in Santiago after the cathedral).

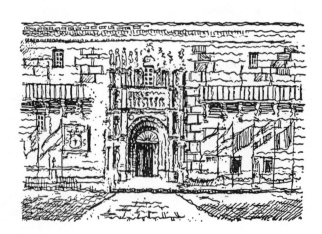

HOSTAL DE LOS REYES CATÓLICOS
Manager: Emilio Martín
Plaza del Obradoiro, 1
15705 Santiago de Compostela
(La Coruña), Spain
Tel: (81) 58.22.00, Fax: (81) 56.30.94
136 rooms, Double: Pts 26,500*
*IVA not included, breakfast Pts 1,800
Open all year, Credit cards: all major
Restaurant open daily
Michelin Map 441, Region: Galicia

Space at the Parador Gil Blas in Santillana del Mar is always at a premium—its popularity is justified because it is truly a jewel. But if you cannot secure a room at the parador, the Hotel Altamira (a 17th-century palace that belonged to Valdivielsos) which is just around the corner offers a delightful ambiance. The style of the Altamira is typical of most of the others in this wonderful medieval town—a three-story building of light-beige-colored cut stone accented by black wrought-iron balconies. You enter from the street into a reception room with a polished cobblestoned floor. A handsome wide staircase with carved wooden banisters leads up to the guestrooms which are pleasantly furnished with wooden headboards and chairs and tables. All bedrooms are equipped with direct-dial telephones and color televisions. The hotel has a small bar with low stools grouped around small tables, a lounge, and two dining rooms—one of the dining rooms is for groups, the other for individual guests. Throughout the hotel there is a scattering of antiques such as benches, mirrors, carved chests, and oil paintings that lend an old-world ambiance. One of the nicest features of the hotel is an enclosed courtyard where guests may dine when the weather is warm.

HOTEL ALTAMIRA
Owner: David Oceja Bujan
Canton, 1
39330 Santillana del Mar
(Cantabria), Spain
Tel: (42) 81.80.25, Fax: (42) 84.01.36
32 rooms, Double: Pts 10,500–Pts 11,000*
*IVA not included, breakfast included
Open all year, Credit cards: all major
Restaurant open daily
30 km W of Santander, 395 km N of Madrid
Michelin Map 442, Region: Cantabria

The Gil Blas, an imposing, 15th-century stone manor with wrought-iron balconies, is named after the infamous character in Le Sage's 18th-century novel. The parador sits on the cobblestoned main square in the heart of the enchanting medieval village of Santillana del Mar, the perfect base from which to explore the nearby archaeological wonders. There are 28 rooms in the main house, plus 28 more in an annex across the road. The entryway into the original house opens into a spacious, cobblestoned inner patio with massive stone walls and superb antiques. There is also a pretty interior garden where supper is served in warm weather. The hallways and charming sitting areas are planked with dark wood that gleams with the patina of age. The beautiful bedrooms are whitewashed and wood-beamed, and furnished with period pieces. If you want to splurge, 222 is a lovely large room with an enormous private terrace. Number 107, a corner room, is also especially attractive. Throughout, the decor is exceptional. Whereas paradors used to have the reputation of rather bland furnishings, the Gil Blas certainly breaks the mold. The interior abounds with splendid antiques which are tastefully combined with sofas and chairs covered with elegant fabrics. Parador Gil Blas is truly a jewel, further enhanced by being located in the quaint town of Santillana del Mar.

PARADOR GIL BLAS
Manager: Cesar Alvarez
Plaza Ramón Pelayo, 8
39330 Santillana del Mar (Cantabria), Spain
Tel: (42) 81.80.00, Fax: (42) 81.83.91
56 rooms, Double: Pts 17,500*
*IVA not included, breakfast Pts 1,300
Open all year, Credit cards: all major
Restaurant open daily
30 km W of Santander, 395 km N of Madrid
Michelin Map 442, Region: Cantabria

Flanked by pretty gardens, the handsome stone façade of the Hotel Los Infantes blends beautifully with the medieval village of Santillana. It is not located in the center of town, but on the main road just outside the pedestrian area. The 18th-century façade of this typical mountain manor was moved stone by stone from the nearby town of Orena and faithfully reconstructed here. Over the doorway are two carved escutcheons—one bearing King Phillip V's coat of arms; the other that of Calderón, the original landlord. The reception area and the first-floor salon are filled with antiques and are charming, with wood floors and beamed ceilings. The breakfast room on the main floor, with its central fireplace, and the good dining room downstairs are not original, but are cozy and decorated with an old-world theme. There are twenty-eight bedrooms in the main house, and twenty more in the annex. The bedrooms, with a few exceptions, are smallish and rather plain, though consistently spotless and equipped with modern bathrooms and tiny terraces overlooking the gardens. The three front-facing doubles with sitting rooms, wooden balconies, and antique touches cost a little more, but are the best rooms in the house. Los Infantes offers reasonable accommodation with historic flavor.

HOTEL LOS INFANTES
Manager: Sra. Marisa Mesones Gomez
Avenida Le Dorat, 1
39330 Santillana del Mar (Cantabria), Spain
Tel: (42) 81.81.00, Fax: (42) 84.01.03
30 rooms, Double: Pts 10,900–18,000
Open Easter to Nov, Credit cards: all major
Restaurant open daily
30 km W of Santander, 395 km N of Madrid
Michelin Map 442, Region: Cantabria

In the 12th century, Saint Dominico built a shelter and hospital on the site of an old palace belonging to the Kings of Navarre. His goal was humanitarian: a wayside hospice for pilgrims who passed through here on their arduous journey to Santiago. Today it houses a recently remodeled parador offering unique accommodation in the quaint old town in the heart of the Rioja wine country. The town of Haro, home to numerous fine bodegas, is only 16 kilometers away. The entrance of the hotel is through a small lobby into a vast lounge, buttressed by massive stone pillars and arches, with a wood-beamed ceiling and stained-glass skylight. The dining room is unusual, too, with dark, rough-hewn wood pillars throughout and the tables interspersed between them. The bedrooms are plain by parador standards, though they live up to them in size and comfort, with traditional Spanish wooden furniture and floors. Those in the old part are similar in decor to those in the new. Ask for one of the front-facing doubles which have small terraces overlooking the quiet plaza, across to the cathedral and a church.

PARADOR DE SANTO DOMINGO
Manager: Alfonso Sanchez M. Capilla
Plaza del Santo, 3
26250 Santo Domingo de la Calzada
(La Rioja), Spain
Tel: (41) 34.03.00, Fax: (41) 34.03.25
61 rooms, Double: Pts 14,500–16,500*
*IVA not included, breakfast Pts 1,200
Open all year, Credit cards: all major
Restaurant open daily
58 km SE of Burgos, 310 km N of Madrid
Michelin Map 442, Region: La Rioja

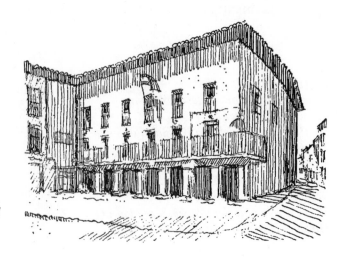

Segovia, with its remarkable Roman aqueduct and outstanding Alcázar, is most frequently visited as a day trip from Madrid. But if you have the luxury of time, you can enjoy Segovia more fully by spending the night there. When deciding on a place to stay, the 19th-century Infanta Isabel can't be beaten for location—the attractive, four-story building with wrought-iron balconies and red-tiled roof faces directly onto the Plaza Mayor. Although the address is Plaza Mayor, the entrance is on a small side street around the corner at Isabel la Católica 1. You enter into a simple reception area with pastel-yellow walls, marble floors, a large crystal chandelier, and pretty prints on the walls. A half-flight of stairs leads up to a small lounge that has a small, rather dated, sitting area enhanced by a large, ornate, antique mirror. More steps lead up to the bar whose walls are covered in a green-and-yellow-patterned design. The guestrooms are surprisingly nice and prettily decorated. Be sure to ask for a room with French doors that open onto a balcony overlooking the square and the majestic cathedral—these are truly special. Although not a hotel that exudes antique charm, the Hotel Infanta Isabel is definitely a winner for location.

HOTEL INFANTA ISABEL
Owner: Enrique Cañada
Plaza Mayor
40001 Segovia, Spain
Tel: (21) 44.31.05, Fax: (21) 43.32.40
29 rooms, Double: Pts 11,340–11,970*
*IVA not included, breakfast Pts 920
Open all year, Credit cards: all major
No restaurant, breakfast only
89 km NW of Madrid, 67 km NE of Ávila
Michelin Map 444, Region: Castilla y León

The Linajes is (not easily) found down one of the tiny stone streets that crisscross Segovia's quaint old quarter, the barrio of San Esteban, which sits on a hill above the modern city. The warm-stone and aged-wood façade of the hotel, known as "The House of the Lineages," is beautifully preserved from the 11th-century palace of the noble Falconi family, whose escutcheon can still be seen over the arched entryway. Inside, with the exception of the pleasantly modern bar/cafeteria downstairs, the hotel conserves an old-Castile flavor, with dark wood, beamed ceilings, and burnished-tile floors. An alcove off the lobby, decorated with antiques, looks into a glass enclosed garden patio on one side and over the open terrace in back, sharing its panoramic views over the city's monumental skyline. There are lovely views from every bedroom, too. In 1996 upgrades were made including new beds in all the rooms, new televisions, new curtains, and new quilts. We have not yet had a chance to inspect the hotel since these improvements were made and look forward to visiting soon.

HOTEL LOS LINAJES
Manager: Miguel Borreguero Rubio
Dr. Velasco, 9
40003 Segovia, Spain
Tel: (21) 46.04.75, Fax: (21) 46.04.79
www.karenbrown.com/spaininns/hotelloslinajes.html
55 rooms, Double: Pts 10,500–10,900
Open all year, Credit cards: all major
Restaurant open daily
89 km NW of Madrid, 67 km NE of Ávila
Michelin Map 444, Region: Castilla y León

Segovia's parador is one of the few ultra-modern offerings within the government-run chain, but, in accordance with its consistently high standards, it is a cut above any other contemporary competitor in service and style. Situated on a hill outside Segovia, the parador commands spectacular panoramas of the golden, fortified city. The hotel's architecture is every bit as dramatic as its setting: huge brick and concrete slabs jut up and out at intriguing angles, topped by tiled roofs and surrounded by greenery. The angled brick-and-concrete motif is carried inside, where black-marble floors glisten beneath skylights in the enormous lobby. Picture windows frame Segovia beyond a garden terrace with a pretty pool. The decor throughout is tasteful, Spanish-contemporary; the feeling open, airy, and bright. The bedrooms are spacious and decorated in earth tones, with pale wood furniture. Each has a balcony that shares the incomparable city view. The combination of the modern and the historical has an unforgettable impact on the guest here, that being the hallmark of Spain's paradors.

PARADOR DE SEGOVIA
Manager: Juan Carlos Morales
Carretera N601
40003 Segovia, Spain
Tel: (21) 44.37.37, Fax: (21) 43.73.62
113 rooms, Double: Pts 18,500*
*IVA not included, breakfast Pts 1,200
Open all year, Credit cards: all major
Restaurant open daily, pool
89 km NW of Madrid, 67 km NE of Ávila
Michelin Map 444, Region: Castilla y León

Constructed on the 14th-century site of the ancient church and convent of Santo Domingo, and next door to the Romanesque cathedral of La Seu d'Urgell (the oldest in Catalonia), this is nonetheless a parador whose byword is modern. But, as with all hotels in this government chain, the accommodations are something special. Of the original building, the stunning old cloister (filled with plants and ivy cascading from hanging pots) has been preserved and converted into the hotel lounge. Graceful stone arches form the foundation of a square central room, several stories high, bedecked with hanging plants. Since our original visit, the hotel has been refurbished and the rooms now are decorated in a Catalan style with mahogany furnishings. The demi-suite 121 costs more, but offers enormous space for the price. The dining room, with its glass ceiling, is sunny, bright, and attractive, as is the indoor pool—a rarity in Spain. Situated in a fertile valley, Seo de Urgel is surrounded by the sierras of Arcabell and Cadi.

PARADOR DE SEO DE URGEL
Manager: Juan Yepes Estebati
Santo Domingo
25700 Seo de Urgel (Lerida), Spain
Tel: (73) 35.20.00, Fax: (73) 35.23.09
79 rooms, Double: Pts 12,500–15,000*
*IVA not included, breakfast Pts 1,300
Open all year, Credit cards: all major
Restaurant open daily, pool
200 km NW of Barcelona
Michelin Map 443, Region: Catalonia

When the need for a fine hotel in Seville—one of the most popular tourist destinations in Spain—became apparent, architect Espinau y Muñoz rose beautifully to the task, creating the Alfonso XIII in an Andalusian style unique to Seville. The talents of local artisans were called upon for hand-crafting the rich interior. Dedicated to its namesake, the Alfonso XIII is reminiscent of an opulent Moorish palace surrounded by gardens, with fabulous artesonado ceilings, marble pillars, graceful Mudéjar arches, and colorful, hand-painted ceramic tiles throughout. The interior patio with its tinkling central fountain is elegant and peaceful, offering the perfect setting for relaxing with a cool drink at the end of a hot day. All of the public rooms are stunning: wide marble staircases lead to expansive landings on each floor, decorated with fine antiques under elaborately carved ceilings. Although some are more spacious than others, the high-ceilinged bedrooms are richly decorated in soft colors and handsome, classic wood furnishings. Many have Spanish "Oriental" rugs, specially made to fit. Some second-floor rooms have terraces over the patio. The Hotel Alfonso XIII is not only the choice of visiting dignitaries, but also the choice of Seville's élite when they entertain. For a deluxe hotel, ideally located for sightseeing, the Hotel Alfonso XIII is tops.

HOTEL ALFONSO XIII
Manager: Jacques Hamburger
San Fernando, 2
41004 Seville, Spain
Tel: (5) 42.22.850, Fax: (5) 42.16.033
149 rooms, Double: Pts 40,000–44,000*
*IVA not included, breakfast Pts 2,500
Open all year, Credit cards: all major
Restaurant open daily, pool
Michelin Map 446, Region: Andalusia

The Doña María has an excellent location in the heart of Seville across from the famous Giralda. Although not a deluxe hotel, it even features a small rooftop swimming pool at eye level with the magnificent spire. On some summer evenings a duet plays beside the pool. The Doña María was originally the palace of Peter the Cruel's administrator and its present owner is the Marquesa de San Joaquín, who still resides here in her private suites and who is personally responsible for the decoration. The lobby of the hotel has character, with a domed ceiling and brick pillars, an intimate, wood-paneled bar, and lots of old-world atmosphere. Its tiny interior garden is glass-enclosed and flanked by suits of armor. The Doña María has added bedrooms over the years, so not all are in the original building. The rooms vary tremendously from antiquated and rather dilapidated to recently renovated. We recommend you request one of the renovated rooms. The location is unbeatable and the price lower than Seville's deluxe category hotels.

HOTEL DOÑA MARÍA
Manager: Manuel Rodriguez Andrade
Don Remundo, 19
41004 Seville, Spain
Tel: (5) 42.24.990, Fax: (5) 42.19.546
61 rooms, Double: Pts 11,000–18,000*
*IVA not included, breakfast Pts 1,500
Open all year, Credit cards: all major
No restaurant, breakfast only, pool
Michelin Map 446, Region: Andalusia

The Taberna del Alabardero (just a five-minute walk from Seville's cathedral) is a real find—almost too good to share. Here you can stay at a remarkably low room rate without sacrificing an ounce of quality, comfort, or ambiance. The charm begins with the exterior, a deep-salmon-pink, three-story building accented with white trim and black wrought-iron grille work. This was the home of Seville's beloved romantic poet, J. Antonio Cavestany. After meticulous renovation, taking great care to leave the original character intact, the home was reopened with the principal purpose of a gourmet restaurant where students from its hotel school could perfect their skills. Under the direction of one of Spain's finest chefs, Juan Marcos, the restaurant earned a coveted Michelin star in 1995. As you enter, you see a café with a bakery on the ground floor. The next level up is the restaurant—a series of intimate dining rooms. The top floor features a large skylight, below which a wrought-iron enclosed gallery opens onto the floors below. Around this gallery are seven guestrooms, named after the provinces in Andalusia. Each is impeccably decorated. Perhaps my favorite is the "Malaga" room, with Pompeii-yellow sponge-painted walls, beds with floral-patterned spreads in soft shades of yellows, rusts, and greens with matching fabric serving as headboards. From the sleeping area, steps lead down to a sitting area in front of a fireplace.

TABERNA DEL ALABARDERO
Manager & Chef: Juan Marcos
Zaragoza, 20
41001 Seville, Spain
Tel: (5) 45.60.637, Fax: (5) 45.63.666
www.karenbrown.com/spaininns/tabernadelalabardero.html
7 rooms, Double: Pts 20,000–25,000*
*IVA not included, breakfast included
Closed Aug, Credit cards: all major
Restaurant open daily
Michelin Map 446, Region: Andalusia

Just 18 kilometers from Seville in distance, yet a world away in atmosphere, lies the beautifully renovated Hotel Cortijo Aguila Real. When the charming Isabel Martinez and her husband bought the property it had fallen into serious disrepair but they saw the great potential of this handsome white farmhouse that had been the showplace of the whole region. In fact, the wealthy landowner who built the cortijo owned all the surrounding countryside—even including the town of Guillena. The Hotel Cortijo Aguila Real crowns the rise of a small hill, and, typical of the Andalusian style, you enter through a gate in the whitewashed walls into a large courtyard. Facing onto the courtyard is the family chapel which now serves as the reception area. Another door from the courtyard leads into an intimate library with prettily upholstered chairs facing the fireplace, a spacious living room, and a handsome dining room (although when the weather is warm, meals are usually served outside). The suites also open onto the central courtyard. The other guestrooms face onto a patio next to the gardens. Each of the bedrooms has a special flower motif which is repeated on the key chain, the fabric in the curtains, and in hand-painted designs on the headboards and dressers. There are many small gardens tucked around the property and also a large swimming pool, and even a private bullring. Another plus, the food is excellent and beautifully presented.

HOTEL CORTIJO AGUILA REAL
Owner: Francisco Venegas
41210 Guillena (Seville) Spain
Tel: (5) 57.85.006, Fax: (5) 57.84.330
www.karenbrown.com/spaininns/hotelcortijoaguilareal.html
15 rooms, Double: Pts 15,000–18,000*
*IVA not included, breakfast Pts 1,500
Open all year, Credit cards: all major
Restaurant open daily, pool
18 km N of Seville, 4 km E of Guillena
Michelin Map 446, Region: Andalusia

Just on the outskirts of Seville, only about 20 minutes by car, you can dwell in utter luxury. The Hacienda Benazuza caters to the rich and famous who want to be discreetly left alone, yet have their every need anticipated and fulfilled. This dazzling white hacienda, dating from the 10th century, belonged to Moorish royalty then, when the Moors were forced from Spain, it came into the hands of the Counts of Benazuza. In the mid-1900s the hacienda became the property of Pablo Romero, who was famous as one of the most outstanding breeders of fine fighting bulls. Today you can fall under the spell of these days long past as you walk the hushed halls, through various small courtyards, and pass fountains and formal gardens planned by the Moors so long ago. Although the niceties of today such as a beautiful swimming pool in the garden, satellite television, and luxurious modern bathrooms have been added, the ambiance remains faithful to the past with superb antiques used throughout. Each of the guestrooms is different. However, whether you are in a suite or a double room, you will find the decor faultless, with beautiful fabrics, quality carpets, antique furniture, and handsome pictures on the walls. The dining room, facing onto the courtyard, is beautiful and serves excellent meals, many of the recipes rooted in Andalusian tradition.

HACIENDA BENAZUZA
Manager: Bernard Wyss
Calle Virgen de Las Nieves s/n
41800 Sanlúcar la Mayor (Seville), Spain
Tel: (5) 57.03.344, Fax: (5) 57.03.410
44 rooms, Double: Pts 42,000–52,000*
*IVA not included, breakfast Pts 1,500
Closed mid-Jul to Sep, Credit cards: all major
Restaurant open daily, pool
27 km W of Seville, 72 km E of Huelva
Michelin Map 446, Region: Andalusia

Make a special effort to include the Parador Castillo de Sigüenza in your itinerary—you won't be sorry. The dramatic stone castle is perched romantically on a hillside overlooking an unspoiled cluster of old stone houses with red-tiled roofs. Happily, there are no modern buildings to interrupt the mood of the 12th century when the castle was a Moorish stronghold. The reconstruction was an overwhelming venture—take a look at the *before* and *after* photographs on the wall (just off the reception area)—you cannot help being impressed with what has been accomplished. Only the shell of the old castle remained, but the original walls have been repaired and the interior has been reconstructed with great care to preserve the original ambiance. Of course there are all the concessions to modern comforts for the traveler, but the decor (although perhaps too glamorous) is great fun. The lounge is dramatic: an enormous room with deep-red walls, blue sofas and chairs, red-tile floor, beamed ceiling, nine massive chandeliers, and a large fireplace. The hotel, following the original plan, is built around a central patio where the old well still remains. The spacious guestrooms are uncluttered and not too over-decorated: the walls stark white, the floors red tile, the furniture tasteful rustic reproductions, and the matching draperies and spreads of fine quality.

PARADOR CASTILLO DE SIGÜENZA
Manager: José Menguiano Corbacho
Plaza de Castillo, s/n
19250 Sigüenza (Guadalajara), Spain
Tel: (49) 39.01.00, Fax: (49) 39.13.64
81 rooms, Double: Pts 13,500–15,000*
*IVA not included, breakfast Pts 1,300
Open all year, Credit cards: all major
Restaurant open daily
133 km NE of Madrid, 191 km SW of Zaragoza
Michelin Map 444, Region: Guadalajara

Next to the ramparts in the ancient fortified town of Sos del Rey Católico, birthplace of the Catholic King Ferdinand, sits a contemporary parador which bears his name. Despite its recent construction, the hotel has a delightful, old-world ambiance and blends harmoniously with the centuries-old buildings around it. The setting is enchanting—surrounded by fertile countryside, resplendent with corn, wheat, and hay. The serenity is interrupted only by the chirping of swallows and the clanking of cowbells. The hotel's location is convenient for exploring the narrow maze of streets lined with low, sunken doorways and stone escutcheons, and for venturing up to the Sada palace where Spain's most renowned king, and Machiavelli's model prince, was born. In the lobby is a statue of the *reyito* (little king) alongside his mother, Juana Enriquez. Upstairs, the view can be enjoyed over coffee or cocktails on an outdoor terrace. Next to the terrace the dining room is attractive with leather chairs, wood-beamed ceiling, and elaborate iron chandeliers. The bedrooms have brick-red tile floors, cheerful, multi-colored striped woven spreads and drapes, pretty brass and glass lamps, and simple iron and brass bedsteads. Room 324 is especially pleasant with a large balcony.

PARADOR FERNANDO DE ARAGÓN
Manager: Miguel Rizos
50680 Sos del Rey Católico (Zaragoza), Spain
Tel: (48) 88.80.11, Fax: (48) 88.81.00
65 rooms, Double: Pts 15,000*
*IVA not included, breakfast Pts 1,300
Closed Dec & Jan, Credit cards: all major
Restaurant open daily
60 km SE of Pamplona, 423 km NE of Madrid
Michelin Map 443, Region: Aragon

The Hotel "La Rectoral" is a deluxe, small hotel tucked into the remote countryside of Asturias. When you arrive in the tiny village of Taramundi, you will wonder if you could possibly be in the right town. However, follow the signs up a small lane and you will arrive at an 18th-century stone house, similar to those you have seen dotting the lovely green countryside in the vicinity. But there is a big difference—this home (originally a rectory for the nearby church) has been totally renovated and now takes in overnight guests. The restoration has meticulously preserved the authentic, rustic mood. The bakery (with the old oven still in the corner) is now a small dining room with a skylight in the roof to lighten the darkened beams and thick stone walls. The dining room is especially attractive, with planked wooden floors, stone walls, and heavy beams blackened with age. Doors lead off the dining room to a wooden balcony where tables are set for dining in the warm summer months. The guestrooms are located in a new wing built in the same style as the original house and are decorated in a sophisticated, modern style with built-in headboards and all the latest amenities. Ask for a room on the ground level with a terrace—these offer a stunning view across the valley to the patchwork of beautiful green fields. For the sports enthusiasts, there is a well-equipped gymnasium, a sauna, and a large swimming pool.

HOTEL "LA RECTORAL"
Manager: Jesús Mier
33775 Taramundi (Asturias), Spain
Tel: (8) 56.46.767, Fax: (8) 56.46.777
18 rooms, Double: Pts 15,000–20,000*
*IVA not included, breakfast Pts 950
Open all year, Credit cards: all major
Restaurant open daily, pool
167 km NE of Santiago de Compostela
55 km E of Villaba
Michelin Map 441, Region: Asturias

The Parador de Teruel, located a little over a kilometer from the city, is a recently remodeled parador, incomparably graced with Mudéjar architecture. Surrounded by appealing grounds sheltering an attractive pool, the hotel has the appearance of a large private home, built in Mudéjar style, with a warm yellow façade and gently sloping tiled roofs. The unusual, somewhat formal octagonal lobby, dotted with antiques, features marble pillars and a high, sculpted ceiling. A massive stone archway frames marble stairs leading up to the bedrooms. The sunny, glass-enclosed terrace off the dining room and bar has the feel of an atrium, with pretty pastel-colored, flowered upholstery and wicker furniture, making it an altogether inviting spot for cocktails or supper. The bedrooms are parador large, with wood floors and woven earth-tone spreads on dark-wood beds. Although this is not a stellar example within the government chain, the hotel is nonetheless pleasant and commodious throughout, and it is unquestionably the best choice of accommodation when visiting the architecturally and archaeologically rich province and city of Teruel.

PARADOR DE TERUEL
Manager: Antonio Escobosa Blazquez
Carretera N 234, Carretera Sagundo-Burgos
44003 Teruel (Teruel), Spain
Tel: (74) 60.18.00, Fax: (74) 60.86.12
60 rooms, Double: Pts 13,500*
*IVA not included, breakfast Pts 1,300
Open all year, Credit cards: all major
Restaurant open daily
149 km NW of Valencia
Michelin Maps 443 & 444, Region: Aragón

The Gran Hotel is located on a tiny peninsula that is connected to the mainland by a narrow bridge. Surrounded by pine trees and with a view of the inlet of Pontevedra, this large, turn-of-the-century hotel whose white façade is accented by yellow awnings appears as a grand old mansion. One of the finest white-sand beaches in Spain (La Lanzada) is a five-minute drive away, and the hotel has its own Olympic-sized saltwater pool, gymnasium, health spa, tennis courts, and nine-hole golf course overlooking the sea. For those who like to try their hand at the game table, there is also a casino just steps from the hotel. Famous among Europeans for decades for its thermal baths, this somewhat dated, spa-style hotel is a reminder of the grand hotels of days gone by. The sparkling-white lobby offers the first taste of the formal public rooms. The vast, grand dining room is dramatic, with a huge stained-glass skylight and gleaming marble floors. One of the most attractive rooms is the sun terrace, looking out to the pool and the inlet (dotted with platforms for the cultivation of mussels). This bright and cheerful sun terrace has a ceiling draped in yellow and white, a motif carried out in the upholstery on the white wicker furniture beside glass-topped tables. The totally renovated modern bedrooms are spacious, catering to the comfort of the many long-term guests who return each year.

GRAN HOTEL LA TOJA
Manager: José Felix Alvarez
36991 Isla de la Toja (Pontevedra), Spain
Tel: (86) 73.00.25, Fax: (86) 73.12.01
198 rooms, Double: Pts 20,000–27,000*
*IVA not included, breakfast Pts 1,650
Open all year, Credit cards: all major
Restaurant open daily, pool
62 km N of Vigo, 70 km SW of Santiago
Michelin Map 441, Region: Galicia

The Hostal del Cardenal, a former archbishop's summer home, is an absolute jewel. As an added bonus, it has a convenient location—on the northern edge of Toledo, with an entrance next to the Puerta de Bisagra (the city's main gate). Your introduction to the small hotel is through a dramatic 11th-century wall and into an enchanting garden with a reflecting pool reminiscent of that found at the Alhambra. Climb the stairs on the right to reach the tiny foyer of the hostal. The stunning stairway, the patio with its lovely fountain, and the cozy sitting rooms embellished with antiques all reflect the hotel's 18th-century heritage. The period furnishings in the inviting guestrooms seem to blend into a tasteful whole. Although smallish, the rooms provide modern comfort with an unbeatable ambiance of past centuries. The indoor dining rooms (which are used only in the winter) are fabulous with their heavy wood beams and fireplaces. In warmer months, meals are served in the garden in the shadow of the medieval walls. The kitchen is outstanding and serves Castilian specialties such as suckling pig. The Hostal del Cardenal has a natural grace and authentic old-world charm frequently lacking in more deluxe hotels. With its gardens, excellent management, and lovely ambiance, this is definitely the finest place to stay in Toledo (and the price is low for value received).

HOSTAL DEL CARDENAL
Manager: Luis Gonzalez Gozalbo
Paseo Recaredo 24
45004 Toledo, Spain
Tel: (25) 22.49.00, Fax: (25) 22.29.91
www.karenbrown.com/spaininns/hosteldelcardenal.html
27 rooms, Double: Pts 11,500*
*IVA not included, breakfast Pts 800 (continental)
Open all year, Credit cards: all major
Restaurant open daily
70 km SW of Madrid
Michelin Map 444, Region: Castilla-La Mancha

The Parador Conde de Orgaz has a choice setting on the hillside across the Tagus river from Toledo, one of the most beautiful ancient towns in Spain. If ever you're willing to pay extra for a view and a terrace, this is the place to do so. The bar and the restaurant also have terraces with a view, so what you are paying for is privacy—your own balcony and view. We think it is worth every penny to see the city change from golden brown to pink in the setting sun. In any case, you will be happy with the rooms—large, comfortable, and tastefully decorated with gaily colored wooden headboards and red-tile floors with pretty rugs. The open-beamed ceilings are especially attractive. Indeed, the newly built, regional-style building is handsome throughout. The impressive, two-story lobby with its giant wood beams is magnificent when viewed from the gallery above which leads to your room. Liberal use of colorful ceramic tiles and local copper pieces adds a delightful touch. There is also a pool surrounded by a pretty lawn. As lovely as the parador is, however, it has one drawback: you have to drive into town.

PARADOR CONDE DE ORGAZ
Manager: Fernando Molina Aranda
Cerro del Emperador s/n
45000 Toledo, Spain
Tel: (25) 22.18.50, Fax: (25) 22.51.66
76 rooms, Double: Pts 16,000–22,000*
*IVA not included, breakfast 1,200
Open all year, Credit cards: all major
Restaurant open daily, pool
2 km S of Toledo on circuit road
70 km SW of Madrid
Michelin Map 444, Region: Castilla-La Mancha

Unlike some of the paradors that are historic monuments, this one in Tordesillas should not be considered a destination in its own right. However, it certainly makes an excellent choice for a stop en route. The hotel is an especially appealing choice during the hot summer months because in the rear garden, facing a lovely pine forest, is an exceptionally large, attractive swimming pool. The Parador de Tordesillas is newly built, but in an old-world style and with many accents of antiques such as hand-carved chests, grandfather clocks, and old mirrors. The exterior is painted a pure white, the windows outlined in tan bricks, and the roof made with a heavy terra cotta tile. The hotel faces directly on the main highway into town, but a green lawn dotted with tall pine trees gives an appealing country air. To the right of the reception area is a large, attractive lounge with an enormous tapestry, fine oil paintings, and a large open fireplace flanked by leather chairs and sofas. The dining room is outstanding: a bright and cheerful room with a wall of windows looking out to a lovely pine forest. The guestrooms are attractive, with traditional wood furniture, wrought-iron reading lamps, and gleaming parquet floors accented with colorful area rugs. One of the nicest aspects of the hotel is that it is immaculately kept throughout.

PARADOR DE TORDESILLAS
Manager: Alfonso Sánchez-M. Capilla
47100 Tordesillas (Valladolid), Spain
Tel: (83) 77.00.51, Fax: (83) 77.10.13
71 rooms, Double: Pts 13,500–15,000*
*IVA not included, breakfast Pts 1,300
Open all year, Credit cards: all major
Restaurant open daily, pool
182 km NE of Madrid, 142 km SE of León
Michelin Map 441, Region: Castilla y León

Mas means an old farmhouse, implying perhaps a simple place to stay. Such is definitely not the case at the Mas de Torrent, a hotel of absolute luxury and stunning charm, idyllically set in the countryside near the beaches of the Costa Brava. The enchantment of the 18th-century, honey-toned stone farmhouse remains, while further enhanced by an outstanding interior design. The walls and vaulted stone ceiling are painted a delicate, muted salmon—an ever-so-appealing color scheme that is repeated in the fabrics and fresh bouquets of flowers. There are several cozy sitting areas, each tastefully decorated with antiques from the region. What was once the kitchen is now the bar, and you can still see the massive chimney for the fireplace and the original deep stone well. A new wing, which blends in beautifully with the original structure, has been added and houses the gourmet restaurant. Ten of the bedrooms are located in the original farmhouse—splurge and request one of these. Each is individually decorated with antiques, each is a dream. My favorite (room 1) has a gorgeous antique bed, exquisite armoire, and large terrace overlooking the pool and garden. There are also 20 guestrooms in a newly constructed garden wing. Although not antique in decor, these are beautifully appointed and have the luxury of individual, private terraces.

MAS DE TORRENT Manager: Gregori
Berengui
17123 Torrent (Gerona), Spain
Tel: (72) 30.32.92, Fax: (72) 30.32.93
30 rooms, Double: Pts 28,000–32,000*
*IVA not included, breakfast Pts 2,300
Open all year, Credit cards: all major
Restaurant open daily, pool
133 km NE of Barcelona, 36 km E of Gerona
Michelin Map 443, Region:Catalonia

As you drive into Tortosa, you will see the Parador "Castillo de La Zuda" crowning a hill at the northern end of town. The location is significant, for this historic parador is nestled into the ruins of an ancient Arab fortress that guarded the city in former times. As you wind your way up the hill, the road enters through the ancient walls which still stretch in partial ruins along the hilltop. Although the architectural style is that of a castle, most of the hotel is actually of new construction with a somewhat traditional hotel look. The dining room is very attractive and strives for an old-world feel with wrought-iron light fixtures and a beamed ceiling. The cuisine features specialties of the Catalan region. Each of the guestrooms is furnished exactly alike with wood and leather headboards, home-spun-looking drapes and matching spreads, and dark-wood chairs and desks. Every room has a balcony and the views from this lofty hilltop setting are lovely in every direction, whether it be to the fertile Ebro river valley or the mountain massif. One of the nicest aspects of this parador is a romantic swimming pool tucked into a terrace framed by the ancient walls of the castle. There is also a children's play yard for those traveling with little ones. The bustling town of Tortosa is not terribly picturesque but the hotel, surrounded by acres of land, creates its own atmosphere.

PARADOR "CASTILLO DE LA ZUDA"
Manager: Manuel Esteban
43500 Tortosa (Tarragona), Spain
Tel: (77) 44.44.50, Fax: (77) 44.44.58
82 rooms, Double: Pts 13,500–15,000*
*IVA not included, breakfast Pts 1,300
Open all year, Credit cards: all major
Restaurant open daily, pool
188 km SW of Barcelona
Michelin Maps 443 & 445, Region: Catalonia

Restaurants, boutiques, and souvenir shops now line the maze of narrow streets that spider-web back from Tossa de Mar's beach, but once you get past the high-rise hotels and condominiums, the heart of the town still retains the feel of its fishing village heritage. Most tourists opt for one of the modern hotels with swimming pool and up-to-date amenities. However, if you don't mind sacrificing luxury for location, the Hotel Diana offers a lot of charm. The setting is prime: the hotel fronts right onto the main beach promenade. A bar, with small tables set outside to watch the action, stretches across the front of the building. Arched windows, dark-green trim, and a white exterior lend a small villa-like atmosphere to the hotel. Within, the hotel has the character of a private home. Marble floors, antique furnishings, grandfather clock, painted tile decoration, inner courtyards, fountains, statues, and stained-glass designs all add a romantic, if somewhat worn, appeal. The simply decorated bedrooms have TV and telephone. Ask for one of the best rooms, such as 306, 307, 206, and 207—the headboards are antique, the bathroom modern, and, best yet, there is a good-sized balcony with a lovely view of the beach and the old fortress on the hill. If you don't expect too much from this two-star hotel, the Hotel Diana is an excellent value.

HOTEL DIANA
Manager: Fernando Osorio Gotarra
Plaza de España, 6
17320 Tossa de Mar (Gerona), Spain
Tel: (72) 34.18.86, Fax: (72) 34.18.86
www.karenbrown.com/spaininns/hoteldiana.html
21 rooms, Double: Pts 6,600–10,200*
*IVA included, breakfast Pts 900
Open Easter to Nov, Credit cards: all major
No restaurant, breakfast only
79 km NE of Barcelona, 39 km S of Gerona
Michelin Map 443, Region: Catalonia (Costa Brava)

Henri Elink Schuurman and his Spanish wife, Marta, bought a beautiful 19th-century farm with two granite houses, an olive press, a winery, and a house chapel 14 kilometers outside Trujillo (on the road to the captivating town of Guadalupe). With patience and love he has tucked guestrooms into the various buildings—taking great care not to disturb the ambiance of the farm (finca) that makes a stay here so special. Of course you must be the kind of person who would chuckle to find a lamb looking through your window in the morning or ducks waddling by your door. Henri (who before retirement was a Dutch diplomat) and his family live in Madrid, but are frequently at the finca where Henri oversees the ongoing project of renovation and Marta (who is an artist and decorator) has created a beautiful ambiance of rustic simplicity. My favorite guestroom (the "red room") is on the ground floor of the main house and has two charming antique iron beds, pretty red-print, country-French-style material on the spreads and curtains, a predominantly red Oriental carpet, and a window overlooking a tranquil garden where dinner is often served. Steps lead from the garden to a swimming pool surrounded by a lawn stretching out to groves of olive, cherry, and almond trees.

FINCA SANTA MARTA
Owners: Marta & Henri Elink Schuurman
Por la carretera de Guadalupe
10200 Trujillo (Cáceres), Spain
(or: Juan Ramón Jiménez, 12-8.º A, 28036 Madrid)
Tel & fax: (27) 31.92.03 or Madrid (1) 35.02.217
www.karenbrown.com/spaininns/fincasantamarta.html
10 rooms, Double: Pts 9,000*
*IVA not included, breakfast included
Open all year, Credit cards: MC, VS
Restaurant open daily upon request, pool
14 km SE of Trujillo on C 524, sign on right
Michelin Map 444, Region: Extremadura

Installed in the 16th-century convent of Santa Clara, the Parador de Trujillo, opened in 1984, blends harmoniously with the Renaissance and medieval architecture in Trujillo. Enter through the outdoor stone patio, and be sure to notice the *torno* (revolving shelf) to the right of the doorway. The original residents were cloistered nuns, and it was by way of this device that they sold their homemade sweets to the town's citizens. Inside, 18 of the hotel's bedrooms were originally the nuns' cells, and retain their low, stone doorways (be careful not to bump your head). These rooms surround a sunlit gallery (whose walls are laced with climbing vines) overlooking a cloistered garden patio with an old stone well at its center. An attached annex houses new bedrooms surrounding another, whitewashed courtyard. Although there is a special flavor to the original bedrooms, the new addition has views of the valley and maintains a traditional Spanish ambiance with pale-wood furnishings, brick-tiled floors, leather sling chairs, and iron fixtures. This parador is a charming spot from which explore the beautiful town of Trujillo and to launch explorations of Extremadura, whose native sons launched their own explorations to the New World.

PARADOR DE TRUJILLO
Manager: José Rizos
Plaza de Santa Clara
10200 Trujillo (Cáceres), Spain
Tel: (27) 32.13.50, Fax: (27) 32.13.66
46 rooms, Double: Pts: 15,000*
*IVA not included, breakfast Pts 1,300
Open all year, Credit cards: all major
Restaurant open daily
252 km SW of Madrid, 88 km NE of Mérida
Michelin Map 444, Region: Extremadura

This parador is installed in a 16th-century palace on Ubeda's monumentally magnificent Renaissance main square. It features no less than three interior patios, one lined by slender stone arches and dotted with outdoor tables, another overhung with its original wooden terraces, and the third converted to a lovely garden. All but the five newest guestrooms are found at the glass-enclosed gallery level, up a massive stone stairway flanked by suits of armor. The hotel has undergone two renovations, resulting in a variety of rooms off the antique-lined hallways, all of them lovely, with gleaming white baths, colorfully tiled floors, and wood artesonado ceilings. Our personal favorites are those overlooking the golden Plaza Vázquez de Molina and El Salvador chapel, largely furnished with antiques (room 112 is especially romantic, with a small corner balcony peeking out at the cathedral). The more recent additions are decorated in a modern style and are more spacious (one has a sitting room for an additional 3,000 pesetas). Detailed attention to faithful historic preservation is obvious throughout the parador's public rooms, with the exception of the recently constructed but pleasant restaurant, whose menu offers an unusually creative variety of dishes. Don't miss a visit to the Taberna, a lounge/bar in the stone basement, whose decor includes huge, ceramic storage vats.

PARADOR "CONDESTABLE DAVALOS"
Manager: José Muños
Plaza de Vázquez Molina, s/n
23400 Ubeda (Jaén), Spain
Tel: (53) 75.03.45, Fax: (53) 75.12.59
*31 rooms, Double: Pts 18,500**
**IVA not included, breakfast Pts 1,300*
Open all year, Credit cards: all major
Restaurant open daily
120 km NE of Granada
Michelin Map 444, Region: Andalucia

Four kilometers west of the sleepy town of Verín, its brooding stone towers visible from afar, stands the medieval castle fortress of Monterrey (the most important monument in the province of Orense), facing the parador of the same name. Reached by driving through green vineyards, the hotel is constructed in the style of a regional manor, having a somewhat severe exterior of cut-stone blocks with a crenelated tower at one end. The Parador Monterrey is perched atop a vine-covered hill and surrounded by lovely views in all directions from its high vantage point. The lobby features warm wood decorated with suits of armor and other antique pieces. Fifteen of the twenty-three bedrooms enjoy the countryside vista, eight overlooking the dramatic castle (ask for 102, 104, 106, or 107). The large rooms are pleasantly decorated in beige and brown, with wood floors and comfortable, contemporary Spanish furniture. The tranquil setting of this parador, along with its pretty pool in the middle of a lovely green lawn and the delightfully cozy reading room with its unusual fireplace, makes it an ideal spot for overnighting, especially if you can squeeze in a visit to the castle and its 13th-century church.

PARADOR MONTERREY
Manager: Tomas Cardo
32600 Verín (Orense), Spain
Tel: (88) 41.00.75, Fax: (88) 41.20.17
23 rooms, Double: Pts 12,500–13,500*
*IVA not included, breakfast Pts 1,200
Open Feb to mid-Dec, Credit cards: all major
Restaurant open daily, pool
209 km NW of Zamora, 182 km SE of Santiago
Michelin Map 441, Region: Galicia

Situated in the pine-green mountains outside the medieval town of Vic (also spelled Vich on some maps), this parador overlooks the reddish, gorge like rock formations and the blue Sau reservoir which is fed by the waters of the Ter river. Its setting is singular in beauty and tranquillity. The hotel is within easy walking distance of an ancient monastery that can be reached only by foot and within easy driving distance of several of the most picturesque villages in the region (Rupit being the most notable example). The building itself has somewhat of an institutional look with a severe façade of pale-gray granite with arched windows, iron balconies, and red-tile roof. The two-story patio/lobby has heavy polished-wood columns, a large modern mural on one wall, and a vast stained-glass ceiling that casts blue and gold light on a shining white-marble floor. One of the nicest rooms is the sitting room with antiques and a cozy fireplace. The wood-paneled bar has a terrace with views over the lake below. Most of the bedrooms have terraces with splendid views over the lovely swimming pool and lawn and on to the hill-ringed lake beyond. The bedrooms are large and pleasant, decorated with wooden furniture and lovely brass and iron lamps. Note: The well-signposted parador is located about 15 kilometers northeast of Vic, off the C153 to Roda de Ter.

PARADOR DE VIC
Manager: Anna María Puigdollers
08500 Vic (Barcelona), Spain
Tel: (3) 81.22.323, Fax: (3) 81.22.368
36 rooms, Double: Pts 13,700–15,900*
*IVA not included, breakfast 1,300
Open all year, Credit cards: all major
Restaurant open daily, pool
80 km N of Barcelona
Michelin Map 443, Region: Catalonia

Hotel Descriptions   291

Although the tiniest of Spain's paradors, the "Condes de Villaba" is a real gem. As you drive into town, you cannot miss this small hotel which is incorporated into a very old stone tower—the only remaining fortification standing in Villaba, which otherwise has lost its medieval ambiance. The ground level holds an excellent restaurant—a romantic room with two enormous iron chandeliers, antlers on whitewashed walls, massive stone floor, and just ten tables. Steps lead up to the reception area encompassing the entire second level. Colorful medieval paintings on the walls and a soaring ceiling give this room a proper castle atmosphere. Each of the next three floors of the octagonal tower has two guestrooms. There is a small elevator, but if you want some exercise, it is fun to wind your way up the stairs to the various levels, peeking out as you climb through tiny slit windows in the thick stone walls. All of the bedrooms are spacious but the even-numbered rooms (2, 4, and 6) are enormous. The decor is extremely attractive, with plain wooden headboards, wrought-iron reading lamps, simple wooden writing desks, beamed ceilings, and pretty area rugs setting off the gleam of hardwood floors. The stone walls are so deep that you must actually walk into them to look out through the original tall, narrow windows.

PARADOR "CONDES DE VILLABA"
Manager: José Ceferino Vázquez
Valeriano Valdesuso, s/n
27800 Villaba (Lugo) Spain
Tel: (82) 51.00.11, Fax: (82) 51.00.90
6 rooms, Double: Pts 16,500–17,500*
*IVA not included, breakfast Pts 1,300
Closed Dec 20 to Feb 9, Credit cards: all major
Restaurant open daily
65 km SE of Ferrol, 140 km NE of Santiago
Michelin Map 441, Region: Galicia

The setting of El Montíboli is nothing short of superb—completely dominating its own rocky peninsula which juts into the sea. The entrance is through a well-kept garden, enhanced by long reflecting pools rimmed by a series of terra cotta jugs which have been converted into merry little fountains. Although of new construction, the exterior reflects Moorish influence, with a stark white exterior and arches incorporated throughout the design. The interior is much more contemporary in feel—sort of a "Miami Beach" look with light streaming in through purple, turquoise, and white translucent windows. In the center of the lobby is a gold-leaf table with an artificial silk flower arrangement. To the right is a sitting area with modern brass and leather chairs. Because the hotel is terraced down the hill, the lounge, bar, conference rooms, and dining room are built at various levels, cleverly designed to take full advantage of the fabulous views. Most of the guestrooms too capture a vista of the sea. In addition to tennis courts, there are two pools, one a gem of a small oval pool crowning a promontory overlooking the sea, and the other next to the beach and tennis courts. Best yet, whereas most hotels would be happy just to have a bit of sand, the El Montíboli has not one, but *two* excellent beaches, one on each side of the private peninsula. Amazingly, the hotel is not super-expensive—for all the amenities it offers, it is a good value.

El MONTÍBOLI HOTEL
Manager: José Castillo Aliaga
03570 Villajoyosa (Alicante), Spain
Tel: (6) 58.90.250, Fax: (6) 58.93.857
53 rooms, Double: Pts 25,000*
*IVA not included, breakfast included
Open all year, Credit cards: all major
Restaurant open daily, pools
3 km S of Villajoyosa, 145 km S of Valencia
Michelin Map 445, Region: Valencia (Costa Blanca)

The Hotel la Casona de Amandi (dating back to 1850) is a typical home of this area—an appealing, two-story white house with a wide expanse of small-paned windows wrapping around the second level and a steeply pitched red-tile roof. It faces directly onto a small street, but there are extensive manicured grounds surrounding it on three sides. Some of the gardens are formal, with a French flair, others have a more casual English look. Inside, the ambiance is very homey, much more like an intimate bed and breakfast than a hotel. The owners live on the property and take pride in seeing that guests are well cared for. The furnishings throughout are antiques, nothing pretentious or decorator-perfect, just fine family pieces displayed as in a real home. The spacious living room is lovely with comfortable sofas (slip-covered in pretty floral fabric) flanking a large fireplace. Antiques abound, but the one that is particularly gorgeous is an enormous 17th-century wooden chest under one of the windows. Breakfast is served in an intimate, old-fashioned little parlor. The guestrooms, like the rest of the house, are decorated in antiques—all are different, but have the same old-world look. Number 1, a twin-bedded room, is especially attractive, with beautiful antique headboards, pretty matching floral draperies and bedspreads, and windows looking out on two sides.

HOTEL LA CASONA DE AMANDI
Owner: Rodrigo Fernández Suarez
33300 Amandi-Villaviciosa (Asturias), Spain
Tel: (8) 58.90.130, Fax: (8) 58.90.129
9 rooms, Double: Pts 13,900*
*IVA & breakfast not included
Open all year, Credit cards: all major
No restaurant, breakfast only
32 km W of Gijón, 39 km NE of Oviedo
1,300 meters S of Villaviciosa
Michelin Map 441, Region: Asturias

Cortés was the conquistador of the Aztec empire in Mexico in 1521. He was born in Medellín, east of Mérida, but was taken on as a protégé by the Duke of Feria, whose ancestors built this wonderful fortified castle in the 15th century. Cortés actually lived here for a short time before embarking for Cuba as an ordinary colonist. The castle has been faithfully restored and put to use as a highly attractive hotel. Virtually surrounded by towers, the exterior is somewhat intimidating, but the tiny plaza in front of it is charming and, once inside, you will love the lounges and public areas with antiques in every available space. There is a glorious chapel with an incredible golden cupola. The central patio, with its graceful stone columns, is equally enchanting. The bedrooms vary somewhat, since they were often installed in the original castle rooms, but they are all attractively decorated with regional furniture and the traditional parador good taste. In 1991 the parador was completely renovated: several new guestrooms were added including three with a terrace and several with a special romantic decor. Sala Dorada (room 314) has a stunning ceiling and room 303 has a Jacuzzi. This parador affords a marvelous opportunity to lodge in an authentic castle without sacrificing a single modern comfort.

PARADOR DE ZAFRA
Manager: Antonio Atalaya Diaz
Plaza Corazón de María, 7
06300 Zafra (Badajoz), Spain
Tel: (24) 55.45.40, Fax: (24) 55.10.18
45 rooms, Double: Pts 16,000–25,000*
*IVA not included, breakfast Pts 1,300
Open all year, Credit cards: all major
Restaurant open daily, pool
135 km N of Seville
Michelin Maps 444 & 446, Region: Extremadura

The Parador "Condes de Alba y Aliste" is a stately stone mansion built in the 15th century by the counts whose names it bears. The exterior is somewhat austere, reflecting the style of the times, but inside, you will be charmed. The elaborate use of antiques with regional furniture makes a terrific impression. The central patio, surrounded by glassed-in, stone-arcaded galleries, is wonderful. Masterful antique tapestries and chivalric banners abound on the walls, and many of the interior doorways have intricately carved façades. Sitting areas are arranged around the galleries and afford a lovely view through rich wood shutters of the interior patio with its old stone well. The hotel closed for extensive renovation in 1995 and reopened in the spring of 1996. Twenty-four new bedrooms were added and the hotel refurbished. This delightful parador has always been one of our favorites, and after its face-lift, is even nicer. Its prime setting in the heart of Zamora has, of course, not changed. It faces onto a small stone-paved square, a convenient hub for exploring the narrow, picturesque streets of the old quarter.

PARADOR "CONDES DE ALBA Y ALISTE"
Manager: Sra. Pilar Pelegrin Gracia
Plaza de Viriato, 5
49001 Zamora, Spain
Tel: (80) 51.44.97, Fax: (80) 53.00.63
51 rooms, Double: Pts 17,500*
*IVA not included, breakfast Pts 1,300
Open all year, Credit cards: all major
Restaurant open daily, pool
206 km N of Salamanca, 257 km NW of Madrid
Michelin Maps 441 & 442, Region: Castilla y León

Maps

Regions of Spain

Santiago de Compostela

Galicia

Asturias Cantabria

FRANCE

Navarra

La Rioja

Catalonia

Barcelona

Castilla y León

Aragon

PORTUGAL

Madrid

Madrid

Castilla-La Mancha

Valencia

Extremadura

MEDITERRANEAN SEA

Murcia

Andalusia

ATLANTIC OCEAN

Málaga

Key Map to Hotels

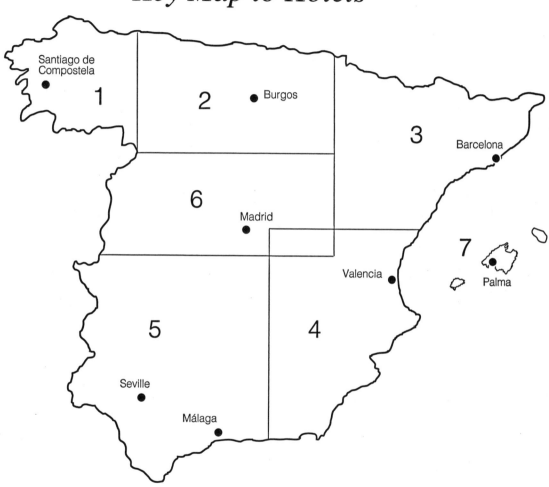

Map 1: Northwest Spain

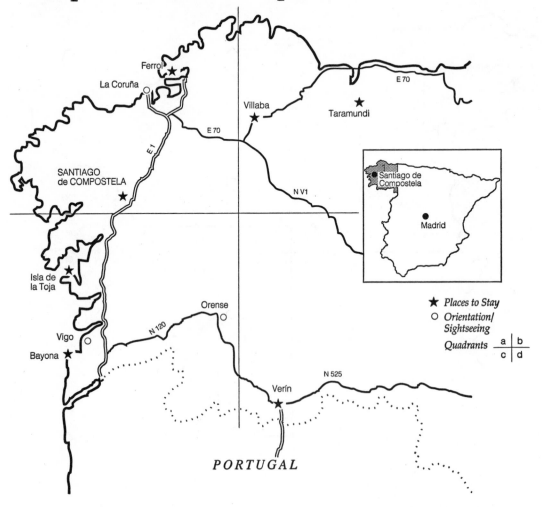

Ferrol ★
La Coruña ○
E 1
Villaba ★
Taramundi ★
E 70
E 70
SANTIAGO de COMPOSTELA ★
N V1
Santiago de Compostela ●
Madrid ●
Isla de la Toja ★
Orense ○
Vigo ○
N 120
Bayona ★
N 525
Verín ★

PORTUGAL

★ Places to Stay
○ Orientation/ Sightseeing
Quadrants

a	b
c	d

Map 2: North Central Spain

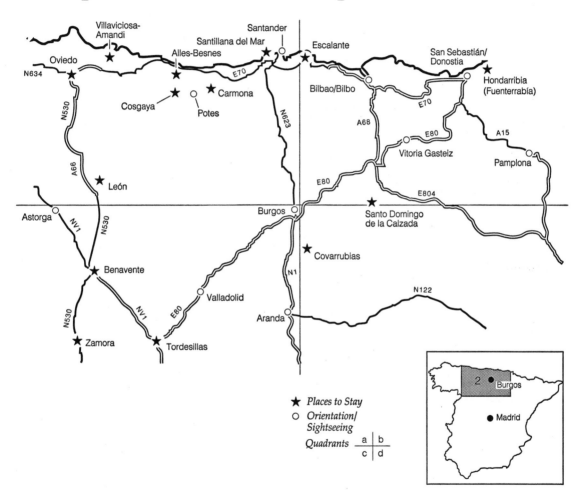

Villaviciosa-Amandi

Santillana del Mar

Santander

Escalante

San Sebastián/Donostia

Oviedo

Alles-Besnes

N634

Hondarribia (Fuenterrabía)

N530

Cosgaya

Carmona

Bilbao/Bilbo

E70

Potes

N623

A68

E70

Vitoria Gasteiz

A15

A66

E80

Pamplona

León

E80

Astorga

NV1

N530

Burgos

Santo Domingo de la Calzada

E804

Covarrubias

Benavente

N1

N530

NV1

E80

Valladolid

N122

Zamora

Tordesillas

Aranda

★ *Places to Stay*

○ *Orientation/Sightseeing*

Quadrants

a	b
c	d

2 Burgos

Madrid

Map 3: Northeast Spain

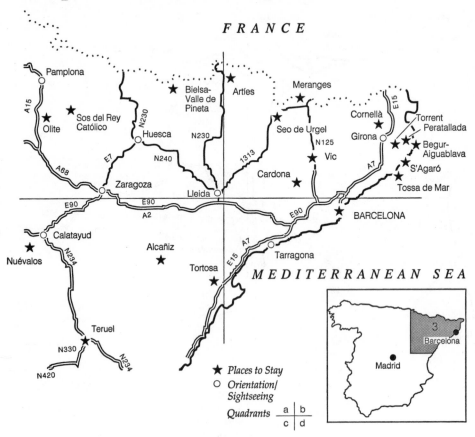

FRANCE

Pamplona

A15

★ Sos del Rey
Olite Católico

N230

★ Bielsa-
Valle de
Pineta

Artíes

Meranges

N230

Huesca

N240

1313

Seo de Urgel

N125

Cornellà

Girona

Torrent
Peratallada

E15

E7

Zaragoza

Lleida

Vic

Cardona

A7

Begur-
Aiguablava

S'Agaró

A68

Tossa de Mar

E90

E90

A2

E90

BARCELONA

Calatayud

Alcañiz

A7

Nuévalos

N234

Tortosa

E15

Tarragona

MEDITERRANEAN SEA

Teruel

N330

N234

N420

★ Places to Stay
○ Orientation/
   Sightseeing

Quadrants | a | b |
           |---|---|
           | c | d |

3

Barcelona

Madrid

Map 4: Southeast Spain

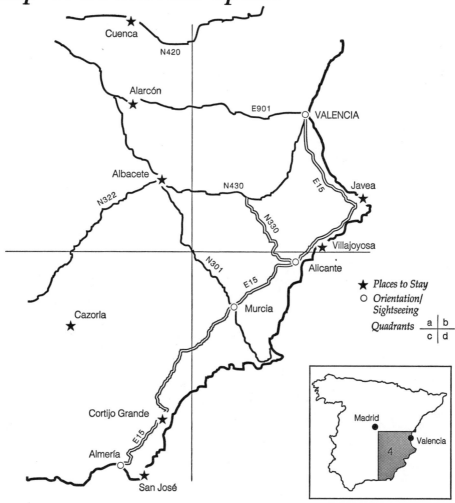

Cuenca

N420

Alarcón

E901

VALENCIA

Albacete

N430

Javea

N322

N330

E15

Villajoyosa

N301

Alicante

E15

Places to Stay

Cazorla

Orientation/
Sightseeing

Murcia

Quadrants

a	b
c	d

Cortijo Grande

E15

Almería

San José

Madrid

4

Valencia

Map 5: Southwest Spain

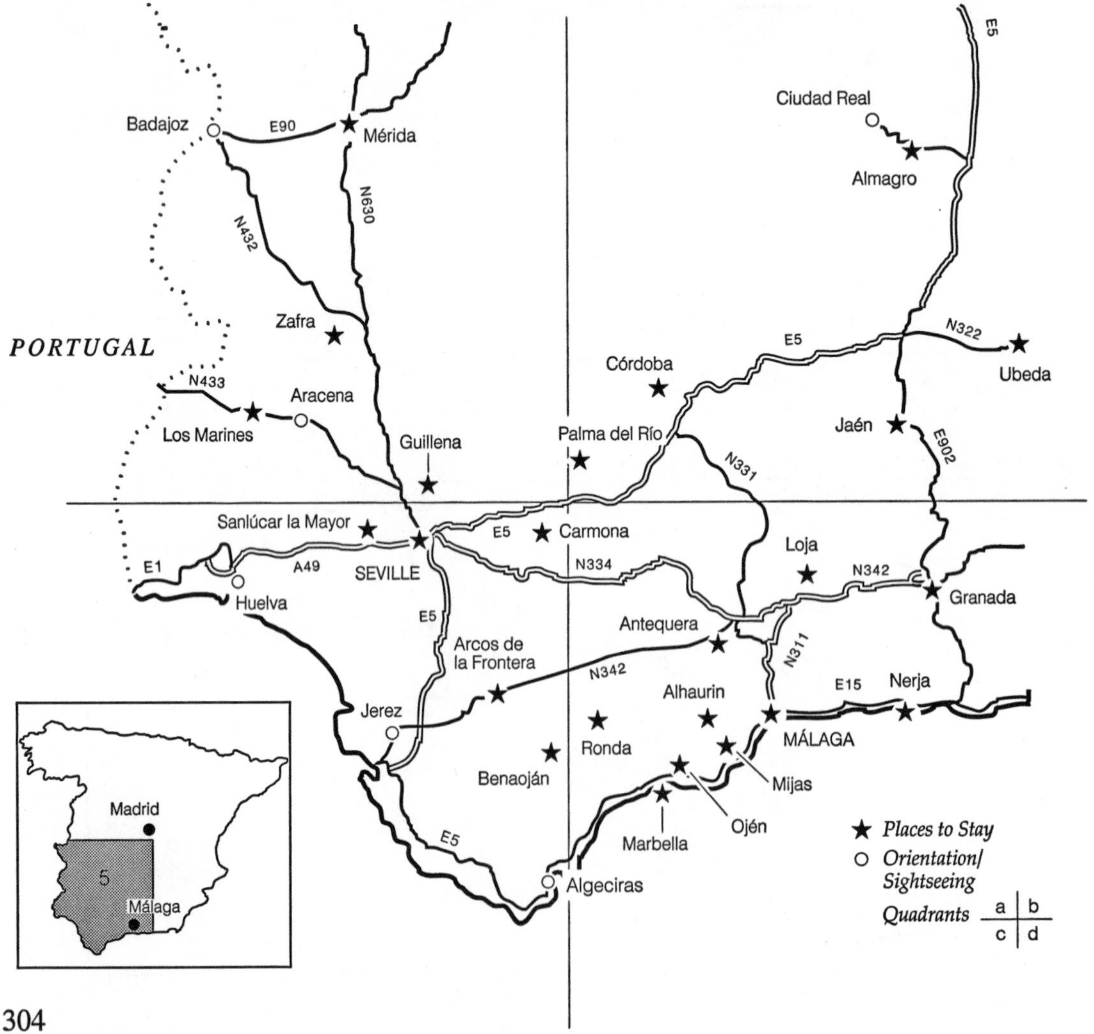

PORTUGAL

Badajoz — E90 — ★ Mérida

N432

N630

Zafra ★

Córdoba ★

Ciudad Real ○
Almagro ★

E5

N322
Ubeda ★

N433
Los Marines ★ Aracena ○

Guillena ★

Palma del Río ★
N331

Jaén ★

E902

Sanlúcar la Mayor ★ ★

E5 ★ Carmona

Loja ★

N342

Granada ★

E1

A49
Huelva ○

SEVILLE

E5

N334

Antequera ★

N311

E5

Arcos de la Frontera

N342

Alhaurin ★

E15 Nerja ★

Jerez ○

Ronda ★

Benaoján

★ MÁLAGA
★ Mijas

Ojén

E5

Marbella ★

Algeciras ○

Madrid ●

5

Málaga ●

★ Places to Stay
○ Orientation/ Sightseeing

Quadrants

a	b
c	d

304

Map 6: Central Spain

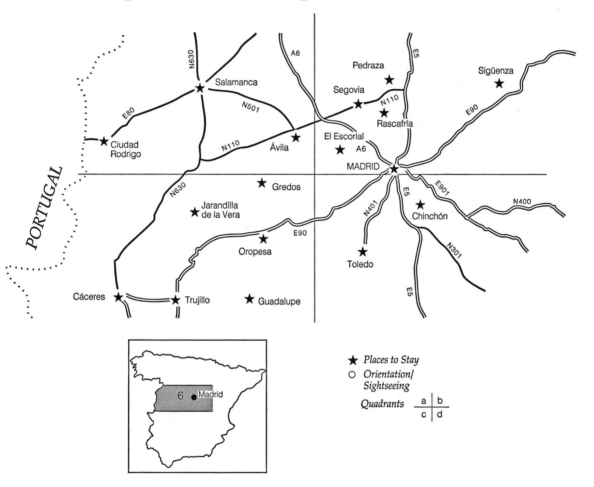

PORTUGAL

N630

E80

Salamanca

N501

A6

Pedraza

Sigüenza

Segovia

N110

Rascafría

E90

Ciudad Rodrigo

N110

Ávila

El Escorial

A6

MADRID

N630

Gredos

Jarandilla de la Vera

E5

E901

N400

N401

Chinchón

Oropesa

E90

Toledo

N301

Cáceres

Trujillo

Guadalupe

E5

6 ● Madrid

★ Places to Stay

○ Orientation/ Sightseeing

Quadrants

a	b
c	d

Map 7: Balearic Islands

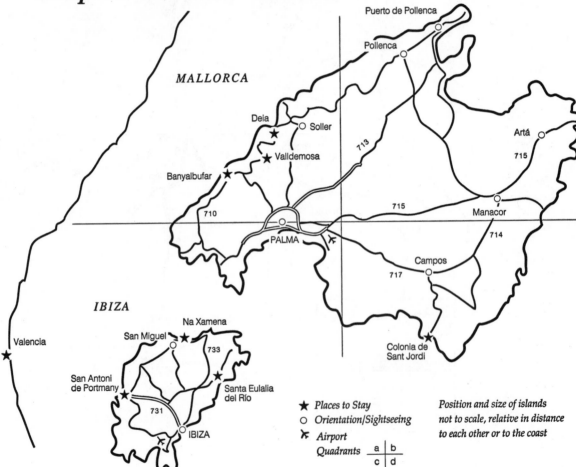

MALLORCA

Puerto de Pollenca

Pollenca

Deia

○ Soller

Artá ○

★ Valldemosa

713

Banyalbufar ★

715

710

715

Manacor ○

☆ PALMA

714

Campos ○

717

Colonia de
Sant Jordi ★

IBIZA

Na Xamena

San Miguel ★

733

San Antoni
de Portmany ★

Santa Eulalia
del Río ★

731

IBIZA

★ *Places to Stay*
○ *Orientation/Sightseeing*
☆ *Airport*
Quadrants

a	b
c	d

*Position and size of islands
not to scale, relative in distance
to each other or to the coast*

Valencia ★

Barcelona

Reservation Request Letter in Spanish and English

HOTEL NAME AND ADDRESS—CLEARLY PRINTED OR TYPED

Muy señores nuestros:
Dear Sirs:

Rogamos reserven para _____   *noches (s)*
We are writing to request (number)   nights (s) at your hotel

a partir del día _____ *de* _____ *hasta el día* _____ *de* _____
Arriving (day)   (month)   departing   (day)   (month)

_____ *habitacion(es) sencilla(s)*
        number of single rooms

_____ *habitacion(es) doble(s)*
        number of double room(s)

con cama extra ____ *con vista al mar* ____ *con terraza* ____
with an extra bed   sea view   with a terrace

con vista al patio ____ *con vista a la plaza* ____ *en la parte antigua* ____
facing the patio   facing the plaza   in the old part

Somos _____ *Persons.*
We are (number of) persons in our party.

Les rogamos nos informen sobre la disponibilidad de habitacion(es), el precio de la(s) misma(s), y el depósito requerido. En espera de su respuesta les saludamos, atentamente,

Please advise availability, rate, and deposit needed. Awaiting your reply, we remain, sincerely,

YOUR NAME AND ADDRESS CLEARLY PRINTED OR TYPED.

Index

SHARE YOUR REVIEWS WITH US

We greatly appreciate first-hand evaluations of places in our guides. Your critiques are invaluable to us. To keep current on the properties in our guides, we keep a database of readers' comments.

Please list your comments about properties you have visited. We welcome accolades, as well as criticisms.

Name of hotel or b&b _____ Town _____ Country _____

Comments:

Name of hotel or b&b _____ Town _____ Country _____

Comments:

Your name _____ Street _____ Town _____ State _____

Zip _____ Country _____ Tel _____ e-mail _____ date _____

Please send report to: Karen Brown's Guides, Post Office Box 70, San Mateo, California 94401, USA
tel: (650) 342-9117, fax: (650) 342-9153, e-mail: karen@karenbrown.com, www.karenbrown.com

SHARE YOUR REVIEWS WITH US

We greatly appreciate first-hand evaluations of places in our guides. Your critiques are invaluable to us. To keep current on the properties in our guides, we keep a database of readers' comments.

Please list your comments about properties you have visited. We welcome accolades, as well as criticisms.

Name of hotel or b&b _____ Town _____ Country _____
Comments:

Name of hotel or b&b _____ Town _____ Country _____
Comments:

Your name _____ Street _____ Town _____ State _____
Zip _____ Country _____ Tel _____ e-mail _____ date _____

Please send report to: Karen Brown's Guides, Post Office Box 70, San Mateo, California 94401, USA
tel: (650) 342-9117, fax: (650) 342-9153, e-mail: karen@karenbrown.com, www.karenbrown.com

SHARE YOUR DISCOVERIES WITH US

Outstanding properties often come from readers' discoveries. We would love to hear from you.

Please list below any hotel or bed & breakfast you discover. Tell us what you liked about the property and, if possible, please include a brochure or photographs so we can share your enthusiasm. We keep a permanent database of all of your recommendations for future use. Note: we regret we cannot return photos.

Owner _____ Hotel or B&B _____ Street _____

Town _____ Zip _____ State or Region _____ Country _____

Comments:

Your name _____ Street _____ Town _____ State _____

Zip _____ Country _____ Tel _____ e-mail _____ date _____

Please send report to: Karen Brown's Guides, Post Office Box 70, San Mateo, California 94401, USA
tel: (650) 342-9117, fax: (650) 342-9153, e-mail: karen@karenbrown.com, www.karenbrown.com

SHARE YOUR DISCOVERIES WITH US

Outstanding properties often come from readers' discoveries. We would love to hear from you.

Please list below any hotel or bed & breakfast you discover. Tell us what you liked about the property and, if possible, please include a brochure or photographs so we can share your enthusiasm. We keep a permanent database of all of your recommendations for future use. Note: we regret we cannot return photos.

Owner _____ Hotel or B&B _____ Street _____

Town _____ Zip _____ State or Region _____ Country _____

Comments:

Your name _____ Street _____ Town _____ State _____

Zip _____ Country _____ Tel _____ e-mail _____ date _____

Please send report to: Karen Brown's Guides, Post Office Box 70, San Mateo, California 94401, USA
tel: (650) 342-9117, fax: (650) 342-9153, e-mail: karen@karenbrown.com, www.karenbrown.com

KB Travel Service

Quality * Personal Service * Great Values

- Staff trained by Karen Brown to help you plan your holiday
- Special offerings on airfares to major cities in Europe
- Special prices on car rentals with free upgrades
- Countryside mini-itineraries based on Karen Brown's Guides
- Reservations for hotels, inns, and B&Bs in Karen Brown's Guides

For assistance and information on service fees contact:

KB Travel Service

16 East Third Avenue
San Mateo, California, 94401, USA

tel: 800-782-2128, fax: 650-342-2519, email: kbtravel@aol.com

---

For additional information on places in the Karen Brown's Guides, visit the following websites:
www.karenbrown.com and www.innsandouts.com

✈ UNITED AIRLINES

is the

Preferred Airline

of

Karen Brown's Guides

and

Karen Brown Travel Services

Seal Cove Inn

Located in the San Francisco Bay Area

Karen Brown Herbert (best known as author of the Karen Brown's guides) and her husband, Rick, have put 20 years of experience into reality and opened their own superb hideaway, Seal Cove Inn. Spectacularly set amongst wild flowers and bordered by towering cypress trees, Seal Cove Inn looks out to the distant ocean over acres of county park: an oasis where you can enjoy secluded beaches, explore tidepools, watch frolicking seals, and follow the tree-lined path that traces the windswept ocean bluffs. Country antiques, original watercolors, flower-laden cradles, rich fabrics, and the gentle ticking of grandfather clocks create the perfect ambiance for a foggy day in front of the crackling log fire. Each bedroom is its own haven with a cozy sitting area before a wood-burning fireplace and doors opening onto a private balcony or patio with views to the park and ocean. Moss Beach is a 35-minute drive south of San Francisco, 6 miles north of the picturesque town of Half Moon Bay, and a few minutes from Princeton harbor with its colorful fishing boats and restaurants. Seal Cove Inn makes a perfect base for whale-watching, salmon-fishing excursions, day trips to San Francisco, exploring the coast, or, best of all, just a romantic interlude by the sea, time to relax and be pampered. Karen and Rick look forward to the pleasure of welcoming you to their coastal hideaway.

Seal Cove Inn • 221 Cypress Avenue • Moss Beach • California • 94038 • USA
tel: (650) 728-4114, fax: (650) 728-4116, e-mail: sealcove@coastside.net, website: sealcoveinn.com

CYNTHIA SAUVAGE was born in Denver and graduated from the University of Colorado where she earned a degree in Spanish and French. Cynthia has traveled extensively throughout the world and lived in Mexico, Spain, and France. Her special love is Spain, and she is well acquainted with its culture and customs. Cynthia lives in Denver, Colorado, with her husband, David, and their two sons, Evan and Michael.

RALPH KITE, for many years a professor of Hispanic Literature, resides in Colorado. Since his retirement from teaching, he has continued his career as an author of textbooks on the culture and language of the Spanish-speaking world.

CLARE BROWN has many years of experience in the field of travel and has earned the designation of Certified Travel Consultant. Since 1969 she has specialized in planning itineraries to Europe using charming small hotels in the countryside for her clients. The focus of her job remains unchanged, but now her expertise is available to a larger audience—the readers of her daughter's country inn guides. Clare lives in Hillsborough, California, with her husband, Bill.

BARBARA TAPP, the talented artist who produces all of the hotel sketches and delightful illustrations in this guide, was raised in Australia where she studied in Sydney at the School of Interior Design. Although Barbara continues with freelance projects, she devotes much of her time to illustrating the Karen Brown guides. Barbara lives in Kensington, California, with her husband, Richard, their two sons, Jonothan and Alexander, and daughter, Georgia.

JANN POLLARD, the artist responsible for the beautiful painting on the cover of this guide, has studied art since childhood, and is well known for her outstanding impressionistic-style watercolors which she has exhibited in numerous juried shows, winning many awards. Jann travels frequently to Europe (using Karen Brown's guides) where she loves to paint historical buildings. Jann lives in Burlingame, California, with her husband, Gene.

Travel Your Dreams • Order your Karen Brown Guides Today

Please ask in your local bookstore for Karen Brown's Guides. If the books you want are unavailable, you may order directly from the publisher. Books will be shipped immediately.

_____ *Austria: Charming Inns & Itineraries* $17.95

_____ *California: Charming Inns & Itineraries* $17.95

_____ *England: Charming Bed & Breakfasts* $16.95

_____ *England, Wales & Scotland: Charming Hotels & Itineraries* $17.95

_____ *France: Charming Bed & Breakfasts* $16.95

_____ *France: Charming Inns & Itineraries* $17.95

_____ *Germany: Charming Inns & Itineraries* $17.95

_____ *Ireland: Charming Inns & Itineraries* $17.95

_____ *Italy: Charming Bed & Breakfasts* $16.95

_____ *Italy: Charming Inns & Itineraries* $17.95

_____ *Portugal: Charming Inns & Itineraries* $17.95

_____ *Spain: Charming Inns & Itineraries* $17.95

_____ *Switzerland: Charming Inns & Itineraries* $17.95

Name _____ Street _____

Town _____ State _____ Zip _____ Tel _____ email _____

Credit Card (MasterCard or Visa) _____ Expires: _____

For orders in the USA, add $4 for the first book and $1 for each additional book for shipment. California residents add 8.25% sales tax. Overseas orders add $10 per book for airmail shipment. Indicate number of copies of each title; fax or mail form with check or credit card information to:

KAREN BROWN'S GUIDES
Post Office Box 70 • San Mateo • California • 94401 • USA
tel: (650) 342-9117, fax: (650) 342-9153, e-mail: karen@karenbrown.com

For additional information about Karen Brown's Guides, visit our website at www.karenbrown.com